Once Upon a
Quinceañera

Also by Julia Alvarez

FICTION

How the García Girls Lost their Accents
In the Time of the Butterflies
¡Yo!
In the Name of Salomé
A Cafecito Story
Saving the World

ESSAYS

Something to Declare

POETRY

The Housekeeping Book
The Other Side/El Otro Lado
Homecoming
Seven Trees
The Woman I Kept to Myself

FOR CHILDREN

How Tía Lola Came to ~~Visit~~ Stay
Before We Were Free
The Secret Footprints
finding miracles
A Gift of Gracias: The Legend of Altagracia

Once Upon a
Quinceañera

COMING OF AGE
IN THE USA

Julia Alvarez

Viking

VIKING
Published by the Penguin Group
Penguin Group (USA) Inc., 375 Hudson Street, New York, New York 10014, U.S.A. · Penguin
Group (Canada), 90 Eglinton Avenue East, Suite 700, Toronto, Ontario, Canada M4P 2Y3 (a
division of Pearson Penguin Canada Inc.) · Penguin Books Ltd, 80 Strand, London WC2R
0RL, England · Penguin Ireland, 25 St. Stephen's Green, Dublin 2, Ireland (a division of Pen-
guin Books Ltd) · Penguin Books Australia Ltd, 250 Camberwell Road, Camberwell, Victoria
3124, Australia (a division of Pearson Australia Group Pty Ltd) · Penguin Books India Pvt
Ltd, 11 Community Centre, Panchsheel Park, New Delhi – 110 017, India · Penguin Group
(NZ), 67 Apollo Drive, Rosedale, North Shore 0745, Auckland, New Zealand (a division of
Pearson New Zealand Ltd.) · Penguin Books (South Africa) (Pty) Ltd, 24 Sturdee Avenue,
Rosebank, Johannesburg 2196, South Africa

Penguin Books Ltd, Registered Offices: 80 Strand, London WC2R 0RL, England

First published in 2007 by Viking Penguin, a member of Penguin Group (USA) Inc.

1 3 5 7 9 10 8 6 4 2

Grateful acknowledgment is made for permission to reprint the following copyrighted works:
Excerpt from "The World's Gone Crazy" by Jeff Durand and Tommy Barbarella. Used with
permission. · Excerpt from "Querida Companera" from Loving in the War Years by Cherrie
Morega (South End Press). Copyright © 1983 by Cherrie Morega. Used by permission of the
author. · Excerpts from for colored girls who have considered suicide / when the rainbow is enuf
by Ntozake Shange. Copyright © 1975, 1976, 1977 by Ntozake Shange. All rights reserved.
Reprinted with permission of Scribner, an imprint of Simon & Schuster Adult Publishing
Group. · "Father and Child" (from "A Woman Young and Old") from The Collected Works of
W. B. Yeats, Volume I: The Poems (revised), edited by Richard J. Finneran. Copyright © 1933 by
The Macmillan Company; copyright renewed © 1961 by Bertha Georgie Yeats. All rights
reserved. Reprinted with permission of Scribner, an imprint of Simon & Schuster Adult Pub-
lishing Group.

LIBRARY OF CONGRESS CATALOGING IN PUBLICATION DATA
Alvarez, Julia.
Once upon a quinceañera / Julia Alvarez.
p. cm.
Includes bibliographical references.
ISBN 978-0-670-03873-2 (alk. paper)
1. Quinceañera (Social custom)—United States. 2. Hispanic Americans—Social life and
customs. 3. Hispanic Americans—Rites and ceremonies. I. Title.
GT249C.A45 2007
395.2'4—dc22   2006037561

Printed in the United States of America

for
all the girls
and for
the wise women
who raise them

Education is teaching our children to desire the right things.

—Plato

Invitation

Y OU ARE DRESSED in a long, pale pink gown, not sleek and diva-ish, but princessy, with a puffy skirt of tulle and lace that makes you look like you're floating on air when you appear at the top of the stairs. Your court of fourteen couples has preceded you, and now they line up on the dance floor, forming a walkway through which you will pass to sit on a swing with garlanded ropes, cradling your last doll in your arms. Your mami will crown you with a tiara recessed in a cascade of curls the hairstylist spent most of the afternoon sculpting on your head. Then your papi will replace the flats you are wearing with a pair of silver heels and lead you out to the dance floor, where you will dance a waltz together.

No, you are not Miss America or a princess or an actress playing Cinderella in a Disney movie. In fact, you are not exceptionally beautiful or svelte and tall, model material. Your name is María or Xiomara or Maritza or Chantal, and your grandparents came from Mexico or Nicaragua or Cuba or the Dominican Republic. Your family is probably not rich; in fact, your mami and papi have been saving since you were a little girl or they've mortgaged the house or lined up forty godparents to help sponsor this celebration, as big as a wedding. If challenged about spending upward of five thousand dollars—the average budget—on a one-night celebration instead of investing in your college education or putting aside the money for their own mortgage payments, your parents will shake their heads knowingly because you do not understand: this happens only once.

What is going on?

You are having your quinceañera, or fiesta de quince años, or, simply, your quince. And one day when you are as old as your grandmother and you want to say to some young person, hey, I once was young, too, the expression you will use is *Yo también tuve mis quinces.*

I, too, had my quinces.

You will want to claim that magic age in which a Latina girl ritually becomes a woman in a ceremony known as a quinceañera.

⚬⟋⟍⟋⟍⟍⟋⚬

What exactly is a quinceañera?

The question might soon be rhetorical in our quickly Latinoizing American culture. Already, there is a Quinceañera Barbie; quinceañera packages at Disney World and Las Vegas; an award-winning movie, *Quinceañera;* and for tots, *Dora the Explorer* has an episode about her cousin Daisy's quinceañera.

A "quinceañera" (the term is used interchangeably for the girl and her party) celebrates a girl's passage into womanhood with an elaborate, ritualized fiesta on her fifteenth birthday. (Quince años, thus quinceañera, pronounced: *keen-seah-gneer-ah.*) In the old countries, this was a marker birthday: after she turned fifteen, a girl could attend adult parties; she was allowed to tweeze her eyebrows, use makeup, shave her legs, wear jewelry and heels. In short, she was ready for marriage. (Legal age for marriage in many Caribbean and Latin and Central American countries is, or until recently was, fifteen or younger for females, sixteen or older for males.) Even humble families marked a girl's fifteenth birthday as special, perhaps with a cake, certainly with a gathering of family and friends at which the quinceañera could now socialize and dance with young men. Upper-class families, of course, threw more elaborate parties at which girls dressed up in long, formal gowns and danced waltzes with their fathers.

Somewhere along the way these fancier parties became highly ritualized. In one or another of our Latin American countries, the quinceañera was crowned with a tiara; her flat shoes were changed by her father to heels; she was accompanied by a court of fourteen damas escorted by fourteen chambelanes, who represented her first fourteen years; she received a last doll, marking both the end of childhood and her symbolic readiness to bear her own child. And because our countries were at least nominally Catholic, the actual party was often preceded by a Mass or a blessing in church or, at the very least, a priest was invited to give spiritual heft to the fiesta. These celebrations were covered in the newspapers, lavish spreads of photos I remember poring over as a little girl in the Dominican Republic, reassured by this proof that the desire to be a princess did not have to be shed at the beginning of adulthood, but could in fact be played out happily to the tune of hundreds upon thousands of Papi's pesos.

In the late sixties, when many of our poor headed to el Norte's land of opportunity, they brought this tradition along, and with growing economic power, the no-longer-so-poor could emulate the rich back home. The spin-offs grew (quinceañera cruises, quinceañera resort packages, quinceañera videos and photo shoots); stories of where this quinceañera custom had come from proliferated (an ancient Aztec tradition, an import from European courts); further elaborations were added (Disney themes, special entrances, staged dance routines à la Broadway musicals); and in our Pan-Hispanic mixing stateside, the U.S. quinceañera adopted all the little touches of specific countries to become a much more elaborate (and expensive) ceremony, exported back to our home countries. But rock-bottom, the U.S. quinceañera is powered by that age-old immigrant dream of giving the children what their parents had never been able to afford back where they came from.

In fact, the quince expression notwithstanding, many of us older, first-generation Latinas never had a quinceañera. There was no money back when we were fifteen or we had recently arrived in the United States and didn't want anything that would make us stand out as other than all-American. Or we looked down our noses at such girly-girl fuss and said we didn't want a quince because we didn't understand that this was not just about us.

These cultural celebrations are also about building community in a new land. Lifted out of the context of our home cultures, traditions like the quinceañera become malleable; they mix with the traditions of other cultures that we encounter here; they become exquisite performances of our ethnicities within the larger host culture while at the same time reaffirming that we are not "them" by connecting us if only in spirit to our root cultures. In other words, this tradition tells a larger story of our transformation into Latinos, a Pan-Hispanic group made in the USA, now being touted as the "new Americans."

It's that story which intrigues me. Why when I was invited by an editor to write a book about quinceañeras, I welcomed the opportunity to follow the tradition wherever it might lead me. Given that we Latinos/Hispanics are the new booming minority, it seemed an apt moment to look at a ritual that marks a young Latina's coming-of-age. We, too, are coming of age in the USA, mixing and morphing in ways that I'm not sure we ourselves are tracking or fully understanding. More personally, as my generation, the baby boomers, begins to lose its parents, we become the depository of our old-country cultures. This is an enormous responsibility that challenges us to look critically at ourselves to ensure that what we are passing on is useful to our young people and even true to what we experienced at their age in our old cultures or, for those of us who came here preadolescence, in our new country.

And so, for a year, I immersed myself in this tradition. I traveled to various Latino communities in the United States: Dominican-Americans in Lawrence, Massachusetts, and Queens, New York; Cuban Americans in Miami; Mexican Americans in San Antonio and Los Angeles. Even as I ascribe distinct nationalities to these communities, I have to qualify that these nationalities are mixing with other Hispanic as well as non-Hispanic nationalities. The parents of the quinceañera I attended in San Antonio were Panamanian and Mexican American; of the two quinceañeras I attended in Lawrence, only one was Dominican, the other was Ecuadorian; Monica's quinceañera court in Queens included Colombians, Peruvians, and one Italian-Irish-American.

I also spoke with dozens of girls and their families and members of their courts, with events providers and photographers, with parish priests and youth ministers and choreographers. I talked to Latinas my age and older, Latinas in academia and in businesses catering to the quinceañera market, who observed that the quinceañera has become an even bigger deal stateside than it had ever been back home.

With that elaboration and expense a certain entitlement has set in. Many of the Latina girls I interviewed who responded in writing often termed the celebration "my right of passage." Given that spell-check would not have picked up this transposition, this was an understandable orthographical mistake, but it also seemed an apt description of what happens to traditions in the United States. Rites become rights. New generations feel entitled to what older first generations struggled to obtain for them.

By the same token, this entitlement ethic does not seem to shield our young Latina population from failure. As I read the research, I was alarmed by how our teen Latinas are topping the charts for all sorts of at-risk behaviors: from teen pregnancy to substance abuse to dropping out of high school. What is going on? We are crowning them princesses and meanwhile the statistics are showing a large number of our young girls headed for poverty and failure! Are these the same girls, I wonder?

So, what began as the study of a tradition became a journey of exploration rife with questions and misgivings. I admit that the disjunction between this grand Latina debut and the reality of their lives, the enormous cost of the celebration to struggling families, made me initially skeptical about the tradition. And yet, time and time again as I attended these celebrations I felt deeply moved by something at the heart of the tradition, a desire to empower our young women, a need to ritually mark their passage into adulthood, remind them of their community and its past, and by doing so give them and ourselves hope. Who could argue with that?

How I wished I had had that kind of support as a young teenage immigrant from the Dominican Republic in the early sixties! Not surprisingly, my exploration of this tradition led me back to my own coming-of-age soon after my arrival in the United States. Was it that tricky overlap of a double passage that made my journey from girlhood to womanhood so rocky, strewn with shipwrecks and riddled with many mistakes? What if anything had I learned from that passage that might be of help to young Latinas trying to integrate their dual cultures, each with its own gender handicap, as they passed from girlhood to womanhood? In fact, the more I spoke with young girls and boys, some of them not Hispanic but part of the quinceañera's court and circle of friends, the more I realized that it is not just Latina girls facing this challenge. Our young people are all coming of age in a new global culture that challenges them to integrate myriad worlds and create a coherent personal and communal narrative.

And so, as I attended quinceañeras, I felt as if I were getting a peek into the future as well as the past. A future that—given the demographics—would have, if not a Spanish accent, a Latino flavor. And a past that was my past, growing up in a USA just beginning to wake up to its own identity as a multicultural country with women and minorities demanding equal rights.

Now into a second and third generation we are still celebrating quinceañeras! Is this a testament to the fact that in our struggle for rights, we have not forgotten our rites? Or, given the walloping expense and elaboration of the celebration stateside, is it a more sinister sign of a greedy market making mucho dinero by this oh-so-American supersizing of tradition? As our president advised a nation struggling with how to express our grief for our dead after 9/11, "Go shopping." What other mourning rites could we tap into in that dark time? In this post–September eleventh world, many of us feel a heightened need to provide our young people with ways to access deeper resources than can be found in a mall or purchased with a credit card. We want them to know their roots and traditions and therefore themselves more fully. By the same token we need to review what we pass on to them to ensure that these traditions and practices are useful and appropriate to the challenges they are facing today and will no doubt be facing mañana.

This book is an invitation to a journey into a tradition which might provide insights into some of these quandaries and questions, as well as a glimpse into an increasingly large section of our

American population. I would hope that the journey also inspires readers to muse about their own traditions, about the need for rituals that might serve our young people, indeed all of us, in the many jolting transitions that living any life entails. And for those who like myself are entering into elderhood, this book is an invitation to take up that mantle or mantilla of elders of the tribe, to consider what it means to be at the other end of our young people's coming-of-age. How can we provide them with hope and a light to steer by, which those who were our elders and antepasados once passed on to us?

⚜

But mostly, this book is an invitation to a party.

Specifically, to Monica's quinceañera somewhere in Middle Village, Queens.

Monica Ramos is not her real name and any other identifying characteristics of this young lady have been changed. (Venues, vendors, and attendants that serve any number of quinceañeras and so would not compromise Monica's identity are specifically named.) From the inception of this book, I realized that any criticism of the ritual must not tarnish any one specific celebration nor embarrass any girl or her family. In our native Latin cultures as in many tribal cultures, the relationship of host and guest is a special one, not to be dishonored and misused. I was welcomed at their tables, ate their food, and in some cases I served as the authority on some detail of the ceremony—the meaning of the last doll, the traditional color of the dress, the lyrics of the song "Quinceañera." (By year's end I could field most if not all quinceañera questions.)

I also debated over how to present all the material I had collected about quinceañeras in the course of my travels, interviews, and research. What I found as I began to write up the different journeys to communities and quinceañeras and Q-related events was that I was repeating much of the same information. So instead I made the choice to follow one quinceañera on her special afternoon and night and through that story connect with the stories of other quinceañeras as well as my own coming-of-age. I chose Monica's quinceañera for a number of reasons. First, she was one of the most voluble of the young ladies I interviewed. Second, her quinceañera encountered any number of little snags which provided opportunities to discuss different issues connected with the tradition, including its religious dimensions, expense, trends in the larger culture. Third, and more personally, Monica's quinceañera was taking place only miles from where I had spent my early adolescence, in Jamaica, Queens. Her celebration inevitably triggered memories of myself at her age, facing some of the same challenges as the ones Latina girls face today. Four decades later, what if any insights have I gained into this tradition and time of life? Hopefully, by the end of this narrative, one young girl will ritually have become a woman, and my readers and I will be the wiser for having gone through this special night with her.

And so I apologize to Maritza and Chantal and Xiomara and María, whose quinceañeras I attended, for not making you the stars of this little book, as you might have hoped. Often in salons as your hair and nails were getting done or in studios or formal gardens during your photo shoots, or as we rode from home to church to reception hall in a stretch limo, you asked me what kind of a writer I was. Had I been on *Oprah*? Had I written something you might have heard of? Would your photos be in my book?

I usually disappointed you. I tried to explain that the kinds of books I write are not really about specific people, although, of course, your English teachers are right: we travel through stories inside characters. But even when I am writing about myself, that self is not personal but a creation of language in a story that is ultimately about all of us.

At this point in my explanation, you were no doubt distracted by several curls that stuck out or some pose the photographer was requesting which you thought (and so did I) was over the top. But what I hope is that now, in the quiet maturity of your post-quinceañera life, you will read my book and find in it not a mirror that reflects your very own face but an opportunity to experience your lives through language and story and other points of view and come of age—this time on the page—as a wiser, truer you.

⁂

When I was a young teenager growing up not far from Monica's home, and later in boarding school, I had no idea that I would ever write books, much less write a book about this time of life when I felt totally lost. Recently arrived in the United States, fleeing the dictatorship of Trujillo in the Dominican Republic, I was starting over on all counts: learning a new language, a new culture, a new way of being an American girl.

Upon our arrival in New York City in 1960, my father contacted an American doctor who had visited the island for a medical conference years back. Dr. Deluccia and his wife, Nancy, themselves first-generation Italian-Americans, became our helpers in our new country. Dr. Deluccia guided my father professionally as Papi applied for his medical license and took his boards. We were indebted to this kind man and his flamboyant, vivacious wife. When my parents did not understand some document or procedure or when they wondered where we should rent a home or what kind of car to buy, it was always, *Why not call up Dr. and Mrs. Deluccia and ask them for their recommendation?*

One evening a few months after our arrival, the Deluccias invited the whole family out to dinner. In deference to us, the restaurant was Spanish, and prior to leaving the apartment, Mami had cautioned us to let her choose our dinner from the menu. Perhaps since this was the Deluccias' treat, Mami was worried about the expense. Midmeal a floor show began: two flamenco dancers strutted onstage, the woman in a long white dress with red polka dots, a slit up one side, a red mantilla on her shoulders and a comb in her hair. Her male partner wore a sleek black outfit and a black, wide-brimmed hat. As they danced with passion and skill, the audience cheering and clapping, I felt a surge of ethnic pride. These were Spanish people, kin to us, commanding attention and applause. We were no longer poor spics whose accents were taunted in the playground; suddenly, through these dancers, we were lifted up, a beautiful, soulful people with a rich culture, the stars of the night.

Soon after the show was over, the female dancer came round with a basket of Barbie-type dolls dressed just like her. She stopped beside my chair and tilted her basket toward me. I thought she was inviting me to pick the doll I wanted, and so I did, though I could feel my mother's eyes beaming a warning at me.

Later that night, after we had parted company with the Deluccias, Mami gave me a thorough scolding. Those dolls were for sale, expensive souvenirs. My father had insisted that Dr. Deluccia allow him to pay for my extravagance. I don't remember how my mother said the issue of payment had been settled. But from then on, my ownership of that doll was shot through with ambivalence.

Every time I saw her, perched on the dresser in the room I shared with my sisters, I recalled the beautiful, passionate dancer and my moment of intense and vindicated ethnic pride. Never mind that she was a Spanish dancer, not a Dominican one. In that premulticultural America, that was close enough. But the doll was also a reminder of how I had stupidly mistaken the peddling of wares for a symbolic gift from one of my own. I did not yet know that I had embarked upon an adventure in which this doll might well be the symbol of the end result: a popular American icon, Barbie, dressed up like a Spanish lady, the mixtures and combinations that would take me—and the United States—several decades to sort out. After all, it was not until 1980, when I was thirty, that the first black and Hispanic Barbie dolls began to appear on the shelves of Wal-Mart and Target.

She comes to mind now, my doll of many faces (shame and pride, American and Spanish, expense and loss), because dolls came up often in the course of this book—from the traditional última muñeca ("last doll") the quinceañera receives to the quinceañera in her flouncy dress with a tiara in her hair: a life-sized doll herself!

As I worked on this book I myself collected three tiny doll figures as charms to remind me of aspects of coming-of-age as a girl. I found these dolls on a trip to a toy store while buying my granddaughter her Dora the Explorer backpack. They are manufactured by Papo, a French company, but the exquisitely detailed dolls are, as the fine print reads when you turn them over, made in China. Even our dolls embody our global, racial, and ethnic mixtures!

The first Papo doll is a "dancing princess in pink," and I suppose I picked her out because she represents the subject of my journey, the quinceañera herself.

The second figure is a fairy in white with a lifted wand, tipped with a star: the godmother every girl needs to internalize to make her dreams come true.

The final figure does not seem to belong in the same universe as the other two: she is dressed in male trousers, her head covered in a white wimple held down by a flat silver crown. She is lunging forward, sword in hand, her red cape swirling around her.

Only with the hindsight of womanhood do I fully understand how necessary this last figure is to complete the trinity of princess and godmother that the fairy-tale quinceañera embodies. She is the woman warrior, whom I first encountered in my late twenties in Maxine Hong Kingston's memoir by the same name. To be female in today's United States—not to mention the world—continues to be an uphill battle against sexism, gender inequalities in wage earnings, threats to our equal rights, as well as against internal furies and naysayers that still try to hold us back. But the touch that I find most endearing about this warrior taliswoman is not her plucky armed demeanor but the left hand she holds out to balance her lunge with the sword in her right: five teensy flesh-colored fingers, vulnerable and open and inspiring tenderness, a hand to hold a pen or a briefcase or a scalpel or another hand.

As I write this in my home in rural Vermont, a state with one of the smallest Latino populations (5,504 out of a population of 608,827, according to the 2000 census), I am aware of a whole new underground population on neighboring farms. In fact, our county of Addison now has 400 illegal Mexican migrant workers doing the milking jobs on dairy farms that would go under if this cheap and round-the-clock workforce were deported. In other words, there is no corner of America that is not fast becoming a multicultural community.

Some of these workers traveled here with their wives and girlfriends. Recently, during a baby shower for one of these women, I brought up the tradition. "Just in case the baby is a girl," I joked, "we'd better start thinking about her quinceañera." The young women's faces lit up. The soon-to-be mami's smile spread wide.

Suddenly, in the midst of a foreign country and an even more foreign state, Vermont in midwinter, there was a tie that took them back to their little pueblos and familias in faraway Mexico. And even though only one of the four women had had a quinceañera, each one could recite all the elaborations: the long dress, the change of shoes, the last doll, the Mass, the dance with the father . . .

"Every girl grows up with the illusion that one day she will have her quinceañera," another young woman, also pregnant, explained. The others nodded.

"So, if you have daughters, will you celebrate their quinceañeras here in their new country?"

The women fell silent, for in the uncertain days that lie ahead, who can imagine what might be possible?

May this book be part of that imagining of a bright and promising future for all our daughters. May they grow up feeling as special as princesses, as empowered as fairy godmothers, and as fiercely committed to the struggle for equality of all people as women warriors.

Once upon a quinceañera

I'm sitting in my room at the Pan American Hotel feeling pretty much like Cinderella before her fairy godmother shows up. I drove down from Vermont early this morning, a five-hour drive that had taken me six hours since I'm not used to finding my way through the urban labyrinths of parkways and expressways with exits popping up out of nowhere to this multicultural, multilingual, multimulti area of Queens where forty years ago my own immigrant adolescence was spent.

I've driven down here to attend Monica Ramos's quinceañera. The plan was that I would phone the Ramoses as soon as I arrived and they would come and get me so I could follow the quinceañera in the last few hours of her preparations. But I've been calling the family home number and Monica's father's cell number for the last half hour and nobody answers. Maybe it's the busy floral pattern of the hotel bedspread or the scented air freshener recently sprayed in the room, but I'm beginning to feel lightheaded with misgivings. Did I come this far just to spend a night in my overpriced room at the Pan American, only to have to turn around tomorrow morning and drive back to Vermont without even a glimpse of this Queens quinceañera?

Like many USA-born Latinas, Monica, whose parents were both born in the Dominican Republic, is actually celebrating her quinceañera on her sixteenth birthday. This is just one more ad-aptation of the old-country tradition which has now survived more than four decades on American soil. But with a persistence unique to this immigrant group that seems to retain at least some of its Spanish and its feeling that "home" is still south of the Rio Grande even into a second and third generation, Monica calls her sweet sixteen a "quinceañera sort of."

Monica's quinceañera had sounded great over the phone. It was going to be so special, she told me during several long-distance conversations. Open, friendly, easy to talk to, Monica was one of the most verbal and forthcoming quinceañeras I interviewed. She didn't want a party at first, but she was finally won over by two things: the chance to dress up in a beautiful princess gown and the opportunity to give a speech in front of her whole family and all her friends. Monica's party will include the lighting of seven-teen candles, each one dedicated to a special person with a little speech about why this person is so special to her.

"There's always an added candle, dedicated to someone ab-sent," Monica explains about the extra candle. "Mine's going to be dedicated to God for giving me such a special life."

Monica has told me that she is a devoted Catholic. I have to bite my tongue so as not to point out that a candle meant for someone absent is perhaps not the best category for a God who I'm sure Monica believes is everywhere. But it's hard enough to get these young ladies to confide in a virtual stranger without peppering them with prickly questions. As one young lady told me when I pursued a line of questioning about how exactly she thought she was going to go from being a girl to being a woman by having a quinceañera, "This is becoming annoying."

Instead I asked Monica if her quinceañera was going to have a theme. Themes are popular: the quinceañera is a butterfly, emerg-ing from a flower. The quinceañera is a princess, sitting on a throne. The quinceañera is a cowgirl, with a court of boys sporting lassos. The quinceañera, like a magician's trick, rises up out of a trapdoor in a puff of smoke.

"Mine is all based on Disney characters," Monica announced excitedly. The girlfriends in her court were going to be Sleeping Beauty, Snow White, Jasmine, Belle . . . "We're going to do like a little play where my prince is going to find my heels on the dance floor and bring them to my dad to put on my feet," Monica gushed on.

Before hanging up, I asked Monica what her quinceañera meant to her. Although she had been quite garrulous about the party details, Monica seemed stumped by the question. Every quinceañera I've asked has given me the same pat answer. Claudia in Lawrence, Massachusetts, a short, stocky girl in sweat pants, pressured by her mami to have a quince party; Ashley in San Antonio, a popular, petite girl with a string of girlfriends who had celebrated or were in line to celebrate their quinces; Leticia in East L.A., who ran off with her chambelán seven months later—all of them echoed Monica as if reciting the mantra of quinceañeras: "I'm going from being a girl to being a woman." When I pressed Monica about what this meant, she answered vaguely: "It's like part of my culture."

"So, did your mother have a quinceañera back in the D.R.?" I wondered.

Monica wasn't sure. "Mami!" she called out from her end of the phone. "Did you have a quinceañera?" The answer came back, "A quinceañera quinceañera, no, mi'ja."

I found out about Monica's quinceañera only four days ago in that word-of-mouth way so reminiscent of our home cultures. A Dominican student's Colombian friend has a mother who owns a flower shop in Queens that does a lot of quinceañeras, and she (the mother) was doing Monica's flowers and also providing some of the props, and she told the Ramoses about me. By the time I got word back that the Ramoses would be happy to have me attend Monica's party and, phone number in hand, I called them, they were into that forty-eight-hour countdown usually associated with weddings in which everyone is racing around, hyperventilating, arguing, bursting into tears, and the bride is threatening to call the whole thing off. In fact, Monica's party is taking place soon after the headline story about the runaway bride, Jennifer Wilbanks, who disappeared days before her wedding in Duluth, Georgia. As I sit in my hotel room, waiting to get through to the Ramoses, I wonder if no one is answering because Monica has run off. Perhaps she will be the first runaway quinceañera to get national media attention.

On the phone, a very generous Mr. Ramos ("José, por favor!") had offered to pick me up at the airport should I come by plane. "I wouldn't think of it with as much as you have to do," I declined. In part, I thought it wise to have a way to get from the church, where a Mass or blessing would precede the party, to the Dance Club, where the ceremony, supper, and dance would take place, and back to the hotel at a reasonable hour, as these parties tend to go on past the Cinderella stroke of midnight. Bringing my own wheels will turn out to be an inspired decision in more ways than I would ever have anticipated. But at the moment, I am wondering if the long drive has been in vain as none of the messages I've left on Mr. Ramos's cell phone or home phone have been returned. Foolishly, I have no address, no other way to contact the family. I look out the grimy picture window of the Pan American past the back parking lot toward street after street of fenced-in row houses, and I know, with a sinking heart, that this is not the kind of neighborhood where everyone knows everybody else.

An hour goes by. It's Friday, so back in Vermont, my husband is still at work. I had suggested we both fly down, wimpy city driver that I am, and make a weekend of it, but before I could finish outlining the fun of two nights at the Pan American Hotel, my husband was shaking his head. He'd had enough of quinceañeras, thank you. "You've only been to a few," I argued, feeling vaguely wounded at his obvious disenchantment with one of *my* cultural traditions. "I've been to four and that's three too many," he countered. I don't know if it's his thrifty German-Lutheran roots, but from the beginning he has looked askance at these over the top celebrations, many of them costing much more than working-class families can afford.

His skepticism about this tradition is also my own. The incredible expense; a girl encouraged in the dubious fantasy of being a princess as if news of feminism had never reached her mami; the marketing of a young lady as attractive, marriageable goods. Why not save the money for education? I've snuck in that question in all of my interviews. Why not have coming-of-age celebrations for boys as well as girls? But still, every time the young lady makes an entrance through her archway, or curtains part and there she is, sitting on her swing or a throne or a carousel horse, while the whole familia and roomful of friends applaud her, my eyes tear up and my throat catches. The tradition, whatever its trappings, is homing in on a need to acknowledge and celebrate these new arrivals in the field of time. From my spot in the crowd I am torn between optimism for this tender, young being emerging from the cocoon of her childhood and a sense of dread that the world she is entering, unlike the fantasy she is enjoying this one night, will not allow for such winged flight.

The sad state of Hispanic girls

Reading about the state of adolescent girls in America can only deepen that sense of dread.

In her best-selling book *Reviving Ophelia: Saving the Selves of Adolescent Girls,* Dr. Mary Pipher, a clinical psychologist who has been treating girls for more than thirty years, notes that something happens to spunky, lively American girls when they hit adolescence. They become muted, lose their self-esteem, doubt their abilities, underperform in the classroom, and become easy prey to substance abuse, risky sexual behaviors, and depression. And adolescence is beginning earlier than ever. The average age of onset of menstruation among middle-class white girls in the USA today is twelve (even younger among Hispanic girls) in contrast to fifteen or sixteen in the late nineteenth century. Girls are becoming sexually mature and in many cases sexually active while they are still children. And this early maturation is taking place in what Dr. Pipher terms a "girl-poisoning" culture, "a sleazy dangerous tinsel town with lots of liquor stores and few protected spaces." The pressures and demands of contemporary adolescence are enough to make even the strongest girls keel over and lose their spirit.

Not only have physical and social pressures on young girls intensified, but they are less protected and less nurtured than they were a century ago, according to Joan Jacobs Brumberg, who ends her book *The Body Project: An Intimate History of American Girls* with a rousing call to what she terms "girl advocacy." Ironically, this lack of protection is an outgrowth of our previous generation's feminism. "In the late 1960s and 1970s, the traditional notion that women needed special protections because of biology was discredited." Feminists, among whom Dr. Brumberg includes herself, backed off from any special supervision or guidance for girls. And so, these young girls are left stranded in a popular culture that bombards them with artificial, airbrushed ideals of what they should look like, a culture of violence, drugs, and sexual pressures in which their bodies are "the primary currency of the realm." Many are losing their way. "In the U.S. girls under fifteen are at least five times more likely to give birth than girls of the same age in other industrialized countries."

But all of this turns out to be the brighter side of the bad news compared to the situation among young Latinas. In a study conducted by the National Coalition of Hispanic Health and Human Services Organizations (COSSMHO) titled *The State of Hispanic Girls,* young Latinas topped the charts in rates of teen pregnancy, suicide attempts, school dropouts, and substance abuse. It's no wonder: as of 1996, the study notes, "more than 40 percent of all Hispanic children under the age of seventeen were living in families with incomes below the poverty line." The results read relentlessly grim: "It is chilling . . ." (close to one out of every three Hispanic female high school students has seriously considered suicide); "Regrettably . . ." (Hispanic girls have school dropout rates higher than any other ethnic group: 30 percent between the ages of sixteen and twenty-four have dropped out of school without reenrolling or earning a high school equivalency degree); "It is dismaying . . ." (Hispanic girls lead their counterparts in the use of illegal substances); "More dire is the finding . . ." (Hispanic female students are more likely to have started drinking alcohol before age thirteen); "Most disturbing of all . . . It is also disconcerting . . ."

What on earth is there to celebrate? Why are these girls having quinceañeras? Perhaps, beyond these thickets of statistics, things aren't all that bad? But in fact, according to the COSSMHO study, these are "conservative estimates," as the Youth Risk Behavior Surveillance data was collected from high school students, by which time many Hispanic girls had already dropped out. (Out-of-school Hispanic females are even more at risk than their school-bound counterparts.) Since Hispanics are the largest growing minority population, and since more than one in three Hispanics are under the age of eighteen, these figures represent a significant part of our girl population.

In part this is why I got hooked into writing about quinceañeras. If the situation is indeed this bad, shouldn't our community en masse and each of us individually rush to rescue our girls? How many of these one-night princesses will end up going in the opposite direction of the Cinderella fairy tale: from ball gowns and tiaras and quince parties to life at the bottom of the American heap? As the authors of *The State of Hispanic Girls* wonder, "These surveys prompt us to ask an important question: has Americanization become hazardous to the health of Hispanic adolescents?"

The answer seems to be affirmative: "long-term residence in the United States significantly increased rates in all disorder categories, with particularly dramatic increases in the rates of substance abuse." And yet, the study also found that those girls who do take wing succeed in part because of protective cultural beliefs and practices that provide an important buffer against depression and risky behaviors. And so, in fact, the quinceañera celebration, while endorsing a questionable and often expensive fairy-tale fantasy, also involves an investment of time, energy, and attention in a young person, which can pay off in ways that can't be so easily dismissed. It's worth remembering the old adage about how our strengths are often so tied up with our failings that we'd better be careful where we snip and what we cut off.

Fallout

I figure that rather than sit around in my Pan American Hotel room, waiting for the Ramoses to call me back, I might as well do a little scouting of my old neighborhood. Nice thing about cell phones: I can carry my portable means of access with me. Not that it has done me much good so far.

According to the Latina girl at the front desk, it's real easy to get to 179th Street in Jamaica from where we're at on Queens Boulevard. "You basically just go down the road till you hit Hillside Avenue." I consider asking her if she had a quinceañera, but her patience seems to have a one-question timer on it, which runs out when I ask if she has a small map since I tend to be a visual person.

She does not.

But her instructions turn out to be picture-perfect: I drive down Queens Boulevard, make a left at Hillside, and soon the neighborhood starts looking familiar. All the storefronts have changed: where there was a candy store, there's now a dry cleaner. The grocery store has been replaced by a bank. Dr. Gold's dentist office is gone. The Dillers' house has been spruced up. The trees are taller. But the neighborhood still has that familiar look of a childhood friend in middle age—you see glimpses of the young girl surfacing in her lined face.

My family moved to Jamaica, Queens, in 1963, our third year in the United States. My parents had actually lived in the States before, during an earlier, failed emigration. They had returned home in 1950 when I was a month old. Now ten years later, they were back. But this time, they had no choice but to stay. My father's involvement in a plot against the dictator Trujillo had been uncovered and we had narrowly escaped with our lives.

The first couple of years were difficult. The world we knew had ended, and now we were struggling to stay afloat in the overwhelming newness of everything. Money was tight. My father had to apply for his medical license in order to practice. Would he get it before the loan from Mami's parents ran out? Would he get it at all? We rented an apartment near Columbia University from a professor going off on sabbatical, then sublet a house in New Hyde Park—every year a new neighborhood, a new school, a new place to get used to even as we were still trying to get used to a whole new world. We clung together as a nuclear family, all of us suffering from profound culture shock.

But by our third year, things were looking up. My father had gotten his license and was working seven days a week in a clinic in Brooklyn. Back home on the island, the political situation remained iffy; even after the dictator was deposed, there were coups, military takeovers, civil unrest. The illusion that someday we would go back was over. We were here to stay. We bought our very own house in Jamaica, and began to put down roots in this country.

And so, this neighborhood, not far from where Monica will be celebrating her quinceañera, is where my sisters and I began to surface as American girls. Of course, this began to cause trouble in our family. My sisters and I wanted to hang out with our friends, sleep over at their houses, attend their parties, wear clothes like theirs—skirts that were too short, tops that were too skimpy, raggedy jeans. We were arguing, answering back, sneaking around. My parents would definitely have agreed with the conclusions of the COSSMHO study: long-term residency in the United States was beginning to ruin their girls.

My mother, who became the primary parent now that my father was always working, resorted to punishments, ultimatums, and when those methods didn't work, she tried scare tactics. Constantly, she warned us about the dangers in this new country: we could not trust anyone; the only people who would always be there for us was our familia. Punto, end of discussion. Daily, we heard stories garnered from newspapers and TV of muggings and murders; girls found raped; girls found strangled; girls found raped and strangled only ten blocks away. I think I learned about rape before I fully understood how normal sex actually worked.

And yet, while trying to maintain control over our sexuality and behavior, my parents also stressed the importance of education, of doing well in school—where, in contradiction to the rules at home, we were being taught to think for ourselves, express our opinions, stand up for what we believed in. We began to feel totally at sea, torn between loyalties, *entre Lucas y Juan Mejía,* the Dominican expression for neither here nor there. On the one hand my parents fought to protect us from the assimilating, alluring, corrupting influence of American culture, but on the other hand they pushed us to excel and succeed in this new world where the old mainstays would no longer be available to us as Dominican girls from a nice family.

This bicultural double bind—which three decades later would be recast in the popular media and public school curricula as the multicultural richness immigrants bring to the melting pot, by then renamed "the American mosaic"—this bind was the Gordian knot that my sisters and I soon found ourselves unable to untie. Of course, it would have helped had we moved into a Dominican community which might have acted as a buffer zone and helped us maintain our traditions and language, those protective cultural beliefs and practices that the COSSMHO study found kept girls from risky or—my mother's rewording—bad behaviors.

But it would be another decade and a half before the huge wave of Dominican immigrants splashed onto the shores of Nueva York in Washington Heights, Queens, the Bronx. Another decade before our fiercely ethnocentric Central and Latin American and Caribbean identities were subsumed under one bureaucratic umbrella, "Hispanic." In 1973, the Nixon administration's O.M.B Statistical Directive 15 would give Americans five categories in which to box themselves racially and ethnically: "Black"; "White"; "Asian / Pacific"; "Native American / Eskimo"; "Hispanic."

Another decade of mixing and politicizing, and by the eighties we ourselves began to claim that that's who we were. And although some took issue with the name and preferred calling themselves "Latinos" instead of "Hispanics," the bureaucratic brainstorm had turned into a reality: we had become La Raza, one people.

But that was ten, fifteen years into the future. In 1963, America was still steeped in the Red Scare, just crawling out of the McCarthy years, just beginning to hear its darker masses yearning to breathe free within its own borders. In our own neighborhood, a black family moved in across the street from our house. They received threatening phone calls, so we heard. A police car patrolled our block. The father was a professional, the superintendent of something; the daughter, a girl about my age, was also held in the strict confines of her family, not permitted to come out and play.

Was this success: you moved up and out of your element, and then you clung to the few who had come with you because they were all that was left of what you had lost in your climb to a brave new world? Pale as we were, hadn't my sisters and I been told by passersby on the street who heard us talking loudly in Spanish: *Spics! Go back to where you came from!* There had been several incidents at my school, older boys spitting at me, throwing pebbles at me, chasing me down the block, accusing me of being a Commie because they had overheard me say that our island was next to Cuba, where the dreaded Castro was getting ready to launch a bomb against the United States.

But though the wave of multicultural consciousness with its accompanying political correctness was decades away, another tide was already turning, one that would not wait ten, fifteen years: my sisters and I were becoming teenagers. My older sister turned fifteen, but there was no question of throwing her a quinceañera. What family was there to invite except two old paternal aunts up in the Bronx? What community was there to gather together to mark one of its own going from niña to mujer? As for our American friends—my mother did not even allow them inside our house. These were girls without our costumbres, girls who were a bad influence, girls whom my mother could not control as she hoped she could still control us. (Ha!)

And so for her quince, my older sister got the ring my mother had been given by her parents when she turned fifteen. My sister was also now allowed to wear a little makeup—pale lipstick, a brushstroke of blush. The other privilege that came with turning fifteen, shaving her legs, we had circumvented months before when the three oldest sisters had gone down to a drugstore on Hillside and bought a large tube of Nair and depilated our legs. Technically, we had not disobeyed Mami since the prohibition was that we could not *shave* our legs until we turned fifteen.

Obviously, we found ways around our parents' control, which was all the more extreme for being out of context—frozen in time—the direct result of their feeling under siege in a world they did not trust.

I began to plot my escape. Periodically, I would run away from home, roaming the little shops down on Hillside Avenue. Once, I called Pan American, the airline that had brought us to New York, for information on how much it might cost to fly to Australia. *Australia?* Why not fly back to where I had come from? Why Australia? Recently, my father had taken us to see a film, *On the Beach*, about nuclear war, the end of the world, the northern hemisphere destroyed. The last uncontaminated stronghold is Australia. Gregory Peck falls in love with Ava Gardner, as fallout moves across the Pacific Ocean. . . .

I was in love with Gregory Peck. Maybe he would love me back? After all, Ava Gardner looked "Spanish" (what we said back then instead of "Hispanic" or "Latina"). Maybe he preferred dark women? But it was more than romance that captivated my attention. The film was riveting, terrifying, in part because I was living in that same emotional key. I understood the feeling of a world ending. Of not knowing if disaster would be averted or if the fallout cloud would slowly move to where love had momentarily saved you.

The Pan American operator humored me, a girl with a pronounced accent trying to buy a plane ticket with birthday money. "It's very expensive to fly to Australia, dear."

Well, how much would it cost?

"Depends, do you want a round-trip or a one-way ticket?"

I didn't know the difference. She had to explain it to me. And here was the crux of what would become my ongoing dilemma, the Gordian knot I kept reknotting myself: I wanted a round-trip ticket even though I was never ever coming back again.

And now, here I am forty-two years later, driving down Hillside Avenue, the street I used to roam when I ran away from home. It always ended the same way: I stuck it out until supper time when I knew my father would be coming home from work and be sent out with one or another of my sisters in search of me. I'd spot the black Mercury turning onto Hillside, my father would honk the horn, my sister would roll down the window and holler, "JULIEEEEEEEEEEEE!!! You better get in the car!" The whole street seemed to stop and stare at us. We were proving them right, loud spics making a scene. We didn't belong here. We should go back to where we came from. No wonder I wanted to run away to Australia and marry Gregory Peck and watch the world end in his arms.

꘎

Every girl should have one

I wish I'd had Isabella Martínez Wall to call up and talk to back when I was a young teen in need of rescue and an infusion of self-esteem.

Based in Los Angeles, Isabella is the founder of a one-stop quinceañera Web site cum advice column, bellaquinceañera .com. She's also an actress, a former Miss Dominican Republic, a successful fashion model, and founder of Someone Cares International, a nonprofit that is described on her Web site as "benefiting needy children" in her native country. Speaking by phone with this passionate and inspirational woman, I feel the same unsettling mixture of amazement, caution, and yearning that I feel toward televangelists. Can somebody really believe this? And if so, why can't I?

I learned about Isabella from a Dominican contact at Disney World, whom I had called to find out more about the Disney quince package. She described Isabella as an "awesome, full-bodied Latina" who is doing amazing things for young Hispanic girls. According to my contact, Isabella had actually found that young girls who had quinceañeras didn't drop out of school, didn't get pregnant, didn't get in trouble.

"Really? I mean, statistically?" I shot back. Here you go, I thought, peppering these kids with questions. But a quinceañera panacea seemed too good to be true. I'd just barely surfaced from *The State of Hispanic Girls* with a sense of dread in my heart, which was also making me want to grab for a cure.

"I don't know," my contact said. "Talk to Isabella, she'll tell you."

Ah, my people, I thought. Statistics are for the gringos. We trust testimonials, what our hearts and telenovelas tell us. I had just attended a lecture by Dr. James Martin titled "The Meaning of the 21st Century." Solutions to world problems didn't have to be costly or complex, the information technology guru explained. In Mexico, a vanguard group of TV producers who understood the dangers of population explosion had started a campaign to bring down the birthrate by introducing female leads who practiced birth control into popular telenovelas. Initial results showed the campaign was working. Better than pamphlets or science classes or lectures like Dr. Martin's.

When I reached Isabella, after the initial honorifics, "So you're the author!" "So you're the beauty queen!" I asked her about this claim I'd heard that quinceañeras really turn girls around. Not that I wanted an analysis or anything academic, I added, thinking maybe I was sounding too much like a doubting-Thomas gringa. But with all those statistics still heavy in my heart, I wanted to hear why she thought quinceañeras were so effective. "Well, let me tell you." Isabella laughed right out. "There's nothing academic about a quinceañera!

"What I mean is there's no textbook about how you have to do a quinceañera," Isabella went on to explain. She hears from a lot of young ladies on her Web site, where she offers free advice, a kind of Ann Landers to Latina girls.

"They write me, and they ask, can I wear a short dress? Does it have to be white? Can I have a court with only my best friend and my sister? I tell them, listen, there are no rules. The most important thing is to make this celebration yours, totally yours. I try to educate them, I talk to them, the site is highly interactive. Quinceañeras are about creating strong women. Our girls need all the help we can give them."

It's funny how you are sure you are going to end up on the

other side of an opinion from someone, and it turns out you're in each other's court. Never would I have guessed that a former beauty queen promoting a princessy fantasy would turn out to be a crown-carrying feminist. But how on earth can this quasi beauty pageant cum mini wedding make an Amazon out of a stardust girl?

"I have seen it happen!" In fact, it happened to Isabella herself. As a teenager growing up in the Dominican Republic, she hit a wall. "I was smoking, drinking, I had body issues and identity problems." I'm dying to ask her to be specific, but she is on a roll. "When I turned fifteen, everybody started having quinceañeras. I mean everybody. Quinceañeras know no social or class boundaries. You might not have the money but you have a quinceañera for your daughter. The family is making that statement. We might not be rich but we value our daughter."

Isabella's quinceañera turned her around. "It made me feel so special." In fact, she credits it with leading her down the path to being crowned Miss Dominican Republic. "I've been there," Isabella says. "I had that moment. But how many women in the world get to feel like a queen? How many?"

Not this skinny, undersized Latina for sure, I have to agree.

"Well, that's the first reason to have a quinceañera," Isabella says. "To have that experience and not because you're marrying someone."

The second reason comes from her own experience. "Being fifteen, let's face it, it's a tough age. Your body is all over the map. You wonder who you are. Who your friends are. Where you're going. You can get lost for sure. What better time in your life to have your family, friends, community come together and create a support system for you for the rest of your life?"

Isn't that asking an awful lot of a quinceañera?

But Isabella dismisses my skepticism. "About two years ago, I realized that I had a mission: to promote this important ritual. And yes, I've seen it turn girls around. I don't have statistics, this is not academic, like I said, but girls who have quinces, think about it, they're spending a lot of time with their moms, shopping, talking about life. Their friends are coming over to do rehearsals. I mean, a room full of fifteen-year-olds learning dance steps right under your nose. Parents are always complaining they don't know what to do when their daughters hit puberty. *Hel*-lo?! Here's something to do. Give her a wishing well.

"Of course, we've got to take the quinceañera a step forward," Isabella adds. Before, the whole quinceañera thing was about a girl being of marriageable age, goods to be displayed. But now we can invest this old tradition with new meaning.

"We can create a support platform for that young lady that she can have to look back upon for the rest of her life. That moment when she stands dressed like a queen with her mom beside her looking in the mirror, for that moment, if only that moment, she knows she is all right just as she is. She is the queen of her life if she can hold on to that feeling."

In fact, Isabella thinks quinces are so special, the tradition should come out of its ethnic closet and become an American phenomenon. "I don't care what class or group you come from," Isabella claims. "Every girl should have one."

When I hang up I feel that uplifted feeling that must be why folks pick up the phone after watching a TV evangelist and put a donation on their charge card.

Rendezvous with a soon-to-be-crowned queen of her life

Back at the Pan American Hotel, I get lucky: I dial up the Ramoses' home number, and a young man answers.

It's José Jr., "Joselito," who has flown in for his little sister's party from North Dakota, where he's stationed with the air force. He has no idea where everybody is. But he gives me a lifesaving string of cell phone numbers, including Monica's and her older sister, Silvia's, as well as their father's, which I've been calling without success. I try them all and finally get through on Silvia's number. "I'm the writer," I tell her. "I don't know if your sister told you? I'm working on a book about quinceañeras." I might as well be saying that I'm a silkworm farmer from China or that I analyze the molecular structure of DNA in a lab in Canada. It makes no sense to her, but this is no time for bafflement. "We have a problem," Silvia says. "I've been trying to reach one of my friends. We need a ride home and Papi's picking up the cake and Mami's still having her hair done and the limo is coming at five-thirty and we've got to get dressed or we'll never make it to the church for the six o'clock blessing. Could you maybe come get us?"

I live in Vermont, I want to tell her. I don't drive well in city traffic. But the need is so straightforward, the voice so plaintive. Besides, I just survived the drive to Jamaica, so I'm feeling confident.

"Where are you now?" I ask. That's the bad thing about cell phones. Silvia and Monica could be anywhere. Queens is a maze of expressways and boulevards and little neighborhoods. Does she know what she's asking for?

They're at a salon not far from where I tell them I am. ("What's the name of this place?" I hear Silvia asking folks at her end. Incredibly, no one is really sure.) "It's R.L. Coquette Unisex." Silvia has walked out to the sidewalk with her cell phone and is reading the name on the awning. There's the faint roar of traffic, crowd sounds, a siren going by. This could be twenty minutes from now. An accident I've caused.

"Okay," I agree, gulping down my terror of urban traffic. Silvia is sounding too desperate. She gives me instructions on how to get there, but they turn out to be a nondriver's instructions: she has me taking a one-way street going the wrong way, then turning left onto a street which, she's correct, is on my left, but with a median and oncoming traffic between me and it.

But this is a quinceañera, a fairy tale with a happy ending, and so I turn left at a posted no-left-turn and disobey a couple more traffic signs, and drive down a street full of shoppers, and there they are. You can't miss two girls in jeans and T-shirts with elaborate Marie Antoinette hairdos like mismatched Mr. Potato Heads waving frantically at you.

Silvia, the older sister, is eighteen, honey-skinned with streaked blond hair, shorter and plumper than Monica, who is tall and pale with a tiara in her dark hair. She is indeed a beauty, a little gawky in her skinniness, with large, expressive eyes and a tendency to giggle after everything she says. (I did notice this on the phone and dismissed it as initial nerves with a stranger, but it turns out to be the way Monica speaks to almost everyone except family members.)

Very briefly, as I'm double-parked on this narrow street, I run inside to meet the girls' mother. Rosa is sheathed in a black plastic cape as a woman brushes some foul-smelling chemical on sprigs of her hair sprouting out of what looks like a cap of aluminum foil. Rosa must be in her forties, good-looking, but with the embarrassed smile of someone caught by a stranger in a moment of private grooming. Back outside, we clamber into my car just as the sky lets loose and it starts to rain.

"Oh, no, one more thing!" Monica groans.

It turns out that everything that could go wrong at the last minute has gone wrong. The limo company that was supposed to transport Monica and her court burned down just a few days ago. If it hadn't been for Joselito lining up another limo, they would have had to go to the church and then the dance hall in the family car. Then, the elaborate cake (actually three cakes with bridges to a fourth cake with tiny couples lined up on each of those bridges, the quinceañera on top of the center cake) wasn't ready when the woman said it would be ready. So her father had to go get it right when he was supposed to be picking up the girls and their mother, who will still need a ride home when she's done. To top it off, the photographer just phoned in that something has come up, and he can't shoot the party after all.

"How can he do that?" I say, falling in with the drama of the event. I stop short of offering my services, using my husband's digital camera, which I just learned how to operate. I'm beginning to understand. Part of the fun is to be attended to by hired professionals, handlers who constitute a kind of retinue around the young lady so she feels important. I hate to tell Isabella but it's as if there is a textbook: you have to have a limo; you have to have a stylist do your hair; you have to be paparazzied by a photographer and a videographer, who will create the movie of your special birthday; you have to have a court of damas and chambelanes who have learned their dance steps from your choreographer. Later, after the blessing at the church, when her priest asks who I am, Monica pipes up, "She's my author."

We pull up in front of a modest, white clapboard house, a rental it turns out. The Ramoses have the downstairs. An Anglo couple lives upstairs with several little white dogs they are walking down the front steps as we start up. They are so cool in their greetings, I find myself feeling slighted on Monica's behalf. How can people not make a fuss over a pretty girl with a tiara in her hair? But as I find out more about who all have been packed in the Ramoses' apartment this past week (a cousin, his wife, a baby, a toddler, Monica, Silvia, their older brother and parents, and four couples and one escort in the living room practicing dance steps), I can guess where the tension lies. I think of the many years I lived in rentals, at the mercy of neighbors, avoiding whenever possible apartment houses next to day-care centers or rambunctious one-size-fits-all families like the Ramoses who would make it impossible to have a quiet room of my own at home.

Inside, the little kitchen is homey with knickknacks. There's a semblance of order in the living room/dining room; the TV is turned on to a sports program no one is watching. But down the hall it's bedlam in the bedrooms: outfits strewn on beds, makeup cases spilling their contents on chests of drawers, boxes with what look like party favors, shoes and clothes underfoot. The mess looks like a teenager's bedroom except all three bedrooms are this way, even the one in which the cousin's wife is trying to dress her pint-size little boy, Tavito, in a tiny, white tuxedo.

Somewhere Monica finds her dress, her slippers, her long, white satin gloves, and, shedding her old clothes onto the chaotic pile on the floor, she is transformed! She really does look like a princess in her white gown twinkling with sparkles. The poufy floor-length skirt makes it seem as if she's gliding on air as she moves around the house.

But where on earth is her court? They were all supposed to be here by now to be picked up by the limo that is also not yet here!

It's still raining outside, and her mom hasn't called to be picked up at the beauty parlor, and anyway, her dad isn't back yet. Mr. Ramos, a heavyset man about my age in a soiled T-shirt, sweating profusely, came in briefly but had to run out again on another errand. Monica is on the verge of tears—this will totally ruin her makeup! She paces up and down the narrow hall, her scepter/cell phone in hand, trying to summon the principals in this drama that doesn't look like it's going to be pulled off at the last minute.

Now let us praise the famous quinceañera dress

While we are waiting for Monica's court to arrive, let's turn our attention to the single most important aspect of a girl's quinceañera, her dress.

Mami might be worrying about the tablecloths or what to serve with the filet mignon in the burgundy wine sauce; and Papi's worrying about whether to go ahead and shell out a thousand bucks or more for a stretch Hummer limo as his little girl insists on riding into womanhood in a tanklike vehicle that looks like she's going to storm the Bastille, not just become a lady. But the girls I spoke to, every one of them, mentioned the princess dress as one of the biggest reasons to have a quince. Of course, being good Latina girls who don't want to sound shallow and materialistic, they also spoke of the importance of the church ceremony or their abuelita flying in from Guadalajara, or, in Monica's case, her speech dedicating each of her candles. But the detail on which they lavished the most interview time and vocabulary was their really awesome, really beautiful, really expensive dress. (Price was often mentioned, and not price as in "I got such a bargain!" but as in "It cost me $496," down to the last dollar and sometimes cents.)

Nelly in Lawrence, Massachusetts, for example, whose quinceañera I happened upon when I stopped by St. Mary's to check out the church where most girls in the area have the religious part of their service, was downright laconic in a subsequent phone interview. Yes, she had wanted a quinceañera forever. No, her mami never had one. What did her quince mean? She was going from girl to woman, what else? It was obvious Nelly didn't have much to say, but when I asked about her dress, I could feel her voice soften, and the words began to flow. It was white with a lace bodice and trumpet sleeves and a full Cinderella skirt with lots of gathers and lace in the front, and oh yes, how did I know? The sleeves were part of a fitted bolero-type jacket which she could take off, and then the dress turned into a strapless gown with a sweetheart neck! She had bought it in a store after falling in love with it. It had cost $549.95.

If that seems like a lot of money for a party dress, it's a bargain when you compare it to the price of a wedding gown, which is what quinceañeras used to buy before the special-occasion dress companies started making quinceañera dresses. Lisa Chang, daughter of the owner of Mary's Bridal, one of the major specialty dress companies, told me that about twenty years ago, they started to hear back from bridal shops that Hispanic girls were coming in and buying wedding gowns and cutting off the train. So, they said, heck, "you want no train, we'll make you no train." Now they have their very own BELOVING quinceañera collection.

In fact, some girls still buy wedding gowns and have a seamstress cut off the train! Yes, it happens, according to Juana Reyes, who sews almost exclusively for quinceañeras in Lawrence. Juana comes from a long line of seamstresses: her grandmother, her mother, and her aunts were all costureras back in the Dominican Republic. Juana never had a quince herself, nor did anyone in her poor campo. All the more reason why she considers it a waste to buy a wedding gown and then cut off the train. But the alternative is worse. Some quinceañeras who come to her for alterations insist on leaving the train on the white gown. "What do they have to look forward to as brides?" Juana laments.

The average quince dress will cost you anywhere from $250 (the cheapest quote I got from Juana herself, who can make you a dress for that precio if you don't want too many details) to . . . well, you can go into the thousands, especially if you buy that wedding gown and cut off the train. A new national magazine, *Quince Girl,* did a survey of its readers and found the average cost to be $500 to $700. The rule of thumb in a world where there are no rules, and, as Isabella noted, no textbooks on the ritual, is that the dress will represent 5 percent of the total cost of your celebration.

Of course, there are more reasonable alternatives. Many girls who still have ties to their native countries will sometimes buy their dresses there. For a hundred dollars they can have a gown made to order or buy a ready-made one that would cost twice or three times as much here. In Miami, it's popular to rent your dress from the same studio that does your photo shoot. For $800 to $1,000 you can get a rented dress as well as an album of photos shot in the studio and at some other chosen locations. Esthersita Pentón-Nodarse, author of *Sólo para Quinceañeras* and an expert in all things having to do with quinces, says she can find a girl a rented dress for about $100 if that's all she wants to spend. Of course, if the studio doesn't stock the dress you like or you want it in a weird color like avocado, you might end up paying up to a hundred dollars more. The studios Esthersita took me to visit in

Miami had cavernous storerooms packed with hanging gowns. (These are big dresses: they take up a lot of space.)

Occasionally, older, passé fashions are weeded out, dresses with capes (which used to be popular) or with high collars and far too much coverage for the modern girl. When this occurs, these establishments know to call Esthersita, who packs up the old gowns and sends them to Havana along with fans and tiaras so Cuban girls can have their quinces, too. Notwithstanding socialism and the scarcity of all goods on the island, this bourgeois celebration is flourishing. In fact, so popular is this hand-me-down-quince-dress trade that upon the urging of a friend, I briefly considered tracking a dress from Florida to Cuba. But I soon realized it would be a thankless task. No girl wants to be reminded that her quince dress was some other girl's princess gown. Sometimes history is best kept in the past.

In fact, if you rent, there's a staff of seamstresses at these photo studios who will not only alter but also personalize the dress within limits: maybe you want spaghetti straps with little rosettes added onto the top or some embroidery on the white skirt or a sash at the waist in your party's theme colors—nothing that will destroy the dress, for the next girl also needs a blank slate to elaborate her princess fantasy upon. The seamstresses Esthersita and I happened upon were working away in the back rooms of studios, surrounded by racks upon racks of gowns, chatting amiably.

"It's a happy business we are in," Cindi Freeburn of David's Bridal remarked to me in an interview, "dressing women for the milestone moments of their lives." David's Bridal carries a full line of special-occasion dresses, from First Communion dresses to wedding gowns. "We're a perfect fit with the Latina market," Cindi explains. "We start dressing the young Latina girl for her First Communion. If she has a good experience with David's, she's going to come back seven years later for her quinceañera dress. Then, three years later, she'll need a prom dress, and then a few years after that, an older sibling might be getting married and she'll come in for her bridesmaid's dress, and eventually her wedding dress. We've seen the Latina population grow and explode in the last seventeen years and David's Bridal has grown with it. You could say that our two paths are aligned." David's Bridal doesn't make a specific quinceañera dress because the company doesn't want to pigeonhole the Latina girl into a particular type of dress. "She can shop the whole store, bridal gowns, prom gowns, bridesmaid's dresses." That said, there is a certain quince look: a big, poufy, floor-length skirt and a fitted bodice, a princess-ballerina style, which is what the traditional dress most resembles.

The dress transforms the Latina girl into a princess at least for one night. "But it's actually not just a Latina issue," according to María Hinojosa, author, journalist, and TV anchorwoman. "At least in the West, it's part of the popular culture. Little girls want to be princesses. The pretty dress, the love affair with pink." In fact, in many of our old countries, the quinceañera dress was traditionally pink to distinguish the young girl from a bride, who wore white, and the celebration itself was know as "la fiesta rosa." In fact, some diehard traditionalists still insist the dress must be pink. "If she chooses another color, she's not really a quinceañera," Salvador Suriano, a photographer and native from El Salvador who has been shooting quinceañeras in Queens for more than twenty-five years, told me. "It's more American, like a sweet sixteen."

But in the transport to the USA, the color of the dress has become, along with a lot of other things, democratized. According to Esthersita, the changeover to white came about in the sixties, when girls from the exiled Cuban community in Miami would go shopping for their quinceañera dresses in the only places that sold fancy dresses, bridal shops. Along with Mary's Bridal, the other specialty dress companies got wind of this. Morilee, Maggie Sottero, Alfred Angelo, and a company with the unlikely name—for quinceañera dresses—of the House of Wu all now stock quinceañera gowns in every color imaginable, from bridal white to traditional pink to flaming red.

"The bottom line is that the quince dress has to have a fun, girly look," Trina Chartier at the House of Wu summed it up during an interview. In fact, as you page through the thick, glossy catalogs of these dress companies, the way you can tell the quinceañeras from the brides is not only by the tiaras in their hair and their big "throwback" dresses, as Tonya at Needleman's Dress Shop in Burlington, Vermont, described them, but they are all smiling, every one. They are girls who are fun to be with and who want to have fun—the good clean kind of fun. In fact, they seem totally oblivious to their desirability, their budding bosoms, their pretty shoulders, their little waists and poufy backsides. They dimple, they twinkle, they giggle, they smile coquettishly back at you. So different from the demure, pensive brides who refuse to make eye contact or the pouting, sullen chicks in the other special-occasion dress lines who glare back at you as if in challenge, *What you looking at, girl?* Quinceañeras look like happy girls, and a lot of their happiness has to do with the beautiful dresses they are wearing.

Which is why it's surprising to find that in most of the young adult literature about quinceañeras—this being the genre that readily lends itself to this subject—the dress is treated as a big bone of contention. In *Estrella's Quinceañera* by Malín Algería, for instance, the horrible tangerine dress with ruffled rumba-dancer sleeves and way too many gathers is featured on the cover, front center. Below it, the caption reads: "This fifteenth birthday party is headed for disaster."

"I felt like I was drowning in orange sherbet," complains Estrella, the young protagonist who is not looking forward to her quinceañera. But by the end of the novel, Estrella has come around to see the importance of tradition, a change-of-heart plot twist also common in the genre. Looking at herself in the mirror, wearing "the dreaded quinceañera dress," she has to admit, "it truly looked beautiful." Her punk Anglo high school friend, Sheila, delivers the highest compliment she is capable of: "You're like a total rock star."

In *Sister Chicas,* three Latina authors, Lisa Alvarado, Ann Hagman Cardinal, and Jane Alberdeston Coralin, each writing from the voice one of the three main characters, tackle the subject of the quinceañera. Taina is turning fifteen, and her looming quinceañera forms the main plot of the novel. She, too, runs into problems with her mom over her dress. Mami wants "an ugly lace explosion . . . a white Disney horror," which she claims is traditional, nixing "the sweet coral temptation of my fleeting freedom" that Taina wants to wear. But coral is too close to "puta red," which is totally out for a quinceañera, her mami informs Taina. As the final chapter approaches with the culminating celebration, Taina comes up with a great solution. Listen up, all you girls out there who might be finding yourselves in a similar impasse with your mamis. Taina decides to wear the "cake-topper dress to the misa at the Church of the Sacred Heart, and the coral silk moiré for the party at La Reina Borinqueña, following at least one part of some unwritten tradition."

Quinceañera dresses form the backdrop of Diane Gonzales Bertrand's *Sweet Fifteen,* as the protagonist is not Stephanie, the quinceañera, but Rita, a seamstress who makes quinceañera dresses. Rita is downright fierce when it comes to the sanctity of a quinceañera dress. At one point, when Stephanie suggests that she stop making the dresses because they are a lot of trouble, Rita responds:

> "I'd never stop making quince dresses." Rita's tone was firm. "Few places sell them anymore. And those that do try and make them serve double duty as wedding dresses to save money. A quince gown should look like a special dress for a teenager." Realizing that her adamance might be mistaken for anger she paused then stared down at her plate. "I just enjoy making the quinceañera dresses . . ."

Though the young adult literature might be giving the quince dress a bad rap, every girl I talked to had nothing but good things to say about her dress. It might be that these books are written by adult authors who can now look back at their teen years with a sense of irony. An editor recently sent out a call for submissions of stories by older Latinas about their quinces: "As hard as you may have tried to forget that nightmarish quinceañera your parents forced you to have or perhaps you really wanted for ambitious reasons of your own—this anthology will smack you in the face with those white taffeta-tainted memories." Taffeta-tainted memories. That is the voice of experience, looking back at the excesses of our youth which we always want to say were our parents' fault.

But sometimes not having those taffeta memories to blame on our parents creates its own kind of burden. Poet Gwen Zepeda, who grew up in Houston and did not have a quinceañera in 1986, when she turned fifteen, told me during an interview that for at least ten years after her fifteenth birthday she was still sorry about it. Even after she had her first child, she'd put herself to bed counting the fourteen girls who might have been in her court and picturing the big, beautiful dress she would have worn. Carolyn Ramos, a former student now in her thirties, also laments the fact that her mami refused to let her have that luscious excess of a party with its over-the-top dress. "She was too consumed with feminism to see past the historical significance of quinceañeras," which she felt made girls into "marriage (servitude) material." But Carolyn "wanted desperately to be draped in a frosted cup-cake dress lovingly sewed by my abuelita." Instead, she got money in the bank toward the college education that resulted in her going on to law school. A practical American coming-of-age, dollars and sense, sans the dress.

Ah, the dress.

Let us now praise those famous (some would say infamous) quinceañera dresses. The lavish lace concoctions that make you look like a many-tiered wedding cake; the puffy sleeves that might be wings you are growing to fly away into womanhood; the full skirts ("the fuller the better," according to Lisa Chang of Mary's Bridal, "gowns in our BELOVING line have seven layers of tulle in the skirt and a circumference of 210 inches at the bottom"), taffeta torrents with cascading beadwork and organza skirts with scalloped hemlines and side rosette pickups and split-open pep-lum skirts shimmering with embroidery, flounces and ruffles and gathers under which you will wear a hoop or elaborate crino-lines. A kind of chastity device, if you will, which makes sense since virginhood is being celebrated here. In fact, one quince dos-and-don'ts advice column warns girls to keep in mind "whether you'll be able to go to the bathroom by yourself. Can you lift your dress without help? If not, can two people—and your dress—fit into the stall?"

In contrast to the big skirt, the bodice is snug, showing off the young girl's bosom with any number of sweetheart necklines and coy closures, including a corset bodice with "a buttoned-down modesty piece" (so modest, in fact, it's impossible to guess what is being buttoned down and hidden). For the sassy gal, there are plunging V halter tops and strapless gowns and bare backs and corset bodices with crisscross ties that suggest the intimacy of an undergarment. In order to placate Mami and Abuelita, and, God knows, the priest, there are any number of shawls and little bolero jackets and soft shimmering mantillas to bring back old Spain, and demure wraps to give the illusion of coverage, even "detachable trumpet gauntlets," which once the actual party starts you can hurl down as a challenge to anyone who tries to rein you in!

The time has come to dance, dance, dance all night! To help you at this dancing stage of your party some dress companies are now making gowns with detachable skirts, which you can strip off after the formal part of the presentation, and underneath there is a chic miniskirt in which to dance the Macarena or any hip-hop number you want. (Another good compromise if you and your mami disagree on traditional or modern dress.) Some quinceañeras don't bother with a two-in-one dress but instead have several changes of outfits as the night progresses, a kind of trousseau sans the wedding, which fits in with other bridal aspects of the quinceañera.

"About three a.m., I took off the ball gown a seamstress had made me," Liz Bueno, a student at Middlebury College, explained as we paged through her album, "and I changed into a more slutty dress that was easier to dance in."

"Was that okay with your parents?" I wondered.

Liz shrugged, as if to say, who cared? She was a woman now and could (sorta) strut her stuff.

It might as well be a fairy tale

We left Monica wandering the halls of her parents' duplex, wondering if her court would ever show up. Ten, fifteen minutes tick by, which must seem endless when you are a young girl dressed in a princess gown, having to wait on attendants who are supposed to be at your beck and call.

I decide that rather than tail the stressed quinceañera asking questions, I'm going to go sit in the living room out of her way. The TV blares, some baseball game I should probably know about as it's tantamount to disloyalty to be Dominican and not avidly follow the careers of our own. On the wall hang three large portraits, one of Silvia in her graduation cap and black gown, another of Joselito in his air force uniform, and the third of little Monica in her First Communion dress and veil. Presumably, the latter will be updated by one of the quinceañera in her tiara and gown if an alternate photographer can be arranged at the last moment. In front of the couch on a low coffee table are seven ceramic figurines with elaborate dresses and featureless faces. I smile, recognizing them. This bit of Dominican lore I do know about. There was a time when these dolls were very popular back home. People collected them, gave them as gifts. Their trademark oddity is the blank face in contrast to the elaborate gown. But the Ramoses' collection has a further odd touch: the dolls' centers are hollow, revealing butterflies or tiny bells or little birds inside. The nursery rhyme comes to mind: what are little girls made of?

Monica, for all her jitters and faith in fairy tales, is a strong girl with determination and grit, I can see that. She has told me that she wants to be two things, a lawyer and a poet, but will probably end up being a lawyer because, like her mother says, "Monica tiene mucho carácter." Monica knows what she wants and she goes for it. Not only is she on the honor roll, she's also a student leader, well liked by her teachers and peers. Silvia also did well in school, but ever since graduating a year ago, she has been drifting, most recently ending up in Tennessee, babysitting for her cousins, who are now visiting. "Yeah, yeah," she answers vaguely when I encourage her to keep on studying. Silvia used to dance beautifully, but the money for lessons ran out. As did the money for Monica's piano lessons. They are talented girls on the cusp, but they will need that extra push and those added pesos to get them aloft. Their parents are rightly proud of their brains and their beauty, but their futures are iffy. Mr. Ramos, a carpenter, is currently out of work. Mrs. Ramos does not work. I have to do everything in my power not to blurt out, "Then why go to the expense of throwing your daughter a big quinceañera party?" Besides, I already know the answer. This happens only once. Poverty, on the other hand, can last a lifetime.

Monica finds me sitting in the living room and plops herself down on the floor in front of the TV, her dress splayed out around her. "It's all going to turn out, you'll see," I assure her. Since when did I get a crystal ball? I wonder. But then, as if I have entered a magical fairy-tale realm where such rescues can happen, the front door bursts opens and in steps a large blond woman with a flushed face, dressed in a long pink gown and sporting a tall crown and a sizable wand. "Claire!" Monica is on her feet in a second, rushing into the arms of this apparition, who hugs her, then holds her at arm's length, "Oh my god, you look so beautiful!"

"I'm the girls' godmother," the woman introduces herself. I laugh because who else could she be? The meter maid, the limo

driver? "I mean I really am their godmother," she explains, looking me over, no doubt wondering what I've been hired to handle
that I'm going to charge this working-class family's too much for.
Claire is an old, close friend of the Ramos family's and, indeed,
godmother to both Monica and Silvia. "We go way back. I've
known these girls from day one." More than once, it turns out,
Claire has provided support, advice, and, yes, sometimes money
to keep the girls on track.

"They're so lucky to have you," I will say to her before the
evening is out.

I know whereof I speak. You come to this country and those
parental figures who had been guiding you toward adulthood
are suddenly looking to you to show them the way through this
U.S. maze. Or worse, they insist on still leading, and they don't
have a clue where they're going since they're following some old-
country map for a place that only exists anymore in their cora-
zones. You're fourteen, fifteen, feeling torn, feeling lost, feeling
oh so blue, and can only hope that a teacher steps forward, a
neighbor takes a shine to you, or a family friend pulls you aside
and tells you she sees something in you that you can't yet see in
yourself. So tenuous is the line between falling and flying. It might
as well be a fairy tale.

Santería solution

Finally, in the summer of 1964, our fourth year in the United
States, my mother gave up on punishments and threats and
hired a santera to cleanse our house. There had to be some bad
spirits hanging around for her to end up with four strong-willed

daughters challenging her left and right. Olga, the santera, was a Dominican who lived somewhere up in the Bronx, and she came by subway one Saturday to remedy what was going wrong.

One look at us, and I don't think she needed santería powers to know what the problem was. Three teenage daughters and the fourth not far behind entering the America of the sixties: the music, the drugs, free love, women's liberation—a confusing time to be coming of age even if you were a native, and here we had come from a backwater little dictatorship still stuck in the nineteenth century when it came to opinions on what a girl was allowed to be or become.

One look at her, and I felt mortified by this figure I might have respected or at the very least dismissed with no ethnic angst a few years back. But now I was seeing her through American eyes, a creature of excess, a Latin caricature. Olga's face was overly expressive; her white kerchief was tied around her head, bandage style; her eyebrows were plucked and then thinly drawn too high on her forehead; her lips were a garish red—she kept pressing them together, making a mess of her mouth.

Olga unpacked several potions and lit candles and burned herbs, and my sisters and mother and I trailed behind her as she went room to room in the house, uttering incantations. As the procession headed downstairs to the basement, I detoured and went outside. It had to have been summer because that's when my mother's nerves got really frayed with four daughters hanging around the house full-time. The backyard had been recently mown, making it look shorn, smaller, even more forlorn. I lay down on that cut grass, looking up at the sky, feeling desolate, lost. Where did I belong? The old world of the island now seemed claustrophobic, like being home with Mami and Papi all the time. And yet, this new U.S. world was full of strangers who smelled and looked and acted in ways that were so different from ours.

Ways that said our way was low-class and shameful and loud. I mean, if my classmates at school even knew what was going on right now inside our house!

That moment in the backyard, looking up through the limbs of the trees, was definitely one of the low points of my early adolescence. I was fourteen and had no story in my head of who I might become. Tabula rasa, prime candidate for all kinds of trouble. And that's what Olga was warning my mother about as I reentered the house and joined the group around the kitchen table. There was danger lurking. What kind of danger? Danger as in men who were not good for us, danger as in drogas, danger as in the wrong kinds of friends. Mami looked around the table at four sets of eyes being rolled back at her. Tonight, when Papi came home from la oficina, the talk would be about sending us back home to the island—the new threat—to live with our aunts and cousins until we passed through this dangerous period of puberty.

But that didn't happen. My parents did decide to send us away, but not to the D.R. Instead, Mami contacted the headmistress at a boarding school she had attended in Massachusetts for two years. She explained our situation. We had escaped to America. We had just bought a house. We could not afford the full tuition. Would partial scholarships be possible until Papi got on his feet? I don't think she mentioned that her daughters were possessed by demons that were making them undermine her authority. Mami received a cordial reply from Mrs. Crane with application forms for her two oldest girls, the other two were too young. My mother sat my older sister and me down at the kitchen table and told us to write an essay about why we wanted to go to Abbot Academy.

I didn't want to go to Abbot. A fantasy escape to Australia when the world had already been destroyed by fallout was one thing, another thing altogether was being sent away to boarding school. Living with strangers who smelled, looked, and acted different from me, under constant scrutiny with no place to hide. I saw myself being swallowed up by a country that still scared me—its muchness, its power, its cruel blond beauty. My mother's warnings had not gone in one ear and out the other, as she was always accusing. I looked over at my sister, who was busily writing her essay. "You want to go to boarding school?" I asked in disbelief.

My sister gave me that withering look she reserved for what she called my stupid questions. "No, I don't want to go to boarding school! I just want to get out of here."

My fair lady

I did not know that I was about to enter a world of fairy godmothers, smart female teachers who would provide me not with what was lost forever—roots, belongingness, safety—but with a craft in which to sail and a grand narrative of adventure.

Miss Stevenson, especially. Miss Stevenson, whom I tracked down a few years ago, who had married, earned a PhD, raised three children. She was now the head of the English Department at Union College, close to retirement. When I reunited with her, I was surprised at how little this slightly distracted older woman in a dark coat full of dog hair and a refrigerator door full of snapshots of her children held down by magnets reminded me of my mythic Miss Stevenson. But then she threw her head back and laughed that unforgettable, half-taunting, half-reckless Miss Stevenson laugh.

When I first met her at Abbot, Miss Stevenson was a young woman fresh out of college, a wild card in our buttoned-down boarding school. From her table in the dining room came boisterous laughter, girls having fun. Same thing in her classroom. You never knew what Miss Stevenson was going to do.

Once we were studying *Pygmalion* and she was impressing upon us that Eliza's speech was scandalous, and not just because of her Cockney accent. The word "bloody," for example. Did we realize how nasty an expletive that was back in Shaw's polite Victorian society?

Yeah, yeah, we nodded. It was a warm spring day. The tall windows that looked out on the circular driveway were open.

"You don't believe me, do you, ladies?" She mocked us, drawling the syllables in "ladies." Her southern accent always got heavier the more animated she became.

We nodded that we believed her. We'd believe anything Miss Stevenson said. The whole class was in love with her. Some of us broke the rules and snuck out of our dorms at night to hide behind the hedge in front of the faculty house and look up at her light. One time I remember her stopping at the window and looking out. Oh my god, had she seen us? We broke out in giggles.

"Who's out there?" she called.

If a low point of my adolescence was lying on the grass in our backyard in Queens feeling rootless and adrift with some santera talking our mother into sending us back to the island, then a high point would have to have been this moment of looking up from behind the hedge at Miss Stevenson's window and feeling the thrill of being alive now that I had a person whom I wanted to be like.

That day in our *Pygmalion* class, Miss Stevenson called one classmate after another to the board to write the dirtiest word she knew. The first few girls were unsure if she was in earnest. "Damn," they wrote. "Hell."

"Tame, Miss Moore!" Miss Stevenson mocked. "That's the dirtiest word you know, Miss Hoover?" she challenged. "Miss Elmenhurst, would you kindly help Miss Hoover out." The words got dirtier. "That's better," she said grinning. "Much better." Even now, remembering that day, I feel my breath catch. I knew I would die if she called on me! I didn't know enough dirty words in English to save my life much less my pride in front of Miss Stevenson.

The board was soon filled with all the obscenities a bunch of fourteen- and fifteen-year-olds in the mid-sixties in an all-girls boarding school reading *Pygmalion* in English class could come up with. What Miss Stevenson did next still seems inspired. She climbed on top of her desk and called out the words on the board in a half-Cockney, half-southern accent. We looked at one another nervously. She was going to be fired! We bolted out of our chairs and rushed around, closing the windows. Miss Stevenson laughed that wonderful laugh and swore on. When she was done, she very calmly stepped off the desk onto her chair and then the floor. "Well, ladies," she concluded, "do you now understand how nasty a word 'bloody' was back in Shaw's time?"

"Yes, Miss Stevenson!"

Three decades later, I was invited by Miss Stevenson to give a reading at Union College, and afterward a dozen or so guests were having supper over at her house. I told this story and everybody laughed. That sounded just like Ruth! But Miss Stevenson said she didn't remember ever doing such a thing. Did she remember looking out of her faculty apartment window one night and spotting a bunch of girls spying on her? She didn't remember that either. How could she not remember? The faculty house across the street from Draper? The classroom in the round tower that gave onto the circular drive?

Finally, I let it go. (*This is getting annoying,* the young quinceañera had said about my insistent questions.) But I was troubled. Had I made up my mythic Miss Stevenson because I needed her agency so much in my life? Or perhaps I had misunderstood the way fairy godmothers work? They make only a brief appearance—so you can internalize them—before they disappear into their own ordinary lives.

One-(very small)-size-fits-all script

My first year at Abbot did for me what Isabella Martínez Wall's year of going to quinceañeras and having her own quinceañera did for her. It gave me a new community to belong to, a narrative I could follow into adulthood. Instead of a family and community rallying around the quinceañera's transformation into a woman, planning and preparing sometimes for a year for that symbolic pageant marking her passage, I had a community of classmates and female teachers and coaches and housemothers honing my skills, encouraging my talents, preparing me for being what Isabella Martínez Wall would call "queen of my own life."

Incidentally, I was also turning from fourteen to fifteen, and, needless to say, away at a school where we were the only Latinas (the closest thing to us was a German girl whose parents lived in Guatemala and an American girl whose father was posted in Venezuela), I did not have a quinceañera. Nor was much made of my fifteenth birthday: a cake in the dorm, a phone call from my parents, a card with a check for twenty-five dollars. My older sister had already gotten my mother's ring, and away at school I could shave my legs and wear makeup without asking anyone for permission.

But although some psychological elements of the American quinceañera and my first Abbot year were the same—a community grooming a young lady for her entry into womanhood—the content of that grooming was significantly different. We Abbot girls were encouraged to develop our minds, not leave our brains parked at the door of our gender. In fact, the plaque at the front gate encouraged us to ENTER INTO UNDERSTANDING, SO YOU MAY GO FORTH TO NOBLER LIVING. Nobler living! True, many of my Abbot classmates would eventually marry and have children (this was, after all, the mid-sixties), but it was assumed we would all go to college first. (Out of a class of seventy-eight girls, only one, my roommate, did not go to college, but married her longtime boy-friend instead.) And since many of our teachers were unmarried women, making their own way in the world, the subliminal mes-sage was clear: we were to be smart, resourceful, independent women.

This new narrative of female possibility was groundbreaking and bracing even for my American classmates. "Although Colum-bus and Cabot never heard of Abbot," one of our school songs began. A good thing, too. Those old-world explorers would not have approved of young women taking over the helm of their journey through life and discovering their own new worlds.

In contrast, the typical quinceañera enacts a traditional narra-tive that is, let's face it, a one-(very small)-size-fits-all script corset-ing a full-bodied female life. The young Latina is dressed up in finery not unlike a bride, her father is changing her shoes, claim-ing that first waltz, then passing her on to a brother or uncle or grandfather, until finally she ends up in the arms of her escort to a round of applause. The quinceañera is like a rehearsal wedding without a groom, and it sends a clear message to the Latina girl: we expect you to get married, have children, devote yourself to your family. It's no wonder that girls end up getting pregnant soon after celebrating their quinces. Jaider Sánchez, a hairdresser and dance coach for quinceañeras in Denver, mentioned in a re-cent interview that out of seven quinceañeras he instructed in 2005, four have already invited them to their baby showers.

And so, although it gives her a momentary illusion of power (the princess rhetoric, the celebration of her sexual power, her youth, her beauty), in fact, the ritual enacts an old paradigm of the patriarchy increasingly (in the USA) pumped up by a greedy market. In a fascinating book titled *Emerging from the Chrysalis: Studies in Rituals of Women's Initiations,* Bruce Lincoln, who teaches at the University of Chicago Divinity School, amplifies Arnold van Gennep's classic theory about rites of passage as they apply to females. According to van Gennep, who coined the term, rites of passage are ceremonies within cultures that enable an individual to pass from one well-defined role to another. Male initiation rites of passage involve the stripping, testing, and reintegration of the young man into the sociopolitical adult society.

But what Bruce Lincoln found was that female initiations follow a different pattern: the girl is decked in ceremonial finery, often layer on layer is piled on her, a magnification that confers on her cosmic status and participation in a mythic drama. "Rituals of women's initiation claim to transform a girl into a woman, [they] claim to renew society by providing it with a new productive member." During the ceremonies, the initiant is "regarded as having become a deity, a culture heroine, the link between past and future." So far so good, but Bruce Lincoln goes on to suggest that this mythic power is a substitution for actual power, a pie in the sky versus options and opportunities in the here and now:

> The strategy of women's initiation is to lead a woman's life . . . away from the sociopolitical arena, introducing her to the real or imagined splendors of the cosmos instead. To put it in different terms, women's initiation offers a religious compensation for a sociopolitical deprivation. Or to put it differently still, it is an opiate for an oppressed class . . .

Cosmic claims notwithstanding, the desired result of the ritual is to make a girl ready and willing to assume the traditional place of a woman as defined within a given culture. . . . The strategy is that of placing women on a pedestal, carried to its outermost possibilities: speak of her as a goddess to make of her a drudge.

Although the young quinceañera is being crowned queen, the ritual doesn't change anything. It merely casts its net of glittering meaning over what might be a dismal situation: "It is rare that a ritual can alter the basic ways in which a society is organized," Bruce Lincoln concludes. "Nor do rituals shape the way in which people live as much as they shape the way people understand the lives they would lead in any event."

Even if she is at the bottom of the American heap, if the young Latina girl can believe the fantasy—that her condition is temporary, that she is a Cinderella waiting for that fairy godmother or husband to endow her with their power—then she can bear the burden of her disadvantage. And as years go by, and the probability of her dream becoming true lessens, she can at least pass on the story to her daughter.

Maybe that is why I get tearful at quinceañeras. I'm watching the next generation be tamed into a narrative my generation fought so hard to change. Why I feel like a snake in the garden, because here I sit in their living rooms or in their rented halls, eating their catered food, celebrating with la familia, and I am thinking, Why spend all this money enacting a fantasy that the hard numbers out there say is not going to come true?

❧

Quinceañera expo

At the Quinceañera Expo in the Airport Convention Center in San Antonio, little girls are walking around with tiaras in their hair, oohing and ahing at the fancy dresses, the pink balloons, the wedding-cake-size cakes, the last dolls encased in plastic, the fluffy pillows with straps for securing the heels in case the page trips as he bears them to the altar to be blessed by the priest.

At a cordoned-off area at the rear of the hall, Victoria Acosta, a fourteen-year-old local pop sensation, is singing into a microphone as she dances and gestures with her free hand. "Crazy, crazy, crazy, I think the world's gone crazy!" Her next song, "Once Upon a Time," is dedicated to "all of you out there who have had your hearts broken." "All of you out there" is a semicircle of pudgy preteens sitting on the floor, mesmerized by the slender, glamorous Victoria with her long mascara'd lashes, her glittery eye shadow, her slinky black outfit and sparkly silver tie. "You bet I'm going to have a quince," she tells me during a break between songs, although I don't see why. She seems to have already made her passage into womanhood quite successfully.

There isn't a male shopper in sight. In fact, the only men around are manning booths or working the floor:

a couple of boy models, one in a white tuxedo with a pale pink vest, the other in a white suit with a yellow vest;

a grown man in a military uniform, a popular escort outfit with some girls, he tells me;

a dj in a cowboy hat who plays loud music while his sidekick, a skinny boy, hands out flyers;

Seve, the clown (who come to think of it might be female
    under all that face paint and bulbous, attached nose);

Dale of Awesome Ice Designs (for $350 you can have the
    "Fire & Ice Sculpture" with the quinceañera's picture
    embedded in a central medallion of ice);

Ronny of VIP Chocolate Fountains, whose wife, Joanne,
    does most of the talking. (Did you know that you can
    run chili con queso through the fountains for a Mexi-
    can theme at your daughter's quinceañera? The young
    people still prefer chocolate, as you can imagine);

and Tony Guerrero, the owner of Balloons Over San Antonio
    ("We Blow for u").

Add the two photographers at Tilde (Photography, Invitations, Videography), Mr. Acosta (Victoria's manager-dad), the
guy with a Starbucks urn strapped to his back, and Manuel Villa-
mil at the Primerica Financial Services booth—and that makes
for just over a dozen men in a crowd of about three hundred
women of all ages here to shop for some member of their family's quinceañera. The hall is so girl-packed that the discreetly cur-
tained BABY CHANGING/NURSING booth seems extraneous. You
could breast-feed your baby out in the open and still be within the
strict bounds of modesty, like peeing without shutting your stall
door in the ladies' room because everyone inside except the little
toddler in Mommy's arms is female.

I feel as if I've wandered into the back room where the female-
ness of the next generation of Latinas is being manufactured,
displayed, and sold. A throwback vision, to be sure. Lots of pink-
lacey-princessy-glittery-glitzy stuff. One little girl wheels a large
última muñeca around while her mother follows, carting the
baby sister, who has ceded her stroller to a doll bigger than she is.
"How beautiful!" I bend down to admire the little girl's proud

cargo. "Is that for your quince?" The little girl looks pleadingly toward her mom. "It's her cousin's," the mom says, gesturing with her head toward a chunky teenager carting a large shopping bag and lolling at Joanne and Ronny's booth, scooping her tooth-pick of cake into the chocolate fountain. The little girl looks for-lorn. "I'm sure you'll have a last doll, too, when you have your quince," I console her. She gives me a weak smile in return. Why on earth am I encouraging her?

Crazy, crazy, crazy, I think the world's gone crazy.

It's not that. It's that after an hour roaming up and down the aisles, I fall in with the spirit of the expo. There is a contagious, evangelical air to the whole thing that sweeps you up and makes you want to be part of the almost religious fervor that surrounds this celebration. I half expect to find Isabella Martínez Wall here, addressing a crowd of wide-eyed teens.

In fact, my guide, Priscilla Mora, reminds me of Isabella. Both women share a crusading enthusiasm for a tradition they believe is one of the best things going for Latina womanhood. Plump and pretty with the sunny face of someone perennially in a good mood, Priscilla has organized six of these expos, and even though some have not been as well attended as she would have liked, her faith is undimmed. When not organizing these expos, she is a quinceañera planner, an author of the *Quinceañera Guide and Handbook,* and most of all a passionate promoter of the tradition. She actually thought up this business at a workshop where par-ticipants had to write down their dreams on little pieces of paper. Then they all put their pieces of paper in a fire and let their dreams go up to God. This isn't just a business, Priscilla explains, it's a calling, part of God's plan for her.

It's from Priscilla that I first hear that when the quinceañera makes her vow in the church, "it's about chastity. You're promis-ing God that you're not going to have sex till you're back at the altar, getting married. That's why it's important that these girls learn all about the meaning," Priscilla insists. Otherwise, the quinceañera "is nothing but a party."

Priscilla's missionary zeal seems to be shared by many of the providers, who tell inspirational stories of why they got involved in quinces. Take Tony Guerrero of Balloons Over San Antonio. Tony grew up real poor in a family of four boys and four girls. ("Are you kidding?" he replies when I ask if the girls had quinceañeras.) A few years ago, Tony gave up his office job to do this because "I just wanted the opportunity to give back something to my community." He loves seeing people having fun, being happy, and hey, if nothing else, "I got myself another entry once I go over to the other side." "Another" because he already has a great-aunt over there. "She promised me she was going to have a spot waiting for me." Ruby of Great Expectations (a photography studio) thinks it's "a privilege" to share this special day with a girl. "I love the idea of rededicating your life to the Lord." (Echoes of Priscilla.) Curiously, the nuns' booth next to Ruby's is empty. "They told me they were coming." Priscilla looks momentarily nonplussed. But her sunny personality bounces back. "Maybe they'll be by later after Mass." This is Sunday, after all. The sisters, it turns out, are the Missionary Catechists of Divine Providence, the first and only religious order of Mexican American women founded in the United States. Their focus on the quinceañera is part of their larger mission as "evangelizadoras del barrio and transmitters of a rich Mexican American faith to the universal Church."

The only heavy hitter at the expo is Sunita Trevino, who was born in Bombay but is married to a Hispanic. At her seminar on financing a quinceañera, Sunita gives us the opposite of the hard sell: the watch-your-financial-back-as-a-minority-woman talk that has me sitting at the edge of my chair. As she talks, Sunita paces up and down the raised platform stage like a lion trapped in a too-small cage.

Sunita works for Primerica Financial Services, but her training is in clinical psychology, which she ends up using a lot as she counsels families about their finances. "I'll tell you," she tells the audience of about a dozen, mostly grandmothers, as this is the only area of the whole hall where there are chairs to sit down, "quinceañeras are high-stress times." A lot of couples come to see her for extra sessions. But the majority of Sunita's clients are single women who are in financial trouble. They don't budget. They overspend. They get into debt. She knows women in their seventies still paying off second mortgages they took out for their daughter's quinceañera. She finds this devastating.

"Nobody sits down to talk to us women! We are playing a money game but no one taught us the rules!" Sunita's own mother came from Bombay to America, thinking her husband would always be there to take care of her, and then her parents separated, and her mother was lost. She had no idea how to take care of herself. Sunita doesn't want to see this happen to any woman. We women are sinking into a hole of debt and the quinceañera is often where we get in over our heads.

Her recommendation to all of us sitting in the audience: pay cash. "If you budget eighteen hundred dollars for flowers, and what you pick amounts to double that, don't do it. DON'T DO IT! Stay within your budget. A lot of women get in trouble at the last minute. They think, oh, I'll go ahead, just this once."

If you end up borrowing money, "please," Sunita pleads with us, "read the terms, read them carefully. What the big print giveth, the small print taketh away. Educate yourselves! Don't think banks and savings accounts are there to do you a favor. Okay, let's see, who can tell me what banks do with your money?" she asks.

None of us grown women in the audience would dare hazard a guess. But a young girl about eleven years old raises her hand and says proudly, "They save it for you."

Sunita shakes her head fondly. "Out of the mouths of babes." She sighs. Nobody laughs. Nobody seems to get the biblical reference that Sunita is misusing anyway. Out of the mouths of babes usually the truth comes. But this young girl is headed for that sinkhole of debt unless Sunita can steer her away from the dangers of borrowing. "No, honey, that's not what they do. They use your money to make money."

The girl sits back in her chair, a chastened, embarrassed expression on her face. Her tiara glints as Sunita explains to her that what she just said is what most people think. But that's why Sunita is here today. To tell us the truth no one else is going to tell us. To get us thinking about these things. "Two hundred fifty families declare bankruptcy every hour of every day in the USA. I know a seventy-nine-year-old retired guy who is now bagging groceries. People don't plan to fail," Sunita explains. "They fail to plan. So, get mad. Get mad and learn the rules."

The girl squirms in her chair, as do the rest of us. After all, we came here in a party mood, not to feel that at the end of our adult lives we will end up as bag ladies, wishing we hadn't started down the road of debt with our own or our daughters' quinceañeras.

Throwing the house out the window

So, how much does a quinceañera cost? You ask any of the party planners and they'll tell you the same thing—anywhere from a hundred bucks for a cookout in the backyard and a stereo booming music for the young lady and her friends to fifty grand

and up in a hall with a party planner, a limo, dinner for a hundred or more.

Everyone talks about this range, but after interviewing dozens of quinceañeras and talking to as many party planners, events providers, choreographers, caterers, I have to conclude that the cookout quinceañeras are becoming the exception. In the past, perhaps they were the rule. In the old countries, of course. In small homogenous pockets—a border town in Texas, a barrio composed solely of Central Americans; in other words, a group still largely out of the mainstream loop, perhaps. But now, as one quinceañera remarked, "If I had to be that cheap I just wouldn't have one. What for?" It is in the nature of the beast to be a splurge, an extravaganza. More than one person describing a recent quinceañera used the Spanish expression for an over-the-top expense: *throwing the house out the window.* They threw the house out the window for that girl's quinceañera.

They threw the house out the window. In a country where the rate of poverty is growing (12.7 percent of U.S. citizens were living below the poverty line in 2004, up from 11.3 percent in 2000), with Latinos forming a sizeable portion of those impoverished numbers (21.9 percent of the Hispanic population was living below the poverty line in 2004 according to a U.S. census survey). Sunita, it turns out, was not exaggerating.

They threw the house they probably didn't own out the window.

Monica's quinceañera was actually quite modest if her estimate of "maybe three thousand dollars" is correct. Why don't I have an exact number? Let me just come right out and say that talking to my people about money is not easy. Maybe if I were an Americana reporter with a stenographic notebook and only a sprinkling of classroom Spanish, I could get away with asking the parents how much they paid for the party. But I'm a Latina. I know the rules. They know I know the rules. To ask my host for the price tag of the fiesta would be una falta de vergüenza. And so, I learned any number of discreet ways to approach the topic. Aproximadamente, how much does a quinceañera cost in your experience? If someone were to throw a party not unlike this one, how much would that quinceañera cost them?

The one person I could openly ask this question turned out to be the quinceañera herself. But though fifteen-year-old girls are really good at knowing how much their dress or makeup session cost, they're not so good at knowing the charges for halls, or what it costs to have beef Wellington instead of Swedish meatballs for a hundred people, or what additional charge was made for the linen napkins and tablecloths or the chairs draped in white covers and tied with satin bows, which seem to be de rigueur for anything but the cheapest quinceañera. Fifteen-year-old girls like to throw out huge numbers to impress their friends, but they are not so good at addition—that is, if they paid $250 for a dress, and $250 for the limo, and the hall with a catered meal was $2,500 for one hundred people, not counting the cake made up of four cakes, which was no less than $300, and let's throw in another $100 to $200 for sessions at the beauty parlor, and at least $300 for the photographer and pictures, and because things always come up at the last minute and Mami definitely needs a new dress herself and Papi will probably have to rent a tux and some family members will need help with travel costs, another $500 to $1,000 more—anyhow, I've gone way over the low-end figure of $3,000 that Monica Ramos with uncharacteristic teenage understatement calculated.

And her father was not working.

They threw the rented apartment out the window. Why not? It's not theirs to keep anyhow, just as this American dream isn't as easy to achieve as it seems, so why not live it up, give your little girl a party she won't forget, enjoy the only thing you really have, tonight's good time, before the bills start rolling in.

When Abuelita is no longer a resource

Will Cain is president and founder of *Quince Girl,* a new national magazine targeting the more than four hundred thousand Latinas in the United States who turn fifteen every year. Early in 2006, the magazine sent out a survey asking its readers how much they had spent or were planning to spend on their quinces. The resulting average was $5,000.

I confess to Will that I find that average low given the figures events planners and quinceañeras and their families have been quoting me. I'm thinking of Idalia's quinceañera, which cost her affluent Dominican family $80,000, not surprising given a guest list of more than five hundred and a fully choreographed performance by her court of twenty-eight couples (double the usual number so as not to leave out any friends or cousins) with special effects to rival a Broadway show and mermaid dresses for the girls designed by Leonel Lirio, renowned for Miss Universe Amelia Vega's gown. Granted that's the top end of the Q-scale, but the low end is rising. In Miami, Sofía's dad apologetically confessed that he was "only" spending about $12,000 on his daughter's quince, though his wife corrected him by appending, "Twelve thousand dollars not counting all the food and goodies we fed twenty-eight kids for three months of rehearsals."

"You have to remember that $5,000 takes into account the full spectrum," Will Cain reminds me about the *Quince Girl* average.

"It includes the girl who is spending $25,000 with the one who might spend $1,000. The point is that even working-class folks who don't have a whole lot of purchasing power are going to devote a significant portion of their resources to this one tradition. It cuts across a wide range of strata."

Will himself did the numbers before he decided to launch his magazine. The Latino population is exploding, and it is mostly a young population. "I don't have to tell you about the demographics," Will tells me. "One out of every five teens is Hispanic. And that population is growing at the rate of 30 percent, while the non-Hispanic population rate is just 8 percent."

I'm trying to follow what Will is saying, but the question that keeps tugging at my curiosity is not about Hispanic demographics but about Will himself. Will Cain does not sound even close to a Hispanic name. How did "your run-of-the-mill white boy," as he describes himself when I ask him about his background, end up founding a magazine for young Latinas celebrating their quinceañeras?

Will, who is all of thirty-one—just over twice a quinceañera's age—grew up in Texas surrounded by Mexican Americans and has always been interested in the Hispanic culture. He was also interested in media. So, he decided to put the two things together and came up with the idea of *Quince Girl*. Though it's a shrewd economic decision, Will believes he's also providing an important service for Hispanics in this country.

"The Hispanic community is this very fractured community," he explains. "You have your Mexican Americans and your Puerto Ricans and your Cuban Americans. And the only thing that ties all these separate nationalities together—no, it's not Spanish," he says, anticipating what I might think, "in fact, many in the second and third generation don't even speak Spanish. What ties them together, the one single tie that binds all these cultures . . ."

As he drumrolls toward his conclusion, I'm thinking that Will Cain learned something from growing up surrounded by a Hispanic community: a sense of drama.

". . . is this tradition celebrated across the whole diverse group: the quinceañera. I mean, it is big! And the rest of America is starting to pay attention to it."

"Amen," I say. I'm writing a whole book about it.

As if he can hear my mind thinking, Will adds, "We would not be having this conversation right now if this were not so."

What Will realized was that there was no magazine out there that these girls could consult about the tradition and trends and fashions. "Girls were in chat rooms asking each other about the ceremony, what to do. It used to be you could learn these things from your grandmother . . ." But with immigration and the amount of mobility in this country, la abuelita is not always a resource. Plus it's a different world from the one she grew up in. A different budget. Five thousand dollars is probably more than the grandparents earned in a year back in their home countries.

Does he think the tradition is becoming more popular here?

"Well." Will hesitates. He is rightly cautious about delivering opinions beyond what the numbers can tell him. "The quince tradition has always been important, but there's this retroculturation going on right now—"

"Retroculturation?" This is the first I've heard of the term.

"It's a pattern that's been happening with the Hispanic community," Will goes on to explain. "First generation comes to the United States, and they push to assimilate. They adopt the American culture and norms. Second generation, they want to be all-American. Many don't even speak Spanish. They aren't that familiar with the culture. By the third generation, they're born and bred here, but they have this special something that makes them unique, their Hispanic culture. They want to learn Spanish—many, in fact, speak more Spanish than the second generation. They make a concerted effort to hold on to their traditions, to establish cultural ties with their past."

Will quotes a study on Hispanic teens "just released today" by the Cheskin Group, an international consulting and marketing firm that has done a great deal of research on Hispanics. The study confirms Will's point that the up-and-coming generation of Hispanic teens is "predominantly bilingual and bicultural," celebrating its ethnic identity and combining it with mainstream teen culture. "They live on MySpace.com and shop at Abercrombie, but they listen to Spanish radio and embrace diversity," a summary of the study reads. Most important for businesses that are considering purchasing the full report with its $5,850 price tag—the cost of your average quinceañera—is that Hispanic teens are

> a bellwether for one of the most important trends shaping the future of the United States—the growth of the US Hispanic population. Clearly, the future is theirs and they know it.

The future is ours and we know it. Meanwhile the present needs to be lived through and paid for.

The difference between boys and girls

How did the quinceañera get to be so expensive? Even the *Quince Girl* average of five thousand dollars is a lot of money to blow on a birthday party.

Kern's Nectar, which has developed a niche market of "untraditional" juices (guava, papaya, mango) popular among Latinos, sponsors a yearly Dulce Quinceañera Sweepstakes: "Fifteen lucky Quinceañeras will be awarded $1,000 each plus a year's supply of Kern's Nectars; the grand prize winner selected at random from this group takes home $15,000."

Why did Kern's Nectar single out this one tradition? "Next to marriage, a quinceañera is perhaps the most meaningful moment in a young woman's life," the press announcement reads. Given such claims, perhaps five thousand dollars is not a lot to spend on a girl's coming-of-age.

I decide to ask the girls themselves about such claims.

In the wood-paneled faculty lounge at Lawrence High School I speak with a gathering of a dozen girls who have volunteered to be interviewed about the tradition. Light streams down from a magnificent stained-glass window, giving the room the hallowed feel of a chapel. At first glance, the robed scholar portrayed in the window could be Aristotle or Plato, but on closer inspection it turns out to be a woman. With one hand clutching a book, the other lifted, palm out, she seems to be setting the example of telling the truth, the whole truth, and nothing but, which is precisely what I am after. Later I find out that this testifying woman is Emily Greene Weatherbee, the first female principal of the high school, in the 1880s.

A century and a quarter later, the room fills with the likes of students that Miss Emily could never have imagined. The young Latinas present are mostly of Dominican and Puerto Rican descent, though one junior varsity softball player in sweatpants and sweatshirt whom it's a stretch to imagine in the girly-girl getup of a quinceañera is of Ecuadorian parentage. Except for one girl who feels "really gypped" that she didn't have one (her mother said the expense was too high), the other eleven girls have all had or will be having quinceañeras before the year is out. A few days before my visit they were reminded to bring their albums along to school. They file in, lugging large pink or white wedding-type albums of what amounts to extensive photo shoots. A few of the empty-handed girls confess they left their albums at home so as not to have to haul such a heavy weight around all day.

After paging through several of these albums, I ask the girls if they consider their quinceañeras as important as their eventual marriages. "I mean if you get married," I add. I do not want to be pushing any assumptions on their life stories.

"That's the thing," Soraya pipes up. Hers is among the largest albums, borne in by her brother, who has carted it around all day for her. "You don't ever know if you're going to get married. I mean you hope you will, but that's not for sure. But you are going to turn fifteen no matter what." The other girls agree.

But if it's just about turning fifteen, boys turn fifteen, too. Why not give them a quinceañera?

"Boys don't need a quinceañera," Madeline, who left her heavy album at home, explains. "Boys are born men but girls turn into women."

I have pondered that statement many times in the last year. The comment highlights that very deep, heavily guarded (at least traditionally) divide in a young Latina's life when she goes from niña to señorita and becomes sexualized. In her memoir, *Silent Dancing: A Partial Remembrance of a Puerto Rican Childhood,* Judith Ortiz Cofer describes how when she became una señorita, she was watched closely as if she "carried some kind of time-bomb in [my] body that might go off any minute . . . Somehow my body with its new contours and new biological powers had changed everything: half the world had now become a threat, or felt threatened by its potential for disaster."

"We never touch the girls," more than one male photographer told me when I interviewed them about the very popular photo shoots in Miami. The full package features young quinceañeras in a variety of provocative poses and outfits, including teensy bikinis. "We tell the mothers, 'Mami, there's a little masita that needs tucking in.' We let the mothers do it." Why was I being assured of this sexual delicacy over and over? Girls hitherto blithely living inside children's bodies turn into women with sexy, enticing cuerpos, and suddenly, it's open season. Meanwhile, boys, born men, who have been taught since day one to prove themselves as healthy machos, are going to prey on them.

When I make these observations to the Lawrence group, the roomful of young girls erupts into excited giggles. Obviously, I'm onto something.

All the girls admit that once they started developing, their parents, especially their papis, were like, *Who are you going out with? Who was that that just called? Whose parents will be there?*

These girls are on the receiving end of the ill effects of machismo, no arguing with that. But what of those poor boys having to perform from day one, if Madeline is to be believed? Often at quinceañeras, I'd spot some little tyke in a teensy tuxedo pushed and prodded to pick up some girl at a dance or given a shot of rum and encouraged to strut around. Contrary to how it's often described, machismo oppresses not just the girls but also the boys. And yet, understandably, would you want your pubescent daughter to be in the company of a grown version of this little macho, unsupervised?

"The quinceañera is the sanctioned way that a nice family says, okay, now my daughter may receive male attention," Gloria González, a Spanish professor at Middlebury College, explains to me about her experience growing up in Guadalajara, Mexico. "We are permitting this and we are monitoring it." That *is* a big moment. In fact, in his song "De Niña a Mujer," which is arguably *the* quinceañera anthem of all time, Julio Iglesias bewails how as a father he has been anticipating this moment when his little girl disappears forever inside a woman. The lament goes on for six pained stanzas. The song makes a daughter's growing up sound like something that's going to break her father's heart.

If so, then why celebrate this loss?

Enter the mothers.

If the father is losing his little girl, the mother is gaining a potential girlfriend. More than one girl in the Lawrence group mentions—and when she does the others agree—that planning their quinceañeras really brought them and their moms close together. "We were deciding about what dress and what decorations and addressing all the invitations. I'd say that I was spending most of my time when I wasn't in school with my mom," Soraya recalls about the months of preparations. "We were already close, but we got even closer."

Even if the ceremony itself focuses on the father-daughter transaction (he changes her flat shoes to heels, he dances her first grown-up dance in public with her), the months of preparations are intense mother-daughter time. Inevitably, this causes fights and disagreements, but even those moments offer opportunities for negotiation and bonding. And it's not just mothers and daughters, but the extended familia of tías, abuelitas, primas who often get involved. Sofía's mom in Miami, Consuelo, explained how in deciding each detail of her daughter's quinceañera her mother, her sisters, and Sofía's girl cousins would all vote. "We'd go into a store and try on dresses or pick out decorations and the whole gang would be giving their opinions." As her mom recounted how special it had been for her to share this experience with her only daughter, Sofía, who had been sitting quietly beside her, began to cry.

"Are you okay?" her father, who had come along for the interview, asked from the other end of the couch. "What's wrong?"

Consuelo, who had been distracted talking to me, turned to
her daughter. In profile they were time-lapsed copies of each
other. Consuelo understood. Tears filled her own eyes as she
reached over and the two women joined hands like little girls
who were going to be best friends for life.

Remote control

Another factor that has upped the price tag of this traditional
celebration is that tricky word "traditional."

Más católico que el Papa, goes a Dominican saying, more Catholic than the pope. Our exported tradiciones mix and combine
with those of other Latin American and Caribbean countries
stateside and become more elaborate, more expensive, more traditional than they ever were back home.

In fact, to have a full-blown traditional quinceañera in our
Pan-Hispanic United States is to have adopted every other Latino
group's little traditions and then some. So that now, Cuban quinceañeras in Miami are hiring Mexican mariachis to sing the traditional "Las Mañanitas." The full court of fourteen damas and
chambelanes, "each couple representing a year of the quinceañera's life," a mostly Mexican practice, is now a traditional must.
As is the changing of the shoes to heels, which seems to originally have been a Puerto Rican embellishment. From the Puerto
Ricans as well, though some say from the Mexicans, came the
tradition of la última muñeca, a "last doll" dressed exactly like the
quinceañera, which the girl cradles to symbolize the "end of her
childhood" or "the child that she herself will be having in the not-

too-distant future" (both explanations given to me by different events planners). The quinceañera might keep this last doll as a keepsake or give it away to a younger member of the family. In one celebration, perhaps inspired by the wedding bouquet, the quinceañera threw her last doll over her shoulder to be caught by a screaming group of little girls, anticipating their own future quinceañeras.

This symbol of bygone childhood is also mirrored in a Central American or Puerto Rican custom (I've heard both) of having a very little girl dress up in a minuscule version of the quinceañera's dress and be "the symbol of innocence." Sometimes she is accompanied by a little escort, though the tradition has now been further elaborated so that "the symbol of innocence" as well as a little prince and princess (slightly older) are part of a full traditional court.

There is also always some sort of photo session to commemorate the event. This is not a custom exclusive to quinceañeras. In our old countries every important life event is marked by a photograph. Your First Communion photo, your quince photo, your graduation photo, your wedding photo. Even in my husband's old German-Nebraskan family, there were the formal portraits shot in a studio, the principals in dress clothes, hair combed and tamped down: a wedding, a christening, a son shipping off to war. Of course, now there are whole albums of the young lady in different outfits, in different locations, a practice that seems to have started with the Cuban community in Miami, where girls sometimes just have the photo shoot and forego the party. Many girls also have videos made, recounting their lives since birth, with still shots and footage of themselves at different ages and credits rolling as if this were a real movie with the quinceañera playing the lead and her parents starring as "padre" and "madre" and Julio Iglesias's "De Niña a Mujer" as the score, of course.

Clearly, the old-country portrait tradition has arrived stateside and, as one Cuban friend put it, "taken steroids."

The tradition of crowning the young girl is often ascribed to the Mexicans, who seem to be the group that has most ritualized the ceremony. But here in America, every quinceañera gets her tiara. The bouquet the quinceañera carries to put at the Virgin Mary's statue at the Mass is also part of the Mexican and Central American tradition, as is the Mass, which our more hedonistic Caribbean party-cultures dispensed with back home. But now the Mass and the Virgin's bouquet have become part of our Dominican and Puerto Rican and Cuban "tradition" in the United States.

One economically sensible and emotionally gratifying tradition that has not been picked up by other Hispanic groups is the Mexican custom of sponsorships by madrinas and padrinos. In a Mexican quince, every aspect of the fiesta from the cake to the dj has a sponsor, which spreads the cost of the celebration around. It is also a touching symbol of the emotional, spiritual, as well as financial investment of a whole community in this young person. Why aren't others adopting this custom?

"It's a point of pride not to go begging for your party," my Cuban friend Carmel confided. But in fact, a lot of informal sponsorships are going on. The grandmother who buys the quinceañera's earrings and necklace, the brother who gives her the birthday gift of paying for the limo, the sister who contributes to the dress. Still, when the twenty or more names of sponsors are read out in a Mexican-American quinceañera, there is a sense of public participation that is not lost on the young lady. "Everybody I knew contributed something," Verónica Fajardo remembers about her quinceañera fifteen years ago. "I felt like I received so many bendiciones, my whole community made it happen!" In actual fact, Verónica's family is from Nicaragua, but she grew up in a Mexican American neighborhood in Los Angeles, so though sponsorships were not part of the custom back home, by the time her quince came around, her family had adopted that tradition.

Sometimes these cultural borrowings are not even coming from fellow Latinos. The tradition of lighting and dedicating candles, for example, seems to have been lifted from the Bar and Bat Mitzvah. In fact many critics see the quinceañera as going the same route as the Jewish celebration. Rabbi Jeffrey Salkin, author of *Putting God on the Guest List: How to Reclaim the Spiritual Meaning of Your Child's Bar or Bat Mitzvah,* compares this moment in time for the Hispanic community to the early 1960s for the Jewish community, when the Bar and Bat Mitzvah ceremonies became increasingly secular and extravagant. "These rites of passage are a way for a minority group to demonstrate that they have succeeded in America."

But given the statistics, our Hispanic community cannot yet lay claim to such wholesale success. For many, the quinceañera becomes an extravaganza that, as Sunita warned, puts the family further into the hole. Marie Arana of the *Washington Post* shared with me stories of visiting migrant camps in the Maryland and Virginia countryside where families with almost nothing would put out hundreds of dollars to throw their girls' quinceañeras. Perhaps these are the cookout parties everybody talks about, the ones that are under the radar because they are taking place in segregated, often undocumented populations? If you do the numbers, several hundred dollars for a migrant worker with no citizenship or papers or cushion of savings might as well be several thousand for a working-class family that owns a car and has access to unemployment benefits and credit cards.

"Today, it's all about supersizing," Nina Diaz, the executive producer of *My Super Sweet 16,* told *U.S. News & World Report.*

(The price tag for a recent quince party featured in one of the episodes was $180,000.) One quince site I happened upon in cruising the Web for Q-lore—just Google "quinceañera" and you will get 8,230,000 hits (if you put the tilde over the "n") or 4,220,000 hits (if you dispense with the tilde)—urged providers to register with their site. "The Hispanic population's buying power is expected to reach $300 billion by 2006. Timing is prime to begin your Sweet 16 and Quinceanera advertising campaign. The demand for more vendors that cater to Latinos is of epic proportions."

Epic proportions; the house out the window; 8,230,000 hits and rising.

"Upholding this coming of age celebration is definitely expensive," Kimberly García concluded in her 1999 article: "Sweet 15: A Financial Affair." In the seven years since her article was published in *Hispanic Magazine,* the trend is growing. Her shocking high-end figure of $15,000 for a celebration would not raise an eyebrow now. More likely, it would elicit an apology, as with Sofía's dad. "Hispanics are likely to make a big spending decision no matter their income level," Lisa Holton reported in an article about quinceañeras for the *Chicago Sun-Times.*

At Disneyland, Denny Nicholas, manager of corporate and wedding sales, says he has seen anything from a modest $5,000 to $50,000 for a quinceañera, the average nowadays being about $12,000 to $15,000. When I ask Denny if he doesn't find this *average* shocking given that the poverty threshold for a family of three is $15,277, he laughs. "By the time families come to me, they've already made the decision that this is what they want. All I do is provide the elements they need to make their dreams come to life." It's just a different world, Denny reminds me. "Kids are growing up expecting so much more." He chuckles, sounding a lot more cheerful about this than I obviously feel. "I joke with my two boys that when I was growing up, the remote control was me standing by the TV and my dad saying, 'Change it to such and such a channel'!"

Dinero vs. money

The supersizing of the tradition might well be blamed on U.S. consumerism, but the spending of money now instead of mañana seems to be our very own bagaje.

"Hispanics tend to make immediate use of their money," writes Rose Carbonell in her article "Dinero vs. Money." As part of her graduate research in Hispanic Marketing Communication at Florida State University, Carbonell studied the different attitudes of Hispanics toward money. She found that "capital accumulation is not a characteristic of Hispanics, especially because being wealthy has a negative connotation . . . as the masses of Hispanics have endured slavery and endemic poverty over the past 500 years, the meaning of wealth has been associated with the experience of others, not oneself."

Initially, I dismissed this as a kind of cultural profiling we do to ourselves as it hath been done unto us, until I found this point curiously echoed by none other than Octavio Paz, the seminal writer on Mexican identity and thought and the 1990 winner of the Nobel Prize in Literature. "Our poverty can be measured by the frequency and luxuriousness of our holidays. Fiestas are our only luxury," Paz writes in The Labyrinth of Solitude. "Wasting money and expending energy affirms the community's wealth in both. When life is thrown away it increases. What is sought is potency, life, health. In this sense the fiesta . . . is one of the most ancient economic forms."

Another way of understanding this phenomenon is an interesting term I found bandied about in academic articles: "cultural
capital." The term, originally coined by French social theorist
Pierre Bourdieu, describes other kinds of assets, not monetary,
that are important for status in a community. A family's throwing
its daughter a lavish quinceañera represents a kind of cultural
statement that counts for a lot more than the dollar cost. Thinking only of "how much it cost" in dollar amount is to simplify a
much more complex and layered transaction. Patricia Saldarriaga,
a professor of Spanish at Middlebury College, turned fifteen in
1975 in the port city of Talara, Peru, where her father was mayor.
Although she did not want one, she was obligated to have a big
quince party because of her father's position.

"*Somos decentes* is a very important concept in our communities," Eduardo Béjar, also a Spanish professor at Middlebury, explains. Eduardo, who grew up in Cuba in the forties and fifties,
recalls how fiestas de quince años were a family's way of main-
taining status. "Ser una familia decente. You work hard, you do
things for the welfare of your family. La quinceañera reflects that:
a way of saying we are decentes."

But why not have both? After all, being Latina/o is about being a hybrid, a made-in-the-USA sancocho of all our different cultures and races and histories and nationalities. Why not be una
familia decente that celebrates a daughter's quinceañera without
going into debt? Throw a fiesta, not the house, out the window?
Our cultural habits and traditions can be revised to work better
for us in the new realities we are facing right now.

But whenever I've suggested restraint to quinceañera parents
and events providers, the refrain I often hear is, "We love to party!"
That's the way we are.

This ethnic profiling persists both internally within our communities and without. It's a reductionist either/or way of thinking

about ourselves that ill prepares us for this new millennium in which the world is shrinking and we are all becoming ever more permeable mixtures of traditions and cultures.

Mami, too, always maintained we couldn't have it both ways. We couldn't be both girls from una familia decente and little Americanitas with minds (and bodies) of our own.

"Why not?" I would challenge. "'I resist anything better than my own diversity.'"

"Don't you answer me back!" she'd scold. "Don't you be fresh with me!"

"But that's Walt Whitman. We're reading him in English class."

That always made her stop.

"You live in this house, you respect our rules!" she'd grumble, more quietly now. What monster had she created by sending her daughter to Abbot? "Who do you think you are?"

"'I am large, I contain multitudes.'" I was finding a new way to defend myself. Technically, it was not "answering back" if I was reciting poetry.

More fairy tales

Monica's court is arriving!

First one in the door is Cindy, who hightails it to the master bedroom to change. She sits on the floor trying to read the instructions for a strapless bra contraption she just bought to wear under her low-cut gown. They look like breast molds, which is precisely what they are, but how do you get them on? I've come to the bedroom to help her dress, but I'm not much help in this department. If you ask me, the slender, waiflike Cindy doesn't need this extra support, but it's not the kind of thing you bring up to a girl dressing up for a woman's debut. Never mind that it's not hers.

Actually, this is a sore point for Cindy. She is the only one of the girls in the court who did not have a quinceañera. She had the dress and everything, but at the last minute, the money was needed for a family emergency back home in Colombia. Cindy will spend a lot of tonight talking about the quinceañera she never had, how magnificent it would have been, more than two hundred guests, at such and such a place. One of her friends in the court will finally turn to her and say, "Why don't you just have it now?" Otherwise, I'm sure, they will be hearing about this quinceañera that never was for the rest of Cindy's life.

Once Cindy has mastered the bra, I am surprised to see her put on a long purple dress. "But I thought you were Snow White." Cindy nods. It turns out that the court couldn't really afford costumes, so they just each picked the Disney character they wanted to be and tried to make the best of it. "I see," I say, trying not to sound disappointed. But the whole reason I drove down from Vermont was because Monica had described an extravaganza that would be great to write about. Who is doing the cultural caricaturing now?

Cindy is explaining that she really dislikes her dress, but it was the closest thing she had to Snow White. Her mami even sewed the gold braiding onto the empire waistline to make it look "sort of medievalish." When three more girls in the court arrive, I ask each one which Disney character she is, then try to figure out why she chose her dress. Kelly, the only non-Hispanic girl in the court (though she did have a big sweet sixteen, modeled after her Latina friends' quinceañeras), says she's Aurora from *Sleeping Beauty,* which I guess explains the pale pink dress, though the halter top and plunging back and very risqué slit that goes all the way up her thigh would not fly in the kingdom. Alicia from Peru picked Belle, and though she is indeed a beauty, tall, with intriguing amber-colored eyes, there is nothing *Beauty and the Beast*-ish about her pale gold gown with spaghetti straps. Finally, Raquel, Colombian and Spanish, is Jasmine, in a blue and beige striped dress that has nothing to do with the world of *Aladdin,* as far as I can tell. About the only thing that ties this motley group together are the way-too-high spiked heels which none of the girls seems yet to have mastered walking in without wobbling.

That's it for the court? What happened to the fourteen girls dressed up as fairy-tale characters? Thinking back to our phone conversation, Monica mentioned only a few Disney characters. I just assumed that, like most fifteen-year-olds pummeled with annoying questions, she lost interest and grew vague midanswer.

But sometimes it is the failure of the attempt that endears you to the person or situation. What started out as initial disappointment at this not being the extravaganza I'd been promised ends up as a feeling of tenderness toward these kids who are celebrating one of their number becoming a woman by playing pretend. I'm reminded of another fairy tale, *The Emperor's New Clothes.* Everyone pretended to admire the emperor's magnificent golden robe, until the little boy called out that the emperor had no clothes.

"I'm Snow White," Cindy had told me, pointing to the gold braiding. "Can't you tell?"

I felt as if I were watching from the sidelines as the naked emperor paraded by. Except this wasn't a vainglorious, powerful man, but a sixteen-year-old girl needing reassurance. I had come down to Queens to chronicle how our traditions are remade in the USA, repackaged and sold back to us as authentic at a higher price. But that mission was gone. Instead Monica and her friends were asking me to join them in imagining that they were fairy-tale characters, Jasmine and Belle and Aurora and Snow White and Cinderella herself.

Isn't that a beautiful robe our emperor is wearing?

"You look so pretty," I answered Cindy, avoiding her question altogether.

The designated fairy godmother

The full court is assembled—the five escorts, four young boys in black tuxedos and Monica's escort, Franz (Colombian-German), in a white one. But the Ramos parents aren't back yet and we're already fifteen minutes late for the church blessing. Cell phone calls go back and forth. Mami is still at the salon, and Papi isn't answering his phone.

"Go ahead to the church, we'll join you there," Mrs. Ramos sends word.

When Silvia hangs up, a call comes in. It's the limo driver. He has been circling the area for the last fifteen minutes but can't find the house. "You're on the next road over," Silvia explains. She talks him through several turns to our street, ordering everyone outside to the sidewalk, so that the driver won't miss the house this time around. But it's raining, hairdos will wilt, dresses spot with raindrops.

"Wait here," I say, running into the rain to get a jumbo-size umbrella I keep in the trunk of my car. How did I end up as the one adult with all these kids? Claire has gone on to the Dance Club to help out with last-minute details; the cousin will come later to the hall with her two little ones. Where is her husband? Where is Joselito?

But for the moment, anyhow, those questions vanish. Instead

of Q-inquisitor, I've turned into the designated fairy godmother. Let the girls play pretend. The fact that this quinceañera fails at its attempt to be the glitzy variety, in fact, saves it. I'd bash anyone who came within an inch of critiquing Monica's quince with my umbrella. How to prevent a custom from becoming one more casualty to a greedy market that swallows up authenticity and spouts out counterfeit goods? The Disneyfication. The supersizing. The demand of epic proportions. Buying power to be harnessed. MySweet16online.com has become "a haven for young girls that are turning 15, 16 . . ." Vendors should tap into this "haven" that has a "huge worldwide presence" with "vigorous web traffic." I can't help thinking of Dr. Pipher's description of our girl-poisoning culture as "a sleazy dangerous tinsel town with . . . few protected spaces."

But you also can't freeze-dry a tradition, insist it remain pure, simple, what it once was. It has to evolve, change to accommodate new situations and generations. How to provide these young girls with an authentic part of their Latino tradition, something they will never forget? ("The most meaningful moment in a young woman's life . . .") By the same token, how to transform those things in the tradition that hearken back to an old-world order that many of us left our native countries to escape? "Education is teaching our children to desire the right things," Plato wrote. And sometimes that involves reeducating ourselves as well so we can rightly teach our children.

I escort the girls two by two to their limo; the boys, waterproof beings that they are, rush down in the rain. Silvia rides with me in my car, in part to direct me to the church and in part to get away from the stress of being the oldest in the bunch, the one in charge. "You're doing a great job," I tell her as she leans back against the headrest and lets out a sigh.

As we pull out behind the limo, the rain stops. The late afternoon sun comes out, though the air is still dewy with moisture. "It's a good sign," I tell Silvia. The perfect atmospheric condition for rainbows to form.

A rainbow in the sky.

A light in the second-story window of Miss Stevenson's apartment. I have to remember it's now my turn to keep it on. Someone else might be looking up from that front lawn.

Taming the beast

We're almost thirty minutes late when we arrive at the girls' childhood parish. The rain has let up. The church is deserted. What'd we expect? While the court waits in the parking lot, the boys jostling one another, the girls worrying their hairdos, Monica and her sister rush over to the rectory hoping the priest will still do the blessing.

Ten minutes go by. I've stayed behind with the court, but I'm beginning to wonder if, as the only adult present, I should help the girls explain that the delay was not their fault. Just as I've made up my mind to go over to the rectory, here comes Monica smiling triumphantly, followed by Silvia and a tall, lanky middle-aged priest in his vestments who looks, frankly, weary. It's supper time on a Friday night, and no doubt tomorrow is going to be a long day: plenty of meetings and events that have to take place on weekends in this working-class parish where families toil long hours, parents doing double shifts, kids holding down after-school jobs.

The priest casts a glance at the lot of us, dressed up too fancy and, in some cases, too risqué, to be entering a place of worship.

To his credit he does not scold or lecture us. "Can we get started?" he asks.

Monica hesitates. Of course, she wants her parents here. But the priest's forbearance has been stretched to the limit. The Ramoses hadn't even gotten home when we left about twenty minutes ago, and they have to shower, dress, and get here. "Go ahead," Silvia covers. "My parents are coming soon."

In we go, filling up just one front pew, while Monica stands at the foot of the altar, looking up at the priest, who looks down from his post on the top step. "In the name of the Father, the Son, and the Holy Ghost," he intones, and we are launched. The priest reads a blessing from a prayer book, the only personalized touch being the occasional mention of Monica's name in what must be a blank for the celebrant's name. I wait for a little homily about coming-of-age, a funny anecdote with a light moral at the end, a reminder to Monica that she is an adult now in the eyes of the church, but it's a no-frills blessing, take it or leave it. Before I can even feel sorry for Monica, the ceremony is over, and the priest is coming down the altar steps to shake hands with each of us. He does not even ask her where her parents are. Perhaps he has come to expect this of families for whom the spiritual aspect of the quinceañera is, as so many priests complain, an afterthought.

As the priest is leaving, I catch him at the side door, reintroduce myself, "Monica's author." Can I ask him about his experience with quinceañeras in his parish? The look that comes on his face is a cross between "Lord, please let this cup pass" and "You've got to be kidding!"

"Sure," he says. "What's up?"

I give him the very short version of what I'm up to: I'm writing about quinceañeras, you know, that Latino tradition of celebrating a girl's fifteenth birthday—

"Monica's not fifteen," he corrects me.

I'm ready for this one. I know, I tell him. That's what's happening now in the United States. Latinos are combining their own quinceañera tradition with the sweet sixteen parties common in this country, a syncretization, not unlike the original Aztec rite some claimed it came from combining with the Spanish colonial presentation at court. It's a mouthful, but I can tell by the way the priest is shaking his head before I'm even done that I'm not going to be given too much of his time.

"You're making stuff up," he says.

I'm taken aback. Do I bash him now with my umbrella? Never mind that I have my own doubts about the tradition. I've become protective of my Queens quinceañera, left stranded by so many adults. "But you just took part in Monica's whatever you want to call it?" I challenge him.

"I'll deliver a blessing for any birthday," the priest explains. "Beyond that, no. We're taming the beast here," he adds cryptically. "The church isn't going to get involved in that." He mentions the inordinate expense struggling families go to. He caved in and did an individual blessing as a sort of favor to Monica, who is a lovely girl and devoted to her faith. Usually, he just blesses the girls during the course of a regular Mass.

The court is milling outside waiting for me. Now's obviously not the time to get into it with the priest, who is voicing, whether he knows it or not, some of my own misgivings about the tradition. "Can I call you and interview you further on this?"

He shrugs. "I've basically told you everything I have to say," he says. "But sure," he says. There's a kindness in the eyes that belies the sharp approach. After all, he did do the individual blessing, even though we were close to a half hour late.

Still, I am surprised when a few days later, he takes my call. "Monica's writer from Vermont," I introduce myself again.

"What's up?" Monica's priest says for hello.

He's a little more expansive today, as if he might have stomped where angels fear to tread a few days back. The church, after all, is supposed to support what it calls "popular devotional practices." Way back in the second Vatican Council (1964) in one of the principal documents drafted, the *Lumen Gentium,* the church was encouraged "to foster and take to herself the customs of its people so that they may enjoy growth and renewal in line with their own proper identity." That's all well and good, Monica's priest concedes, but tradition is a funny thing. He's been in this parish now six years and sometimes, when he questions how something is being done, he's told, that's the tradition, when in fact he remembers when the tradition got started five years ago!

"We've got to track the way this nonsense gets started and feeds on itself," he tells me.

People come to him insisting on a whole set of "rituals" he has never heard about. "Take the marriage ceremony. The church has a simple and beautiful rite. But couples want the lighting of the special candle, the coins and handling of money, the lasso—"

Whoa! I stop him. "The lasso?"

"Oh, yes, the lasso," he says, obviously relishing the chance to explain. "You tie up the bride and groom like cattle and it's supposed to symbolize how their lives are bound up together. Couples insist on these traditions, and then they ask me what it means! This stuff is getting handed down without any understanding of its authenticity or meaning."

As for quinceañeras, the church already has a sacrament for acknowledging the passage to adulthood, confirmation. If the girls want a blessing, like he said, he'll do a blessing. But he's aware that in some parishes, priests are performing more quinceañeras than marriages. Quinceañeras become a major focus. And it leaves out the boys. What about the boys? Don't they get a ritual for their coming-of-age?

Whether or not you agree with him, one thing you have to say about Monica's priest is he'd never fall in with the crowd that pretends the naked emperor is dressed in a beautiful robe. There's something to be said for this plainspokenness in a world where political correctness can make cowards of us all. In fact, after one long and lively conversation with a feisty Q-basher who happened to have answered the phone in a Hispanic Ministry office of a Catholic diocese somewhere in the Southwest, I received a panicked call back. "Please, don't mention where I work," this person blurted out. I promised him/her I would be vague.

Monica's priest sums up by saying it's not just quinceañeras. "Kids are coming to church for their First Communion in limos with photographers in tow. You get invited to a wedding reception and you feel like you need to give the bride and groom a gift of at least $150, and if you're a couple $250 to $300, just to cover what they're being charged for your being there. Imagine, that money could go for the down payment of a house.

"But I'm off on a tangent," he says, winding up. "Spending your nickel."

It's not a tangent, I'm thinking as I thank him. *Taming the beast,* I recall that haunting phrase he used. The beast (the one in the Bible, not in the Disney movie) is Mammon, demon of money and riches and greed. In Milton's *Paradise Lost,* Mammon is the angel who before the fall is forever looking down at Heaven's golden pavement. He sounds familiar, like my papi, like so many immigrants who flee to el Norte in search of that country whose streets are paved with gold.

⌐⌐⌐✥⌐⌐⌐

Sister Angela of the Quinceañeras

The sometimes ruinous extravagance of the quinceañera as well as its nonsacramental status are the major reasons that many parishes are refusing to participate in them.

This latter issue is no small matter in a church struggling with a diminishing number of clergy. "I do as many quinces a year as weddings," Father Jorge Pérez of St. Mary's in Lawrence, Massachusetts, admits. In too many instances, the religious aspect is an afterthought. "We knew perfectly well that most girls were only thinking of the party," Father Antonio Sotelo, the bishop's vicar for Hispanic affairs in Phoenix, explains. "For all they were getting out of the church part of the quinceañera, they could have gone out and done the whole thing in the desert and had someone sprinkle magic pollen on their heads."

To address this "queen for a day" atmosphere, the diocese of Phoenix issued guidelines about a decade ago: girls and their families were to participate in a series of quinceañera classes and retreats. In keeping with this new approach, some parishes decided to conduct only one celebration a year for all their quinceañeras. A few parishes, pleading lack of time and facilities to run classes and retreats, decided not to perform any quinceañera masses at all.

This is a big mistake, according to Sister Angela Erevia, M.C.D.P., who is all for making the tradition a vibrant part of parish life. The initials after her name stand for Missionary Catechists of Divine Providence—the same order that did not show up for Priscilla Mora's Quinceañera Expo! But Sister Angela would have been there. She welcomes any opportunity to spread the word about the quince años celebration, which is what she prefers to call quinceañeras so as not to exclude the boys. Yes, boys. Three years ago, in 2003, she prepared a group celebration for twenty-one young people, eleven girls and ten young men. In fact, four were non-Hispanics: a Sudanese, a Korean, a Vietnamese, and one Anglo-American. I can't help thinking of Isabella Martínez Wall's dream. Everyone in America should have a quinceañera. But Isabella meant every girl in America. Sister Angela is not going to deny anyone a quince años celebration.

"This is a wonderful opportunity to involve young people in their faith community," Sister Angela says when I reach her by phone at a Hispanic Ministry number given to me by her San Antonio–based order. So many folks have told me to talk to Sister Angela and she is often given as a reference in much of the literature about the religious aspects of the celebration that I'm a little starstruck to have her on the line. But Sister Angela is warm and expansive and we are soon off on any number of tangents. It turns out that Sister Angela is now based in Omaha.

"My husband's from Papillion!" I had no idea there were enough Latinos in Nebraska to warrant the Catholic Church having a whole Hispanic Ministry there. In fact, Bill didn't meet his first Latino person until he left the state for his internship in the canal zone in Panama when he was twenty-four. Of course, that was almost forty years ago.

"We're here now, all right," Sister Angela informs me, laughing. A large and growing Latino population, 90 percent of whom are Mexican American.

Yes, she knows all about the controversy over the expense. But she does not let that argument stop her. Some priests and nuns and their families spend a lot on their ordination, and maybe a few years down the line, the priest leaves the priesthood. "You can't control what people are going to spend." But hopefully, if she and the parish teams she trains do their job right and give this event a spiritual dimension, that in itself might take care of the extravaganza aspect.

As an example, Sister Angela cites a group celebration she organized in Dallas a few years back: seventy-five young people! "Each one shelled out twenty bucks and we had a great reception in the church hall afterward."

But the more Sister Angela talks about the spiritual preparation, the Mass and reaffirmation of vows, the downplaying of the fiesta aspect, the more it sounds like a confirmation experience with an old-country name. How much can a tradition be stretched and changed until it morphs into something else? If you take all the Mammon out of the quinceañera and remove the overt sexual promise of many aspects of the celebration and make it a democratic unisex rite, is it still a quinceañera?

"In our old cultures, I mean Aztec and Mayan, even in colonial Mexico and in some areas of Mexico to this day, our young people came of age in a homogenous society for the most part," Sister Angela explains as if reading my mind. "The whole community, its wise men and women, prepared and supported them as they became adults. Now our young people are growing up in a diversity of cultures and faith—who is preparing them? Who is instructing them in family, language, faith, traditional aspects of their lives? The quince años preparation is an opportunity to do just that."

In her contagious enthusiasm, Sister Angela reminds me yet again of Isabella Martínez Wall, and also of Priscilla Mora. If we could only put Monica's priest in a room with these three women! Sometimes the solution is as simple as that. Being thrown together with other points of view can mollify our own views, round us out, add extra lanes to our one-track minds. I remember one of the retreat exercises for quinceañeras in a guidebook sent to me by the diocese of Phoenix. The girls are all tied together with yarn, left hand to right hand around the circle. (Shades of the lasso Monica's priest mentioned.) Then they're given tasks to do: pour punch, pass out cookies, eat and drink, throw cups and plates away with no spills. When they're finished, the ties are cut and the group discusses how we are all one body, how we need to solve a problem collectively. They end by reading 1 Corinthians 12:12–26. "Now the body is not a single part, but many. If a foot should say, 'Because I am not a hand I do not belong to the body,' it does not for this reason belong any less to the body."

On one point Monica's priest and these three women would agree as one body: it takes a community not just to raise a child but to bring him or her into adulthood successfully.

father cathie

In fact, it's not just the Catholics who have turned their attention to the need for meaningful coming-of-age rituals for young people. Reverend Cathie Caimano, an Episcopal priest who runs the youth program at St. Philip's Church in Durham, North Carolina, says her parish decided some years back that it wasn't taking good enough care of its adolescents. And so, inspired by the Bar and Bat Mitzvah, St. Philip's instituted a six-year program called "Journey to Adulthood." One of its key features is Rite 13.

I e-mailed Reverend Cathie Caimano after I read about this rite in a *New York Times* article. Most graciously and promptly, she replied that she'd be happy to speak with me by phone. I thanked her and asked what was the proper way to address her: Reverend Cathie?

"Cathie's fine," she wrote back. "Actually it's father cathie, but that's a long story in itself."

Maybe because I'd recently read Jeffrey Eugenides's wonderful novel *Middlesex,* in which the protagonist is a hermaphrodite, my curiosity was piqued. Was Father Cathie . . . a transgendered Episcopalian priest? How do you ask a priest that over e-mail? How do you ask a priest that, period?

On the phone, Father Cathie is decidedly female-sounding, lively and full of intelligence and good humor. "I tell the kids that manhood and womanhood are gifts from God. Your body biologically matures. But adulthood is our gift back to God. Being responsible, accountable, ethical adults in a faith community."

I love the distinction. I will quote it for days afterward.

"What we're seeing is a big gap between biological coming-of-age and social maturity," Cathie goes on to explain. "True adulthood, meaning marriage, jobs, all the ways we are part of the functioning adult society, well, it's happening later and later. So, there is an extended period of time in which our young people are growing up without any kind of aid provided. Before, there was maybe a five-year gap between biological-sexual maturity and social maturity, but now that period is at least a decade and a half if not more. We at St. Philip's decided we needed to address this vacuum.

"Kids entering adolescence engage in what's known as gender-proving behavior." Cathie has obviously done the research. "It's natural. Young people want to test themselves to prove they're adults. When we don't provide them with rites and rituals, they find them in other places. They get pregnant, join a gang, take drugs, do some violent act to show how tough they are."

The six-year program takes place in three stages, each one lasting two years and culminating in a rite. The first stage is called Rite 13, after the ritual that ends that first stage, when the youngsters are thirteen. "The whole community gathers together to recognize that this child is becoming a man or woman."

"Girls and boys?" I ask. "Equally involved?"

"Yes," Cathie tells me. "It's really funny. When the group starts out, they're twelve and thirteen. The boys are so much smaller, less mature. But by the third stage, they're all sixteen, seventeen, eighteen, and the boys have caught up." At the end of the second stage, spanning from fourteen to sixteen, the young person can choose to be confirmed or not. "Most end up choosing to be confirmed," Cathie adds.

The success of the program has been phenomenal, and not just in her parish. More than twelve hundred Protestant churches have adopted the rite. The New York City publisher that distributes the program's literature keeps sending them hefty royalty checks. St. Philip's still owns the copyright. "It's selling like hotcakes," Cathie says. She sounds both delighted and still surprised by their success.

The need is out there, no doubt about it. I tell her about the growing popularity of quinceañeras. She is intrigued. North Carolina's Latino population is growing by leaps and bounds. But her own parish does not boast many Latinos so she has not had direct experience with this celebration in her particular parish.

"What if a Latino family were to come to you to do a quinceañera?" I wonder out loud. In fact, many Protestant and evangelical churches have instituted rites for quinceañeras as their Latino membership grows. "What would you do since St. Philip's already has a program in place?"

"That is a really good question," Father Cathie says, sounding genuinely thoughtful. "I'd for sure want to honor their tradition. But . . . I guess I don't really know."

"I'll tell you what," I offer. "When you get your first quinceañera, you just call me up and I'll walk you through it."

"Maybe I will." She laughs.

But it's me who contacts her a few months later, still intrigued by that *Father* Cathie. "If you don't mind my asking," I write in an e-mail. "You said it was a long story, but why are you Father Cathie?"

Within a few hours I get a reply. She doesn't mind my asking at all. In fact, she has written a piece on the subject titled "why i am a father." (I've noticed that in all her written communications Cathie uses uppercase only for God. No doubt, there is a story behind that, too.) She lists several reasons for being Father Cathie: "1. i am not a woman priest. i am a priest. the fact that i am a woman is secondary to my vocation. . . . 2. i think it is high time that feminism be expanded to include typically fatherly notions of protecting, providing for, and leading." But my favorite of her reasons suggests why young people would find this open-hearted, playful minister so appealing: "3. i love it when people ask me why i am called 'father'! it has a lightness and unexpectedness that opens itself up to many wonderful conversations about God, gender, and leadership in the church."

And now, about quinceañeras, too.

Rite of shopping

Even among the faithless, the need to mark the passage into adulthood persists into the twenty-first century.

In East Germany, for instance, long after the fall of the Berlin Wall, the ceremony of Jugendweihe remains curiously popular. Originally, it was established in the mid-nineteenth century by the nonreligious to replace the Christian custom of confirmation—the need for ritual proving to be sturdier than the need for a religious faith. The tradition survived into the days of Communism, when it was recast as a government-enforced ritual in which the young people pledged their loyalty to the state. In the last decade of the German Democratic Republic, 97 percent of all fourteen-year-olds underwent Jugendweihe.

With the fall of the GDR, you'd expect the ritual to fall away, too. Not at all! Sixteen years after reunification, one in every three youngsters in the states of the former East Germany signs up to participate in this coming-of-age program run by the Jugend-weihe Association. The participants, thirteen- and fourteen-year-old girls and boys, attend lectures on safe sex, love, body piercing; they take weekend trips to Paris or London; they are counseled on nutrition, fashion, hairstyling; girls visit a gynecologist. The nine-month program culminates in an actual ceremony in which each young person is called to the stage and is given a copy of the Jugendweihe book, a kind of one-volume encyclopedia, and a handshake.

Asked why a tradition associated with the Communist past has proved to be so resistant to extinction, Margrit Witzle, the head of the German Humanist Association's youth section, which administers Jugendweihe, explains: "People all over the world have a need for rituals. We all choose whatever ritual suits our needs."

Choice—that *is* a change. In Sister Angela's homogenous indigenous community, I doubt the young people got to pick what kind of ritual they would undergo to mark their passage into manhood or womanhood. Each new generation underwent the same rite of passage, passed down by the elders. Now, as Isabella Martínez Wall explained about quinceañeras, there is no textbook. Abuelita is gone. You don't even have to be Hispanic to have one. "Indians, Filipinas, Chinese," Angela Baker Brown, who sells a lot of quinceañera dresses and props at Tatiana's Bridal in Queens, counts them off. "It's a Hispanic tradition, but these other groups are going to these parties and wanting one as well."

MTV's wildly popular *My Super Sweet 16* is billed as a reality show about teens "as they prepare for their most important coming-of-age celebrations." Each young lady designs her very own rite of passage. Judging from the focus of each show, a good part of coming-of-age seems to consist of shopping. Every episode follows the young initiant as she shops for outfits with humongous price tags which are chatted about as if they were nothing but Monopoly money. "My dress cost forty-five hundred dollars," young Janelle, one quinceañera covered in the series, boasts to the camera. Ava dismisses the orange-red creation she went all the way to Paris to buy. "It looks like a crayon," she complains. (An expensive crayon at $2,550!) Lavish gifts are proffered by parents and rebuffed as not quite right or not quite enough. One girl wants a Range Rover, not a Mercedes-Benz, "too small and claustrophobic." Another whines that her dad is booking Unwritten Law to play at her party because her first choice, Beyoncé, is a little pricey at $500,000 a shot. The show is full of beeps as the girls F this and F that, including their friends, their parents, the people hired to help them.

The chat rooms are busy afterward with young watchers ragging on these "spoiled brats." This could be heartening, but in fact, events coordinators and party businesses catering to teens have seen a rise in business since the show premiered in January 2005. The show is merely spotlighting a pervasive problem writ in large sums. These kids are stranded in the land of plenty, without direction or a righting sense of their place in a family, community, and the world. Shopping, it turns out, is not a ritual that can responsibly and lovingly help the young enter adulthood.

What struck me as I watched one too many episodes (my husband lasted through half of one) was how these kids kept talking about what they want: they want to be famous, they want to throw a party that will leave all others in the dust, they want to be in control, they want everyone to be jealous of them . . . They want, they want, they want, and all I could think was, *but you have so much!* What on earth could you want? Zadie Smith, in her acknowledgments to the people who were instrumental to the writing of her new novel, *On Beauty,* thanks her husband for the most valued help of all. "Time is how you spend your love," she writes. On some level, these parents, who are spending a fortune on their kids, are not spending enough love on them.

Or enough of the right kind of love. To go back to Plato: "Education is teaching our children to desire the right things." Maybe we're all in need of more schooling in that regard. What are the right things in a world where so many old verities have come tumbling down? What rites/right things do we have (or can we make them up?) to mark important passages in this uncertain landscape of the here and now?

Time is how you spend your love

Time is how you spend your love.

That first summer after I turned fifteen at Abbot, I came home to find that little suit of clothes that always awaits us, no matter our age, outside our parents' front door. I was supposed to dress up as a child and be their hijita again?! Did they really think that someone who had read Saint-Exupéry (in the original) and could recite any number of poems by heart could not go into the city by herself and come home on the subway after dark?

Mami, of course, countered with stories of recent crimes in the neighborhood, rapes and murders that stirred my fears and made me too scared to carry out my assertion that I was old enough to take care of myself.

Aware that they would have outright rebellion on their hands if all their daughters stayed in Queens for the summer, my parents offered to send us back "home" to our tías and cousins in the Dominican Republic, an offer that two of my sisters accepted. I chose instead to accept my father's offer of working at his office in Brooklyn—a narrow storefront on Graham Avenue next to a travel agency with posters on the window advertising cheap fares to Puerto Rico and the Dominican Republic. In part, I wanted my own money so I'd be able to finance whatever my parents forbade me to do as long as they were paying for it. My pay was to be twenty-five dollars per day, with an extra bonus of ten dollars more on Saturdays and Sundays. Oh, yes, the office stayed open seven days a week. How else was Papi supposed to pay full tuition at Abbot after a first year of his girls being on partial scholarships?

The hours were brutal. By five-thirty in the morning we were out of the house in order to avoid traffic and be able to see patients who had to be at their factoría jobs by seven-thirty. Grumpy with sleep, I'd climb into the black Mercury, and we'd drive down the deserted streets of Jamaica to the Grand Central Parkway, changing over to the Long Island Expressway, then onto the Brooklyn-Queens Expressway. I'd stare out the window at miles upon miles of cemeteries on both sides. Our habit was not to talk much; we were both still sleepy, both loners by temperament. One time, no doubt inspired by the landscape, I asked him if he wanted to be buried here or there, and he shrugged as if he didn't really care.

Occasionally, I recited for him—he liked that, but got annoyed if afterward I pestered him with English-class-type questions in imitation of Miss Stevenson. His favorites were "The Highwayman" and "Do Not Go Gentle into That Good Night" and "In Flanders Fields," which seemed appropriate as we traveled through the land of the dead, and Walt Whitman always made him shake his head and snicker.

We'd get to his office by six, and there would already be a few patients waiting at the door, their faces lighting up at the sight of el doctor with his black bag. They were mostly Puerto Ricans and Dominicans, a smattering of every other Latin American nationality, never un americano, and only occasionally un negro americano who would tax El Centro Médico's linguistic capacities, as very few of the nurses spoke any English. The whole business of the office was conducted solely in Spanish.

"Buenos días," the patients would greet us as Papi unlocked the front door.

"Buenos días," he returned. I waited for him to introduce me, but he never did. Maybe he assumed that everyone knew who I was. Or maybe he was still too sleepy, still too caught up in the world of Walt Whitman, or in his own thoughts.

"Are you the doctor's daughter?" someone invariably asked.

I'd nod, matter-of-fact. After all, I was here on my very own merits (reciter of poetry, honor student at Abbot) in a white smock that made me look official and grown-up. But pride in my papi must have shown all over my face. At Abbot among cool, preppy dads during parents' weekend, I was embarrassed by this colorful figure in his three-piece salmon suit and Panama hat whose heavy accent made it difficult for my teachers and classmates to understand what he was saying. They'd smile blankly or politely ask, "What's that?" And Papi would repeat himself in a louder voice as if the problem were not his accent but their hearing.

But here in Brooklyn I claimed him, el doctor, whose patients were sure he could cure them of what was often just a chronic case of homesickness, not unlike his own.

Alvarez Centro Médico was the antithesis of Abbot Academy: a working-class, Spanish-speaking world whose vibrancy, energy, warmth, noise I soaked up. The waiting room was a gathering place. Friends and families of patients came along, bringing food, pictures of distant relatives to show off, notices and forms in English for me to fill out or translate, gifts for the nurses and for la hija del doctor. The radio was tuned to a Spanish station, and when a good merengue came on, the nurses would stop what they were doing to dance a few steps. They'd pull me to my feet, urging me to join them. But I resisted, knowing I'd end up being teased for dancing like an americanita, forgetting I had nalgas and hips and Dominican blood up in that school in Massachoosett!

The nurses were women in their twenties and thirties, though there was an older one, Bigi, in her forties, quite naughty, who filled my ears with everything I pretended I already knew about, and then some. She was not married ("¿Pa' qué?"), had no children, but to hear her tell it, she had a trail of men just waiting for her favors. She kept a handkerchief in her pocket, divided into little squares, each one printed with a position from the *Kama Sutra*. The first time she showed it to me, it took me a second to understand what was being pictured, which made her laugh all the harder.

Periodically, one of the other nurses would remind Bigi that she'd better watch herself, talking about such things in front of la hija del doctor. I'd wave away such ridiculous concern. It was their way of testing my loyalty, I think, of reminding me that I shouldn't tattle on them, for they all told me their stories, stories about love and family and men, about money and children and men, about homesickness and family troubles and men. They taught me procedures I would never be allowed to do in this age of HIPAA regulations and malpractice suits: giving shots, taking X-rays, drawing blood. Who knew if they were real nurses themselves. They had taken "un curso" back in their home countries, though a couple had some formal training and one had actually graduated from medical school in the Dominican Republic.

Sometimes a woman hurried in, eyes worried, asking for Bigi.

I'd call Bigi to the front and she'd whisk the woman away to the so-called injection room in back with the scales and shelves of samples from drug reps and electric canisters for boiling the syringes. A little while later, the woman would come out with an address written on the back of one of my father's prescription pads. Through the grapevine, which spread from that waiting room into the neighborhood, it was known that el doctor didn't get mixed up in illegal abortions, but Bigi knew someone. Or maybe she did them herself, as some of the other nurses whispered.

Sometimes a handsome, young tipo sauntered in. As I took down his history, he'd begin a flirtation, throwing me piropos, asking if I was married. No matter how sick he felt, he was a healthy macho who had to make una conquista.

"You better watch yourself," the nurses would warn if they caught a guy sweet-talking me. "Esa es la hija del doctor!" The doctor's daughter. But Bigi would just wink and flash her X-rated handkerchief at me, making my hand shake and my face burn with embarrassment.

My job was to man the front desk, answer the phone, find patient charts in the packed file cabinets behind me, or fill out one for new patients. Once the paperwork was done, I'd lead them to the injection room, where I weighed them and took their temperature and blood pressure. Then I'd lead them back to the waiting room, where they sat and visited until their turn came to see el doctor in one of the two examining rooms. Of course, there were always the schmoozers and whiners who tried to get me to put them ahead of others with sob stories of children left alone at home, ill mothers and grandmothers, jobs they would lose if they didn't arrive on time. I'd soothe and reassure, explaining the procedure, how others had also been waiting "for hours." But occasionally when someone got overly pushy, I'd call one of the nurses to come from the back and be the barking dog.

After being seen, they'd come out, carrying their charts on which my father had clipped a little piece of scrap paper (the days before Post-its) with the charge. No one had insurance. You paid in cash. An office visit was five dollars—unless shots were involved, which made it eight dollars; X-rays were a little more. I collected the money, sometimes having to send someone down the street to the bodega for change, then gave the payment to one of the nurses to roll into the wad in her pocket.

We'd work until six, six-thirty at night, until the last patient was seen, the wad of money entrusted by the designated cashier/ nurse into my father's hands. Depending on emergencies or calls from patients too ill to come to la oficina, we'd make house calls, walking up poorly lit stairways in dilapidated tenement buildings, my heart beating strong with fear, recalling my mother's stories. If the suburbs of Queens were rife with rapists and murderers, what would a bad neighborhood in Brooklyn turn up? But no one ever touched us. The people of el vecindario took care of el doctor, or so I thought, until years later, when I asked Papi about those house calls and why he thought he had never been mugged or threatened. "I paid for the protection service," he told me.

"You *paid* for it?" I was shocked.

So that's who those slick-looking fellows had been! They always came in pairs, waving off my wanting to fill out a chart for them. They had some business with el doctor. Could I please pass them ahead for un minutico? I'd answer huffily that others were waiting as well, but they were insistent. Finally, I'd go get one of the nurses to back me up, but one glance at these guys, and even the brassy Bigi said it was okay. I'd show them to the teensy, windowless office at the end of the hall where Papi met with drug reps who were also allowed to butt in line. Minutes later, Papi himself would escort the men out, shaking their hands and thanking them for stopping by to saludar.

I lasted all summer at my job, my stash of independence money growing. Papi was proud. He had a daughter who was not afraid of hard work. Even Mami was impressed. But neither she nor my father knew the real education I was getting at El Centro Médico from Bigi and the nurses. Or perhaps though they would have disapproved of some of the things I was learning—the varied positions of lovemaking, that you could get an abortion in Brooklyn—they would have been glad for the true lesson imbibed that summer along with dulces and cafecito treats from the nurses. No matter how far I traveled down the paths that Abbot might open, I needed to keep coming back to where I had come from, to drink at the springs of my culture, practice my Spanish and my merengue, and feel grateful for the time spent with my father in a world that was neither here nor there—which was probably why he didn't care where he was buried, why he always seemed homesick no matter where he was.

Time is how you spend your love.

Something that comes to us from the past

Incredibly, after rushing around for hours, we are early for the fiesta part of the night, which is supposed to begin at eight p.m. Monica and her court decide they'll drive around in their limo until it's time to appear at the Dance Club on Metropolitan Avenue in Middle Village. Meanwhile, Silvia and I head over to the club, passing what seems like an awful lot of cemeteries.

Later, I will Google Middle Village and find out that the town didn't really take off until burials were banned in Manhattan in 1848 and churches bought farmland in the outlying area for new cemeteries. Lutheran Cemetery and St. John's opened in Middle

Village; Mt. Zion in neighboring Maspeth; and in Glendale, Mt. Carmel, New Mt. Carmel, Mt. Neboh, Machpelah, Beth El, and Hungarian Union Field. A real estate assessment of the area notes that "the dead have the best land in the heights above the streets. The living struggle with basement flooding . . . row houses and multi-family homes. . . ." Originally settled by Germans, succeeded by Italians in the early twentieth century, Middle Village has become a multiethnic place, home of Greeks, Italians, Japanese, Chinese, Koreans, Asian Indians, Israelis, Maltese, and many, many Latinos.

The Dance Club is bustling with workers—handsome young guys dressed in black, a very Italian Mafia look to them (shades of Papi's slick-looking visitors). The florist mother of my student has already been by and decorated the hall with white and green balloons. They hug the ceiling, dangling long, silky ribbons; for a moment I have a droll vision of them as spent spermatozoa with limp tails, exhausted from butting up against some impediment. (What hanging out with adolescents for months will do to one's similes!) At the far end of the long, narrow room an arch of white flowers has been set up, holding up the swing on which Monica will sit to have her shoes changed. All the tables sport white tablecloths and floral centerpieces. The green and white cake on which tiny couples are poised, the central cake crowned by a carriage with a quinceañera dancing on top, has been set up on a table in a dark corner, as if to ensure that this colossal confection ("Bigger than my wedding cake," Claire tells me later) does not upstage the quinceañera herself.

The staff is still rushing around, setting up the buffet tables, testing the sound system, stocking the bar. The best-looking of the guys seems to be the one in charge. He has that young man's no-time-for-an-older-woman-who-isn't-my-boss-or-my-mother look in his eyes. Plus, I can see he's busy. Everybody is intent and focused. Obviously, they've done this often before. The club, to the bafflement of Selina, the owner, has become a very happening place for sweet sixteens and quinceañeras in the area.

Up some steps in a kind of waiting area, two couches face each other with just enough of a passageway between them to get to a small office in the rear. Selina is back there now, busy signing up a young Asian couple, who will be celebrating their engagement here. It can't hurt that they have walked in when the place is spruced up and rocking; otherwise the dark, cavernous hall would seem more appropriate for the wake of some deceased dignitary headed to one of the nearby cemeteries than for a celebration.

I'll meet Selina very briefly a little later when she pops out of the office to give Monica a little gift, a plastic pouch with a bath soap and a fluffy, pink sponge. It's unwrapped and has that look of remaindered merchandise at outlets. I imagine Selina keeps a stock of these gifts in a storage closet to hand out to quinceañeras. Her brisk felicitations, the gift delivered without ceremony, the quick exit surprise me. All business and no Latin expansiveness. But then it turns out that Selina is not a Latina as I had assumed from her dark hair, olive skin, and, of course, the name (though she spells hers with an "i" instead of an "e"). "A lot of people think that," she tells me in a later phone call, but no, she is from Bangladesh. She has been running the club with her husband for six years, and 50 to 60 percent of their business is sweet sixteens or quinceañeras. "The Spanish people are the trendsetters for these kinds of parties. The white people pick it up." And not just the party, but everything: the changing of shoes, the lighting of candles, the waltz with the father, the big cake like a wedding. The Latino-izing of American culture is alive and well in Middle Village!

While we wait for everybody, Silvia and I sit across from each other on the two couches. She tells me about her own quince-añera three years ago. It was just a big fun party, no fancy dress or ceremony. She sounds sorry that she didn't go in for the whole ritual. But back then, her family just didn't know as much as they do now. "By my sister's turn we knew what to do."

How did that happen that they went from not knowing to knowing what to do?

Silvia isn't sure. She thinks it was the florist who told them about the swing. Her sister found out about the candles from a friend. Some stuff came from quince chat rooms on the World Wide Web. Abuelita is no longer a resource, as Will Cain noted. And so, what is left is a hodgepodge tradition stitched together, sometimes not so seamlessly, with hearsay, some history, and a lot of keeping up with the Garcías.

It strikes me as odd that the Ramoses should feel such pressure to honor a tradition whose content and origins remain vague. Later, Mr. Ramos will admit that he didn't know much about quinceañeras because his sisters didn't have them; his family could not afford such luxuries back then. His wife's family was better off, but she also only had an outing with some friends, like any other birthday party. Nevertheless, he maintains that it is "an important tradition for our people." When I press him why, he says, "It's just something that comes to us from the past, that we want to give to our children because it's something we never had." He does not hear the contradiction in what he says, and it seems heartless and annoying to continue asking him why.

⌒⌒⊱❦⊰⌒⌒

Tracking down a tradition

Trying to track down the origins of the quinceañera tradition is a little like playing that old party game, telephone. A whispers some news in B's ear, B then recounts the news to C, all the way around the circle. By the time the news has come back to A, and is pronounced out loud, it has morphed into a skewed version of whatever it was that A claims to have originally said.

Many books, articles, and Web sites state that the roots of the quinceañera tradition lie in an ancient Aztec rite. Sometimes the origin is given as Mayan as well as Aztec, and sometimes more generally described as "indigenous." I don't know if it's because the phrase "an ancient Aztec tradition" has a phony ring to it—an alliterative angling for authenticity in ancientness. But when I repeatedly read this claim in too many articles, I begin to search the bibliographies (in the few cases where one is provided) to see what I can find.

Most folks quote as their source Michele Salcedo's *Quinceañera!,* an informative, well-written guide, the best in its genre. Through a series of e-mails, I finally track down Michele Salcedo at the *South Florida Sun-Sentinel,* where she is assistant city editor. She tells me how about a decade ago, she took a year off from her reporting job to study the quinceañera tradition and write a planner-slash-background book. She is gracious and generous with her time, but understandably cannot cite chapter and verse for the source of a detail in a book she wrote more than fifteen years ago. She does recall getting some of her material on origins from "a nun's book." This has to be one of Sister Angela's many manuals where I, too, have read about this ancient Aztec and Mayan tradition.

And so I e-mail Sister Angela trying not to sound like the doubting Thomas I am, and she sends me to some books—Sylvanus Morley's *The Ancient Maya* and Victor Von Hagen's *Los Aztecas: Hombre y Tribu.* I end up inside the compendious *Florentine Codex,* which was assembled back in the 1560s by a Spanish priest, Fray Bernardino de Sahagún, from testimonies given forty years earlier to a mission of Franciscan monks by twelve high priests of the Aztec empire about their traditions. (Think again of the telephone game: a conquered nation as understood by Catholic priests interviewed four decades later by another Franciscan.) Whatever "facts" we know about the Aztecs are several critical removes from a true and living practice.

But Sister Angela is absolutely right that our indigenous American ancestors did indeed acknowledge the passage of young girls into womanhood. What is uncertain is the age at which the ritual took place. We do know that the Aztec maiden was ready for marriage at the age of fifteen. Presumably at an earlier juncture there was a ceremony of some sort. The *Codex* cites long ceremonial speeches in which fathers and mothers publicly admonished their daughters, probably as part of some ritual. The speeches themselves are quite moving to read. The tenderness is palpable. The father describes his daughter's coming-of-age in heart-tugging words:

> It is as if thou wert an herb, a plant which hath propagated, sprouted, blossomed. It is also as if thou hadst been asleep and hadst awakened . . .

Meanwhile, the mother warns "my dove, my little one, my child, my daughter" that life is dangerous and she must be careful. (So my own mami's dire warnings were not so off the mark. It seems a traditional task of mothers to terrify their daughters into good behavior.) "Behold the road thou art to follow," the mother advises:

> On earth we live, we travel along a mountain peak. Over here there is an abyss, over there is an abyss. If thou goest over here, or if thou goest over there, thou wilt fall in. Only in the middle doth one go, doth one live.
>
> Place this word, my daughter, dove, little one, well within the chambers of thy heart. Guard it well.

This is a far cry from Mami crowning her daughter with a rhinestone tiara or Papi dancing with her as Julio Iglesias sings "De Niña a Mujer." But in both cases there is a transmission going on, an acknowledgment that womanhood is upon her and a life of perils and possibilities is about to begin.

Mayans, too, celebrated the onset of puberty with an elaborate ceremony. Again, the age given by sources varies. Part of the female ceremony involved the mother cutting off a red shell that had been tied around her daughter's waist as a child. Presumably the girl was now considered ripe for marriage and childbearing. We can, of course, stretch the comparison and find in the cutting off of the red shell of virginity a parallel to the casting off of the last doll of childhood. But why belabor the point? Down through the generations the human family has celebrated passages in our mortal lives with rites that use the symbols and signs of our moment in time. We don't have to prove the legitimacy of these rites. They are what they are, part of our human legacy.

This push to legitimize the quinceañera by connecting it with an indigenous past is a fairly recent thing. Back in our home countries in the fifties, elite families would have blanched at any suggestion that their presentation parties had any connection at all to an "Indian" rite. "Indigenous heritage was played down in favor of European and North American culture," writes Valentina Napolitano in *Migration, Mujercitas, and Medicine Men*. Instead, "the fifteenth-birthday celebration used the symbology of European culture (for example, waltzes, performances of classical music, maids of honor, and pages)." It was only with the democratizing of the tradition stateside that the supposed Aztec connection began to be talked about. The desire for native credentials demonstrates both a yearning to reconnect with something forever lost as well as what Renato Rosaldo calls in *Culture & Truth* "imperialist nostalgia," a nostalgia for a culture you have dominated, a people you have destroyed.

More traceable are the courtly elements of the quinceañera tradition. "The first elaborate quinceañeras were balls staged by families of means who liked to pride themselves on their Spanish ancestry and manners," writes Maricel Presilla in an article in the *Miami Herald*. Michele Salcedo cites that its origin might have come from a practice of the Duchess of Alba in eighteenth-century Spain in which she would "invite girls on the cusp of womanhood to the palace, where she would dress them and make them up as adults for the first time." The Empress Carlotta of Mexico, a century later, also "invited the daughters of members of her court to be presented as young ladies eligible for marriage." Interestingly, though its origin might have been these courtly presentations, the quinceañera is unknown in Spain. I suppose you don't need a pretend court when you already have a real one.

Not surprisingly, the pageantry of European courts also pervades debutante rituals in the United States. In fact, part of the success of the quinceañera stateside is that it fits right in with the time-honored American tradition of "debbing." Odd as it seems for a supposedly classless Democratic society, America has always had a fascination with wealth, privilege, and royalty, and nowhere is this more apparent than in its debutante rituals. Karal Ann Marling in *Debutante: Rites and Regalia of American Debdom* cites the cotillions, the balls, the proms with their kings and queens, beauty pageants, including the Miss America contest, which she considers a kind of "debutante ritual for the masses . . . Miss America [as] the queen of love and beauty minus the splendid ancestry." Marling concludes, "The threshold to adulthood in America seems to run straight through the court of Queen Victoria in her prime." And with the addition of new immigrants from Latin America, the courts of Spain and France as well!

Marling's descriptions of the posh debutante parties of the early part of the twentieth century sound amazingly similar to some of the flamboyant, high-end Cuban-American quinceañeras in Miami. At Mary Astor Paul's debutante ball in 1906, for example, ten thousand live butterflies from Brazil were hidden in netting suspended from the ceiling. Alas, when Mary Astor's butterflies were released, the heat of the room had killed them all, and down rained thousands of dead bugs on the disgusted guests. This is reminiscent of the Miami quinceañera whose gigantic flower did not open the night of her party and she was trapped inside, and of the quinceañera whose five thousand Bluebird roses imported from Holland had to be replaced at the last minute because they turned out to be too pink.

Like the upper-class U.S. debut which has become democratized (Marling describes "the almost-anyone-can-be-a-deb deb" of our time), so, too, the quinceañera has changed from a celebration for daughters of the elite to a fiesta for all classes. "When I was your age, only rich girls had quinceañeras," Estrella's mother tells her in *Estrella's Quinceañera,* one of the young adult novels mentioned earlier that centers on this tradition.

Most historians trace this shift to the 1960s and the beginning of vast migrations to el Norte's land of opportunity; the tradition soon became an option for middle and lower classes, both here in the USA and back home. Cross-fertilization knows no borders and influences travel without visa or green card. In fact, even in present-day Cuba, the quinceañera is seeing a revival, as Cuban girls dream of parties like their Cuban-American cousins enjoy in Miami. Many stateside families send their old quinceañera gowns and tiaras along with dollars and medicines to their needy relatives.

Certainly the quinceañera found welcome soil in the American consumer culture, where businesses stood to gain from the expensive elaborations of the ceremony. In fact, when the Los Angeles archdiocese issued guidelines back in January 1990 to try to curtail the growing commercialization and expense of quinceañeras, the outcry came not from the parishioners but from Grupo Latino Por Nuestras Tradiciones, which despite its name was made up of many small-business owners. The group's president, Luis Yanez, declared that "for the church, quinceañeras are not important, but for us they are one of the few traditions we have left," and in the same breath he complained that his shop, which supplies everything from the dresses to the headpieces and artificial bouquets and monogrammed cups, had seen a drastic decline from fifty quinceañeras to five since the guidelines were issued.

And so, while the quinceañera is touted as a marker of ethnicity, it is in many ways an ethnicity with a label that reads MADE IN THE USA (or "Remade in the USA," if you will). Even as the younger generations assimilate in every other way to a mainstream culture, they are holding on to this old-country tradition, which is actually being created here. Odd. Or is it?

In fact, this creation of a past that never was turns out to be a common enough social phenomenon. In his book *The Invention of Tradition,* Eric Hobsbawm coins the term "invented traditions" to describe both traditions actually invented from whole cloth (Kwanzaa, the Bat Mitzvah, just to mention a couple) as well as traditions that "emerge in a less easily traceable manner within a brief and datable period, establishing themselves with great rapidity." These invented traditions are likely to appear when a group is undergoing transformation, and they serve as a way to legitimize and galvanize its members by establishing continuity with a past that may be largely fictitious.

This is not to dismiss them as bogus, Hobsbawm is quick to point out. Instead, they are interesting hot spots in a group's evolution where adaptation and self-creation and legitimization are in progress, as well as moving testimonies toward cohesion just as the winds of dispersal are blowing us hither and yon. The cultural anthropologist Karen Mary Davalos in a study of quinceañeras notes how her Mexican American subjects "cluster around remembered or imagined homelands, places or communities in a world that seems increasingly to deny such territorialized anchors in their actuality."

And so, it makes perfect sense for Mr. Ramos to want his daughter to hold on to her roots by doing something that comes to him from a past that never was—at least not for his working-class family prior to 1960. As his daughters grow up in the USA, speaking spotty Spanish and celebrating their quinces at sixteen, this is the one thing he can give them that might remind them of who they are. *One of the few traditions we have left.* A last Latin spin with his little girl because who knows where she'll end up?

"It used to be that you could give your daughter a wedding. But you don't know anymore if she's going to get married or if she's going to live with her boyfriend first like they do here, or if she's going to get divorced and get remarried several times," Mr. Ramos explained to me, a sentiment echoed by many parents.

So you throw her a quinceañera, a mini boda (mini wedding) minus the groom in which Mami and Papi take the little look-alike bride home. No wonder there is an air of leave-taking about the celebration. It's not just childhood that is being left behind. It's the old country as well, in a pageant proposed and paid for by Papi and Mami, whose own ties to their homelands are growing lax. (At the time of Monica's quinceañera, the Ramoses had not been back to the Dominican Republic in ten years.) But these invented and reinvigorated "traditions" connect us once again to our Latinidad. As Maricel Presilla concludes in her article on the U.S. quince, "When I first moved to Miami, I felt judgmental of the excessive spending and overt kitsch of the fiestas de quince. . . . But then I began to realize that this was really a sign of self-expression and creative vitality."

In that case, let the fiesta go on! One caution only: beware lest our traditions, our very ethnicity, be co-opted by those who would use them for their own purposes. And the quinceañera, especially, presents a perfect opportunity for product promotion in the Hispanic community. (Think girls and their mamis, think *shopping.*) Like Kern's Nectar, Maggi, a subsidiary of Nestlé, also sponsors a quinceañera sweepstakes, but with a different twist. The winners of Put-Flavor-In-Your-Quinceañera Sweepstakes must use the prize money toward the dinner part of the festivity, and Maggi has to be used to prepare at least part of the dinner.

So, quinceañeras, beware! Latinos beware! We might end up performing our ethnicity in costumes made in the mainstream market. I can't help but wince in recognition at Marling's description of quinceañeras as too often being "receptions organized along the lines of a debut grafted onto a Broadway musical, a senior prom, and a dream wedding." The way I might wince at an ethnic joke in which I recognize in exaggerated form a cultural trait I'm not very proud of. And yet, our proverbial loudness, lateness, laziness are—in proportion—the enviable qualities of expansiveness, generosity, joie de vivre. We have management of that balance, oh yes we do. It's that power I want for myself and for all our boys and girls.

Backup

Silvia is still awaiting word whether the original photographer has found a replacement. Her little sister's quinceañera is about to start. Somebody better get here in time to photograph her as she arrives.

The air-conditioning is blasting inside the windowless hall. Silvia and I are wearing just our party outfits, though there's a lot more to mine, a long maroon skirt and frilly black top with sleeves, than hers, a short salmon-pink dress with spaghetti straps and almost no back.

I decide to go wait outside in front of the Dance Club. Maybe I'll spot the photographer unloading his equipment and run in to tell Silvia she can stop worrying now.

Metropolitan Avenue on a Friday evening is a busy, bustling stretch full of end-of-the-week shoppers and folks eating out. Behind us lie the quieter streets of Middle Village: modest houses with their wrought-iron fences and lawn ornaments. But here on the avenue, traffic is brisk, shop lights are coming on. To look around is to see multicultural America in a nutshell: Catalano's

Bakery, Colombo's Fruits and Vegetables, Amore Laundromat—
all have names that announce their Italian provenance. Down the
road Gaspar's Quality Meats is more subtle. I'd guess a German
owner. Meanwhile, Zheng's Oriental Express Takeout probably
has some "Oriental" connection. But one puzzling awning reads
NEW CHINA SOFT TACO. I suppose this is not such a stretch in America, where a gown company owned by a Taiwanese man, House
of Wu, has a very successful line of quinceañera dresses.

One thing I don't see and don't remember seeing on my drive
down Metropolitan Avenue is a photography studio, but, then,
many of the services that families utilize for their daughters' parties come from an informal network of friends and family. Cottage industries. No overhead. Mr. Ramos has confided that people
make a lot of fuss about how expensive quinceañeras are. But not
if you know whom to ask. "You can always find someone cheaper,"
he explains.

One very famous photographer, it turns out, is present, in
spirit, at any rate, in Middle Village. Robert Mapplethorpe, whose
frank, erotic male nudes triggered controversy about the public
funding of artworks, lies just down the road in St. John's Cemetery. Mapplethorpe died young, at forty-two, of AIDS complications, and his ashes are buried in his mother's grave. "Maxey," the
stone reads, his own name absent from the tombstone. I wonder
what Mapplethorpe would have made of quinceañeras, as some
of his black-and-white photos of flowers suggest an eye for that
delicate, almost disturbing pubescent beauty of an emerging
blossom. Disturbing because only for this moment, captured in
celluloid, will it be this perfect. "Thou still unravished bride of
quietness," John Keats describes this kind of captured beauty in
"Ode on a Grecian Urn." He goes on to praise the beautiful urn
with its painted scenes of youths cavorting:

When old age shall this generation waste,
Thou shalt remain, in midst of other woe
Than ours, a friend to man, to whom thou say'st,
"Beauty is truth, truth beauty,—that is all
Ye know on earth, and all ye need to know."

Another reason to have your quinceañera pictures taken.

I check my watch, almost eight. A few folks have begun to trickle in. Definitely not the huge crowds Monica's excited previews had led me to expect. As I turn to go in, I feel inside my purse to make sure. My digital camera. A backup. No matter what, Monica is going to have a record of her quinceañera.

Celluloid quinceañeras

Here's a different twist on having a quince party but no pictures.

Pictures, but no party.

It sounds like a riddle, but it's not. Only in America, a land in part made up in the movies, would having a record on celluloid be an alternative to having the actual celebration.

As noted earlier, in our old countries a formal portrait always commemorated those life-marker events that had taken place or would soon take place: the christening, the quinceañera, the graduation, the wedding. But the extensive photo shoot in lieu of a celebration seems a decidedly American invention, albeit one made up by a flamboyant new kind of American, the Latina American.

It's actually a further subset of Latinas who are caught up in this celluloid dream, the young. In this they are like the rest of

American youth culture, who have grown up with amazing coverage. Camcorders, cameras, digital cameras, cell phone cameras: every possible life-marker event has been recorded, including
the very moment of their births, and every birthday thereafter, as
well as every first: first steps, first haircut, first time to successfully use the potty, first day of school. Within a few short years I
have amassed more pictures of my two granddaughters than
there are of my whole extended family growing up in the Dominican Republic. Almost no pictures exist of my own nuclear
family once we arrived in the United States. Our graduation photos, that's about it. Who had time or money or cameras to be recording our struggles, our homesickness? When we (rarely) went
somewhere notable, a monument, a museum, we did not want to
call attention to ourselves, the obvious outsiders, by taking our
picture in so public a place.

Actually, there is one family photo of the four sisters. It was
taken a year after we had arrived, 1961, by a photographer Mami
hired for a portrait to enter in a contest she had read about in a
women's magazine. The most attractive family would win a
year's subscription and our picture in the magazine as well as any
number of other promotional coupons and gifts. (Shades of
Kern's and Maggi and their quinceañera sweepstakes.) The shot
of the four sisters, three of us in that awkward preadolescent
stage, trying out new smiles for an American photographer, still
gives me a pang. Our worried eyes, our coaxed smiles. My little
sister is biting her lip.

But what most amazes me is that my mother thought her girls
were the least bit competitive with the Dick-and-Jane-and-Sally
shots being sent in, the Shirley Temple girls and *Leave It to Beaver*
boys. We look ethnic, we look odd, so many of us so close in age.
One of those Catholic families with no self-control, too many
kids. Back in 1961, being Catholic was "an issue." John Kennedy

had to assure the populace that he wouldn't let the pope tell him what to do. We Hispanics were not even on the American map yet—except in celluloid, the film *West Side Story* opened in 1961. We had not yet been invented by O.M.B. Statistical Directive 15.

And yet my mother must have been convinced that her daughters stood a chance at winning or she would not have spent money on the extravagance of hiring a photographer to come to our house. He lined us up like a barbershop quartet, shoulders facing the camera, hands on each other's elbows. A year's subscription, our picture in a magazine, free gifts, Mami kept reminding us when we wouldn't smile for the umpteenth time. As we learned to say a few years later when she'd get another one of her great ideas, "Dream on, Mami."

Of course, most photo shoots and videos are shot as the events unfold with a pre-event session at which the quinceañera will have her formal portrait in the studio and some shots at a park or other preferred location. It's quite common to blow up one of the formal portraits and post it on an artist's easel at the door for guests to sign with a wish, like the autograph books of yesteryear. Often, the formal presentation begins with a video of the quinceañera's life with shots of her at every age. (So that's why Mami and Papi were taking all those pictures and making those camcorder videos documenting every key moment of their little girl's life!) Just when everyone is teary-eyed and nostalgic, the curtains part, and there she is, the real-life star.

After the festivities, the videographers add the footage they shot of the party itself and of the day's preparations to this video of her life. (How teenage girls can bear to have a camera crew trailing them all day, shooting them as they're putting on makeup or having their hair curled, still mystifies me.) The quinceañera ends up with a complete and compendious DVD of her first fifteen years, culminating in her quinceañera. Some of these videos are quite professionally done with credits rolling like a real movie and a soundtrack with the music that was popular as each year of her life flashes by playing in the background. In a very real sense, the young lady becomes a movie star.

But the development I find more curious is that of having your pictures taken—an extensive photo shoot, including shots of the girl in full regalia—as if you had the party you didn't have. The posh Biltmore Hotel in Coral Gables offers three two-hour slots every weekday for quinceañeras to be photographed in its elegant lobby under the vaulted ceiling amid marble columns as well as outdoors, descending one of their sweeping stone staircases, or standing by the pool surrounded by statuary of Greek gods and goddesses. To all the world it looks like you had your quince at this swanky spot, when in actual fact you paid the hotel only $250 for your session—this is in addition to the photographer's fees. According to Rosie Aramayo, a sales assistant at the hotel, every month is booked solid. The hotel also found it necessary to make a rule about the number of people the girls could bring with them, four people max, including the quinceañera herself, but not counting the photographer.

"You know how we are," Rosie, who is originally from Peru, explains. "If we could, we'd bring the whole family." Usually it's Mami, Abuelita, a tía or a sibling in tow. When I visited the hotel and happened upon one quinceañera being photographed under an arched outdoor passageway, she had a modest retinue: only her mom and a hair/makeup artist, Noel, brushing up her blush, glossing her lips, cocking his head this way and that to be sure she looked picture-perfect before giving the photographer the go-ahead. Noel assured me that quinceañeras were his favorite clients. "I identify with them," he said. And left it at that.

In actual fact, this practice of having your pictures but not your quinces seems to be mostly a quirk of the Cuban-American community in Florida. At Miami High, I asked a roomful of young Latinas how many had celebrated their quinceañeras. Some hands immediately shot up. But some girls wanted a further clarification. Did I mean a quince party or having their pictures, which they considered a ritual in its own right. They readily admitted they hadn't had parties, so there was no sinister desire to fool anyone. It was the fun of make-believe, just as with Monica's pretend court, or the "cover girl" quinceañera party at which the young lady's photo, superimposed on the covers of *Seventeen, Glamour, Vogue,* and a number of other fashion magazines, served as the table centerpieces. We've seen this in our own lives, a gag joke by friends on our birthday, our picture and name gracing the front page of the *New York Times;* or our faces poking out of the cardboard he-man-and-blondie setup at a photo booth at the fairway. For a moment, anyhow, we have made headlines or we are blondes with perfect bodies. The quinceañera with its built-in princess theme seems right in keeping with these fun fantasy schemes.

But if this is a coming-of-age ritual, shouldn't it actually take place? Can pictures meant to document the ceremony replace the event itself? Enrique Muñoz, owner of a studio in Miami that offers any number of options, including the popular package—dress rental, photo shoot at a studio and two other locations, and a finished album starting at one thousand dollars—says many girls and their families don't want to go to the expense or bother of a big party. "But they want to do something to keep the tradition alive." In a very American way, I should add, like fast food, a quickie quince. Actually, it's the longer-lasting effect of a quince that a photo shoot with its resulting album does capture. "They have that memory of what they looked like at fifteen," Enrique agrees. They, too, had their quinces, as the saying goes.

Enrique tells me that just having your pictures taken is very popular in south Florida. He shoots ten to twelve girls a week who are not having parties. He invites me to follow him around for a day while he shoots two of these celluloid quinceañeras.

As for Enrique, he calls himself "a third-generation photographer," part of a dynasty that stretches back to his family's native Cuba. His grandfather started the Muñoz studio in Havana in 1909, "back when photographers were chemists," Enrique adds. "He had to mix all the chemicals for developing the photos. Also, if he wanted to shoot at night, there was no flash, so he had to create an explosion and then let the smoke die down." Enrique's own father was one of five brothers, all of whom became photographers. (There are any number of Muñoz studios throughout south Florida.) "My sons and my nephew are now fourth generation," Enrique adds. As for his father's five sisters, they worked in the family business as well, painting the black-and-white photos in those days before color film. Enrique is now photographing second-generation quinceañeras, daughters of former quinceañera clients. "If you are thirty-nine or under and my studio did your quince pictures, I probably shot them," he boasts.

I'm way past thirty-nine, but I would have loved for Enrique to have taken my quince pictures. A tall, heavyset man, Enrique has that look of someone always about to crack a joke, which he does a lot, joking to get the best out of teenage girls who are tired and sweaty after a day spent traipsing around the extensive tiered gardens of Vizcaya in big, heavy dresses. "Don't give me that St. Brenda's look!" he teases one of the girls. When I ask him what that means, he tells me it's that little stuck-up private-school look. "Quiero verte más Latina!" he calls out to the other girl a little later. I want you to look more Latina. The girl arches one eyebrow at him. Enrique snaps her picture. "Good!" he tells her, not at all what she expected.

"It's that 'S' in the body," he elaborates, trying out the pose, when I ask what he means by looking more Latina. The two girls exchange an eye-rolling look. But both moms and the one grandmother who came along and I burst into giggles. It is a funny sight: a tall, paunchy fellow pretending to be a curvaceous Latina bombshell.

Besides the mothers and grandmother and myself, Enrique has brought along his assistant, Teresita, who arrived in Miami two years ago from Cuba, where she was a medical doctor. If that sounds like a step down in the world, it's worth noting that Teresita's earnings in a day represent more than twice a doctor's monthly salary in Cuba, which tops at $480 pesos, approximately twenty-four dollars. She is efficient and focused, setting up and dismantling shots quickly, carting along a large satchel of props, from parasols to fans to plastic roses, as well as a big collapsible reflector which the last person in our party is enlisted to hold up. He is a young man in a tuxedo, the boyfriend of one of the girls. She has insisted that he be included in some of her pictures.

"Bad idea," Enrique confides in me, a sentiment echoed by every events planner and photographer I interviewed. "It's a beautiful thing," Enrique waxes eloquent, "this quince años ordeal." I don't know if this is a slip, but I don't correct him, wanting to hear what he has to say. "It's something no one can take away from you. You can get married and end up in an acrimonious divorce, and so your wedding turns into a negative experience. You don't want to see those pictures. But not your quinces! It's all yours."

These high school boyfriends are not going to be around forever. "I guarantee you that that's not the guy she's going to marry," Enrique assures me. "But the mother brings him around para complacerla." To make the girl happy. Not all parents will cede on this point. After going through two horrendous quinces for two older daughters—one of whom broke up with her boyfriend-escort a week before the party, the second one had her court unravel when a boyfriend-girlfriend pair broke up in the course of rehearsals and then didn't want to be together in the same room—the mother insisted that for her youngest daughter's quince all the escorts were to be the girls' fathers. "You might break up with your boyfriend, but you're never going to break up with your dad," Mami explained. Given what I've heard about the attachment Latino fathers have with their daughters, I bet the papis were glad.

One thing I can say about this young boyfriend is that he sure is a good sport. Not every sixteen-year-old guy is going to be okay about wandering around a museum park on a hot June day in a tuxedo or posing on one knee before his girlfriend, pleading for her hand, or standing by, holding up a big clumsy reflector for five, ten minutes at a time.

But the girls are also good sports, when you think they already spent the morning at the studio having their indoor portraits taken. There, in addition to an extensive shoot of them wearing their rented quinceañera gown, they also each did a sequence in a second sexy outfit: a shimmering red gown with a plunging neckline for one, and for the other, a long black dress with an aqua side panel, ditto for the neckline. "Do I have to bring out the dog to make you smile?" Eduardo, Enrique's brother-in-law, called out to the girls. "Arf, arf, arf," he'd bark behind the camera. The joking gene runs even in the in-law part of the family. Between shots, Eduardo easily lifted and shuffled some Styrofoam columns around to create a kind of Versailles garden background. Talk about looking like a he-man! After Eduardo finished the indoor shots, it was Enrique's turn to take the girls out for the location shots.

Popular locales for these shoots include the chic Biltmore Hotel, with its two-hour slot, an hour for indoor spaces and a second hour on its grounds. Also very popular is Vizcaya, the former winter home of James Deering of International Harvester fame, now a museum and park. During our three-hour shoot at Vizcaya, I counted ten other quinceañeras having photo shoots as well as two brides. A third popular shooting locale is at a beach or poolside (this is, after all, south Florida), at which the girls are more scantily clad. "Bikinis, you know." Enrique looks like he might be about to crack a joke, but then decides he'd better not. I wait a beat. "All I got to say is if I had a daughter, I'm not sure I'd have my sons shooting her." Enrique has told me he has three sons, who sometimes complain about how they don't get anything for their quinces. As for beach shoots, Enrique attempts those only in the winter. In the warm weather, he just can't see trying to get a hundred folks out of the water to accommodate him.

I tell Enrique what I've heard from my friend Vitalina in Havana. The quinceañera photo shoot idea is spreading there. The girls' outfits run the gamut from ball gown to bikini to a nun's habit. Enrique laughs. No nun's habit requests have come his way yet.

We arrive at Vizcaya late morning in a caravan, as the two girls are dressed in their elaborate gowns and there is no way we could all fit in one or even two cars. In fact, one of the girls balks as we get ready to leave the studio. "I feel like I'm carrying a bathtub around," she complains about the ballooning hooped skirt she is holding up with both hands. "I don't see how I'm supposed to get in and out of a car in this thing."

"Don't worry, " Enrique jokes. "We provide ropes to tie you to the top."

At Vizcaya, the same sequence is repeated as at the studio: several extensive shots of the girls dressed in their white gowns and then, after a change in the bathroom, another sequence in a second outfit. We move about in the heat of the day, taking in key features of the elaborate gardens: in front of fountains, in arched passageways, by a wrought-iron gate, under a statue of a goddess holding flowers, inside a little gazebo jutting out into a bay, descending a sweeping outdoor staircase, ensconced in a roofed gallery, looking out toward the mansion beyond an alleyway of trees.

At one point, as we are waiting for the girls to change, Joel Hoffman, the executive director of the museum and gardens, happens by. Enrique introduces me and wanders off to set up the next shot. Mr. Hoffman and I chat a moment; he tells me he's been wanting to do some exhibit in the museum on quinceañeras. It's such an interesting tradition here in south Florida. When I tell Enrique later what Mr. Hoffman had to say, Enrique quips, "They should do an exhibit. They earn a lot of money from us." It turns out that each girl has to pay a $107 fee for using Vizcaya as the setting for her quince shots—a bargain compared to the $250 the Biltmore charges for two hours, and the girls can spend the day here and invite up to six in their party. Enrique estimates that he brings the park between $40,000 and $50,000 a year in revenue. Multiply that by the ten other quinceañera shoots I counted. I have to agree with Enrique—Vizcaya should mount an exhibit and throw a big quinceañera-themed opening in which all the girls who had only celluloid quinces can come enjoy a real party.

Here's a sampling of poses visitors might see hanging on the walls of this Vizcaya quinceañera exhibit: the now classic poses: the girl with a rose, the girl with a pretty lace parasol, the girl with a Spanish fan. There are also some fancy-footwork poses: the girl rising from the waves dressed in one of those scanty biki-nis, a new take on Venus emerging from the ocean depths. The girl's face dissolving upon ocean waves, looking alarmingly as if she were drowning. The girl's face surrounded by rose petals, presumably a beautiful bloom herself. The girl's face at the bottom of a wineglass. Hmm . . . In one ingenious one, the quinceañera is photographed sitting without a crown. Then she is photographed standing, holding the crown as if about to crown someone. The final shot of the two put together will show the quinceañera crowning herself!

We are done by early afternoon. The girls ride off with their moms. I climb in beside Enrique, Teresita in the backseat. Are we hungry? Enrique wants to know. But before we can answer he has his mom on his cell phone. Mrs. Muñoz, who works as a seamstress at her son's studio, also cooks almuerzo every day for the family on the premises. Besides his brother-in-law, Enrique's sister, his nephew, sundry other family members are part of the studio. "It's a real family business," Enrique tells me. Today, Mrs. Muñoz has made arroz con picadillo y calabaza, a Cuban dish. But if that's not to our liking, Enrique suggests, "we can also do pizza or a big Cuban hero sandwich." His versatility along with his generosity and sense of humor no doubt account for his successful business.

"So, do you consider yourself a sort of poster boy for the American dream?" I ask him before we part. Enrique has already told me how his father fled Castro's Cuba in 1962, leaving behind most of his equipment and photos. Enrique was born a year and a half later, "the day after José Martí's birthday."

Enrique laughs. "Well, I don't know about poster *boy*. But I guess I could be an American success story. I mean I went to college and all." Something he's not sure his father or grandfather ever did, though some of his father's older brothers might have. "But really, I think of myself also in the Hispanic tradition of going into the family business. I mean in three years it's going to be a hundred years."

"Wow!" I congratulate him. A hundred years of shooting

quinceañeras! Whether or not they had a party, thousands upon thousands of Latinas have albums full of beautiful memories, thanks to the Muñoz dynasty of photographers. They, too, can say they had their quinces.

Photograph of a headache

Monica and her court have been dropped off by their limo, which glides off down Metropolitan Avenue into the night. The $250 carriage might as well have been a one-dollar pumpkin as not many of the guests have arrived to be impressed by the conveyance.

The little waiting room suddenly fills to the brim with the court and quinceañera and, mirabile dictu, the original photographer, who decided to show up after all. His is one of those old-fashioned cameras that resounds with a loud, smacking flash. He keeps photographing the quinceañera in ridiculous poses I thought went out with daguerreotypes—including that old classic of a forefinger dimpling the cheek.

Monica is accommodating, flashing her incandescent smile back at the camera. But she is looking a little pale. It turns out she got a bad headache from riding around in the limo with the music turned up so high. Plus, she hasn't eaten anything today. Her whole party, which she is supposed to be enjoying, is turning into one huge headache.

To top it off, the best-looking of the staff, who is to serve as emcee for the evening, wants to know what he is supposed to say. Monica stares at him dumbly, as if she cannot believe he hasn't gotten his copy of the evening's script before now. Music she wants played? There was a CD burned with the waltz and other songs. Maybe her parents are bringing it with them when they come. Where are they anyhow? The photographer keeps snapping away as if trying to capture some quintessential moment of quinceañera angst.

"I'll write it all out again," Monica says, her voice close to tears. Taking the clipboard from the emcee, she begins scribbling what she remembers, calling out questions to her court and Silvia. It's odd to see her writing with her gloves on, odd to see a girl in a princess gown and tiara bent over a clipboard like a schoolgirl intent on doing well on an examination. The list is long. What does each member of her court want said about him or her as he or she enters? Should Monica descend the stairs alone or should she enter on her father's arm, be seated at the swing, and then have her escort come down the steps and find the heels and give them to her dad?

Meanwhile the relentless photographer is at it again. He lifts the skirt of Monica's dress and creates a hood of tulle all around her head. Could she put her chin on the edge of the couch, hands just so, perfect, perfect, hold. Smack! Flash! Monica looks like she is drowning in her dress as the skirt engulfs her face. Where is this photographer from? He's definitely Latino, probably first generation, as he coaches and coaxes Monica in Spanish. Why did he almost not show up? I know from what Silvia has said that he works for a photo shop, but does these special jobs on the side. Probably, he took on one too many jobs, wanting the extra hours, struggling to make his way up the success ladder to become a professional in America.

I remind myself to ask him later where exactly he's from, why he almost didn't come. But when we are finally sitting in this waiting area wolfing down our dinner from paper plates while the official guests dine in the hall below, we maintain a kind of dignified silence, the silence of servants who don't have much to say to each other except to wonder, when will this night end? At some point I ask him if he does a lot of quinces. His mouth is full, so he just nods. But even after he has swallowed his food, he doesn't elaborate.

Later, during the candle-lighting ceremony and the cutting of the cake, I realize something is missing: the smack and flash of the photographer's camera! I wonder if he slipped out to that other engagement that almost made him miss Monica's party. Maybe he had another quinceañera to go to? I think of him nodding at my question, his mouth full of the Dance Club's catered food. He didn't bother to ask me what I was doing there in the waiting area, what service I was providing for the Ramoses, how I was making my own way up the success ladder in America.

The hurricane quinceañera

Pepe Delgado knows what it means to climb up the ladder of hard work to success in America. After serving in the air force for twenty-one years, Pepe went to work for different contractors, most recently Boeing as a "logistic supply manager." Although his family is based in San Antonio, Pepe "commutes" to Alabama to work, not wanting to continually drag his wife and kids wherever a job opens up for him. He has a nice house for them in the suburbs near where he grew up, working in the fields, milking goats, collecting eggs. His father was from Mexico, his mother was American, but "just barely." Born on the U.S. side of the border. Pepe draws a line in the air and then tips his hand over to one side. That close.

The walls of his comfortable two-story house are lined with art and memorabilia Pepe has collected from his posts around the world—rugs from Turkey, a huge painted fan from the Philippines, sand paintings from Egypt. On one of his jobs in Panama, he met his present wife, Sonia, mother of his fourth son, Juan Carlos, or J.C. (Pepe has three other sons from an earlier marriage), and his only daughter, Ashley, whose quinceañera I've flown to San Antonio to attend. Solidly middle-class, Pepe makes a point of letting me know that everything he has he has worked hard to acquire.

Meanwhile, it's been an expensive week in the Delgado family. His little girl is getting everything her quinceañera heart desires, including a mariachi serenade, a Hummer limo, a huge party at the Embassy Suites Cancun Banquet Hall, a video of her life as well as a two-person crew filming the whole day and night of her party, the footage of which will be added to the video so her quinceañera itself will provide the happy ending to her story so far. Unfortunately—not part of the budget—J.C. happens to have smashed his car this past week, and some of the calls Pepe is fielding as he escorts his wife and daughter to appointments and runs any number of errands are with different mechanics who are giving him estimates on the cost of the repair. Pepe flew in on Thursday to help get things in shape, but on Tuesday he's headed back to Alabama to work. Hearing him talk, I can't help glancing out the window and imagining the boy who used to put in long hours within sight of this house he paid for himself. "Do your kids realize how hard you struggled to get here?" Pepe laughs out loud and shakes his head. "They haven't a clue."

Perhaps if it hadn't been for that summer at Papi's office, as well as subsequent summers and vacations when I returned to my job at El Centro Médico, I, too, would have had no inkling of the blood, sweat, and more sweat that goes into raising yourself, and your family, up by the bootstraps into the American middle class. Perhaps, too, this generational divide in the meaning of hard work, so much a part of the immigrant story in America, is brought home so sharply during Ashley's quinceañera because it is taking place as Hurricane Rita is bearing down on the Gulf Coast. The memory of Hurricane Katrina has not yet faded from the popular imagination. Two and a half million evacuees are fleeing the Houston area, panicked that they will become the next round of hurricane victims.

San Antonio, just northwest of where Rita will be making landfall, is flooding with refugees. In fact, I call Pepe the day before traveling out there, wondering whether the quinceañera is still happening. CNN, the major networks, The Weather Channel—all are predicting a second Katrina. Surely, Ashley's party will have to be postponed. "No way," Pepe assures me. Come hurricane or high water, his little girl is going to turn fifteen in royal Latina style.

By the time I check into the Embassy Suites on Briaridge, the lobby has been converted into Rita Refugee Central, as Bill, the young Mexican American at the front desk, says jokingly. Down in the sunken indoor courtyard, a huge television has been set up. Huddled in clusters on couches or sitting around tables on chairs that have been brought in from storage, families watch the screen for news of what is happening to their homes southwest of here. There are shell-shocked looks on faces, hands clutched as if in prayer. "All we got is what you see on our backs," one African American woman tells me, pointing to her two little boys in basketball jerseys with numbers on them. It took them thirty hours to get here from Galveston, napping along the way, eating bread and lunch meat in the car. Another mom with a tiny baby girl says she and her extended family have gotten the last two rooms at the hotel. They drove up from Matagorda, or "Kill the Fat Lady," a name that she utters without a hint of its ironic implications, given the situation. At a third table, a family group with members of all generations speak in Spanish among themselves.

When I lift my camera to take a picture of the lobby as I head up to my room, a couple of the men in this group hold their hands up to shield their faces.

I feel lucky to have a whole room to myself—having made my reservation months ago in order to be in the same hotel as Ashley's party. But my luckiness is tainted every time I descend to face the crowds who are sleeping seven and eight to a room. I wonder how the Delgado family feels, knowing that tragedy is literally just outside the doors of Cancun Banquet Hall, where Ashley will be crowned princess at a party whose cost probably equals Pepe's family's yearly income when he was fifteen. But when I mention this to Pepe, he assures me that we are safe. "I hired some security," he explains as if that were the point of my remark.

Admittedly, I feel distracted at Ashley's coming-of-age. The hurricane quinceañera, I dub her, a title she giggles at politely. "She was so afraid her quinceañera would be a wash," her grandmother explains during supper before the presentation ceremony begins. There are a few no-shows, but amazingly, given the circumstances, the majority of the guests have come to welcome Ashley into womanhood.

Still, the whole night seems unreal, with a terrible storm raging not far from here: the teenage mariachi's surprise entrance during dinner, singing "Las Mañanitas"; the changing of the shoes—not flats to heels, as the ritual prescribes, but heels to taller heels; the crowning by her mom with her hairdresser standing by to adjust Ashley's curls around the rhinestone tiara. At one point, a fellow guest at our table, a woman from Corpus Christi, mishears me—the music is blaring. ("You were always there for me / The tender wind that carried me," Celine Dion sings.) Instead of Vermont, the guest thinks I've come from Beaumont, Texas, which is getting pummeled by Rita. "I'm so sorry," she says, reaching for my hand.

The camera crew is going table to table, asking each guest to say something to Ashley that will become part of her quinceañera video. I try to explain to the young man and his assistant that I don't really know Ashley. Until twenty-four hours ago, we had spoken only by phone. But they insist.

"Felicidades, Ashley," I croon for the camera. "Thanks for including me in your special celebration. May your life be blessed with happiness." I thrust the microphone at the woman from Corpus Christi, who pretty much echoes my sentiments, and so on around the table. No doubt this will be the part of the video of her life that Ashley will fast-forward until she gets to the fun footage of herself and her friends, barefoot, waving their arms and calling out the lyrics of a hip-hop number.

At some point during the party, I decide to go out and check on the weather. I make my way through the lobby with its TV blaring, guests napping on couches, past the front desk, waving at Bill and his colleague Margarita. "How's the quinceañera going?" Bill wants to know. I give him a thumbs-up and ask him how the weather's doing.

"We're not going to have a problem here," Bill assures me. Earlier, I had asked him about the birds that were packed in all the trees that surrounded the parking lot, a jabber of sounds. "What are they?" I wondered. Bill was prepared for any number of questions—was there an ATM close by, where could you get gas at midnight, were there any extra cribs left in storage—but my question stumped him. "They're just, like, birds," he finally pronounced, grinning.

About the weather, Bill is right. Outside, the sky is clouded over and a brisk wind is buffeting the flag on the flagpole, but there is no rain, no sense that southwest of here homes and lives will be destroyed before morning. On a bench to one side of the entrance, a smoker is enjoying a quiet cigarette. The birds, whatever they are, must be asleep, not a sound. I walk past the heavy smell of cigarette smoke into the parking lot and look out at a most surreal sight. Down the hill from Embassy Suites stands a small castle, complete with crenellated turrets and towers, flooded with lights from its deserted parking lot. MALIBU CASTLE, the sign reads, a family park with video arcade games, a miniature-golf course, sprint-car racing, and entertainment for all ages. I've seen it a number of times, on my way in and out of the parking lot, but that was in the light of day.

Now, dramatically lit up, it seems a figment of my imagination, the result of attending one too many quinceañeras. By Tuesday, Pepe will be back at work, Ashley will have had the party of her life, and most of the refugee families whose cars now fill the parking lot will be headed back to Houston and Corpus Christi and Matagorda and Galveston. They will begin to dig out from under and start the long, hard climb up that ladder where success is measured by negatives: not being hungry or homeless or in serious debt. Storm-tossed lives, all right, which, thanks to our hardworking papis, Ashley and I have so far been spared.

El que inventó esto fue muy inteligente

The oldest person I know on this earth is my 102-year-old great-aunt, Amantina Grullón, whom we all call Titi. Until a recent fall sent her to a sickbed and turned her from a bouncy, sparkly eyed imp in sneakers trekking around her hometown of Santiago to a taciturn and bedridden old woman, Titi was a fount of stories and information. A no-nonsense lady who raised three sons, she was never into the glamour-girl, hair-and-nails aspect of female Dominican culture. In fact, she dismissed quinceañeras as silly, a waste of money. Why not go to Europe or New York or even up to la playa for a pasadía with your girlfriends?

But then a wealthy great-grandniece had a big extravaganza of a quinceañera. The country club was converted into an old ballroom, complete with mahogany paneling. In the entryway an exhibit was set up as if in a museum: blown-up photographs of the young lady at each of her previous fourteen birthday parties, and beside each photo, the very dress she had worn that day. Her mother had apparently saved all but the one for her eleventh year, which had disappeared, but a seamstress re-created it from the photograph. Inside the hall proper, flowers in gorgeous arrangements abounded. It was un show.

I expected Titi to scowl with disapproval as her companion-caretaker, Pali, described the jaw-dropping expense of the party, but instead, my old tía smiled. This quinceañera had converted her into a believer, Pali noted.

"Titi, I don't believe it!"

My aunt laughed her old mischievous laugh, obviously enjoying my shock. Yes, indeed, she seconded Pali. She was turned into a quinceañera believer but not for the reasons I might think.

What happened was that she learned that the decorations were done by a friend of the family's; a dozen carpenters were hired to re-create a nineteenth-century Viennese ballroom in the country club's banquet hall; a cousin's granddaughter who had just opened a flower shop made her own grand debut with the arrangements. Everybody was working, earning money, happy. That did it, Titi changed her mind about quinceañeras. "They keep the economy going," she concluded.

I had to laugh (wince?) recalling a quote I read in Marling's book in which one fictional debutante in a 1932 spoof on the social benefits of coming out says, "We helped to give employment during the Depression." In part due to social pressures, postwar American debuts changed from individual balls to group affairs staged on behalf of some charitable cause or other. "High society seemed to have developed aristocratic inhibitions about flaunting one's wealth in wanton display," Marling notes of these toned-down deb parties. This kind of inhibition has yet to affect some ostentatious Latinos. One Cuban-American friend told me about her mother's idea to have the Eiffel Tower lit up in honor of her quince! No hiding our light under a bush, no, señora!

And so, despite the efforts of Sister Angela and Isabella Martínez Wall and Priscilla Mora, the U.S. quinceañera continues to flourish flamboyantly without any ennobling agenda. Unlike Afro-American debuts "in which the emphasis falls squarely on education and betterment," Marling notes that the quinceañera is more akin to the beauty contest: "a staged show, theme parties with semi-professional dance routines, tiaras . . . high heels, big hair, and a sparkly white dress." And unlike the Bat Mitzvah, which developed into a more egalitarian rite in part because of the women's movement, the quinceañera really has not changed much because of feminism. "The quinceañera aims to legitimate and control the sexuality of the pubescent girl. She is ready to be a wife, a sexual being, says the bridal regalia . . . She is Cinderella, off to the ball." And yet, harsh as her critique may be, Marling acknowledges that the quinceañera baby cannot be thrown out with the murky bathwater:

> Whatever its importations from movie and pageant land, the quinceañera is about having a Latino or Hispanic ancestry. Even the most assimilated high school sophomore, in this one rite of passage, acknowledges her ethnicity . . . The quinceañera accurately portrays

old-country expectations even as they come under in-
creasing pressure from contemporary culture at large.
Quincing is about retaining respect for the old ways,
even if they are sometimes honored in startling new
forms.

New forms indeed! Perhaps one of the most popular spin-offs
is the quinceañera cruise. One week aboard a Royal Caribbean
cruise ship built around the theme of coming-of-age. One of the
nights involves the actual presentation ball complete with a waltz
with the fathers and a banquet in one of the cruise ship's big halls.
Over the course of the summer months, travel agencies will do
ten to twelve groups of as few as fifteen and as many as seventy-
five girls. Add to this the parents, the siblings, the extended family
and friends, and, at one thousand dollars per guest, we are talking
about mucho dinero. The group of quinceañeras don't necessarily know one another—so "the community" that is celebrating
the coming-of-age of its young women is makeshift and momentary. Perhaps that is why Oscar Suárez, owner of Cordoba Travel
Cruises & Tours in Miami, which bills itself as "Home of the
Original Quinceañera Cruise," puts a homey spin on his quince
groups: "Let our family take care of your family." The movie-
star-handsome grandfather and his wife and at least one of his
grown daughters accompany all the cruises. "All our trips can
count on the same warm family feeling that has characterized
our quinceañera groups since 1983."

Twenty-five-year-old Maurice Mompoint, also based in Miami, represents a younger generation of quinceañera business
entrepreneurs. His Web site, yourquinces.com, is allied with his
mother's Happy Holidays Travel Agency, which does a large volume of the crucero business. But, as with Don Oscar's quinceañera cruises, Maurice goes along on all his mom's cruises to

ensure they run smoothly. Why does he think they are so popular? "When you think of it, you're actually getting not just a
quinceañera but a week's vacation and family reunion for one
thousand dollars a person! It's a bargain. Sometimes there are
family members you haven't seen in years all reunited on the ship,
three or four generations spending a week together. It's really
special."

Maurice, a bachelor ("good thing!"), was flat out with cruises
this past summer. He did thirteen trips from June 5 to August 7.
"It was back-to-back. I had two suitcases, one with dirty clothes
that went off the ship, one with clean clothes that came onboard."
A mistake happened during one of the transfers, and instead of
getting the correct suitcase, he got the dirty-clothes suitcase. "I
spent a lot of time on that quinceañera cruise doing laundry."

I observe that his job must be ideal for a single guy, what with
dozens of pretty girls along, but Maurice disagrees. Fifteen-year-
olds are way too young. Besides, Maurice is superbusy trying to
keep everybody happy. "I give it ten years," he says cryptically,
and for a moment I think he's talking about how long he can last
at his job. But he says that in ten years, quinces will be a thing of
the past. "The next generation growing up, their parents will all
have been born and raised here. A lot of them won't even speak
Spanish that well. There isn't going to be that grandparent or parent from the old country pushing for the quinceañera." Is he worried about this? Not really. "In ten years, a lot of these girls are
going to be getting married. I've been building my database, and
with a couple of switches, I can turn yourquinces.com into a
wedding site."

I wondered about Maurice's prognosis. Are quinceañeras on a
culturally endangered list? Higinio Muñoz, who is part of the
Muñoz dynasty of photographers that for three generations has
been snapping quinces in Cuba and now in south Florida, does

not think so at all. "For the last forty years of this business, you think, oh, the tradition is going to end with the next generation, but I've now got second- and third-generation girls, and the tradition is not waning. In fact, it's growing. I have Haitian quinceañeras and African American quinceañeras and American girls wanting quinceañeras." He has a point. At www.quinceañera.us.com, where you can register your quinceañera, there are mothers registering little girls who will be turning fifteen in 2015!

But history would seem to be on Maurice's side. After all, generations of immigrants have trod the assimilation path in America, shedding most of their ethnic past, with maybe only a parade left to commemorate those roots, a green cardigan on St. Patrick's Day, a polka night at the Polish-American club. Cuisine preferences probably linger the longest, though truly the only thing left of my husband's German culinary roots is his potato salad, whose ingredients are now so altered by heart-healthy concerns and a vegetarian wife that his great-grandparents, who landed on Ellis Island in the late nineteenth century, would not recognize their creamy, bacon-filled version as kin to our simple potato salad with a dash of olive oil, salt and pepper, and a sprinkling of thyme.

On the other hand, America is now seeing a new kind of immigrant whose ties to a homeland are never completely severed. In his rousing and passionate book *Living in Spanglish: The Search for Latino Identity in America,* Ed Morales explains that the old idea of "Americanization" involved the loss of contact with people from the old country. "But the continuing migration of Latinos to the north has the effect of reinforcing the Latin culture that we would otherwise have lost."

And the travel is not just north but back and forth. In fact, the whole concept of nation-states with set borders you cross and leave behind is not the way the world really works anymore, according to Michael Dear, head of the Geography Department at the University of Southern California. In "Postborder Cities/Postborder World?" he notes how people, money, communication, and culture are all moving in new currents and combinations. Globalization is creating a new kind of mobile and mutating world citizenry. Perhaps Sister Angela and Isabella Martínez Wall and Priscilla Mora will have their wish exponentially granted, and every girl and boy in the world will have a quinceañera.

Even Las Vegas is getting into the act! Any number of chapels now list quinceañeras along with weddings in the packages they offer. For $500, A Special Memory chapel will fix you up with a bouquet, photographers, music, and a nice service in the chapel with a minister "who can do the whole thing in Spanish." For an additional $200, you can have monarch butterflies released as part of your ceremony; the doves are a little cheaper at $150 for ten. I think of Mary Astor Paul's Brazilian butterflies: there really is nothing new under the American sun.

Disney packages; extensive photo shoots; quinceañera sweepstakes; three new quinceañera reality shows on Spanish language television; cakes as big as a wedding cake—there's a whole production machine out there ready to transport our young into adulthood. With or without butterflies or a priest intoning a blessing in Spanish.

Speaking of cakes, Monica's colossal creation was made by a woman somewhere in Queens who is referred to by everyone simply as Miguelina. I call her, curious as to what she thinks of this tradition from which she makes her living. I expect to hear high praise for quinceañeras, much in the manner of Grupo Latino Por Nuestras Tradiciones. *They are one of the few traditions we have left.* But Miguelina keeps having me call her back because she has a cake in the oven or she has a cake to deliver or one she's decorating. Mostly, she sounds suspicious of anybody having the time to write a book, much less interview her. She won't give me her full name or an exact location where I might send her a copy of one of my books. I suspect she's an illegal alien conducting a business that's probably under the table. Whatever her reasons for secrecy and delay, after the third rescheduling, I start to feel as if I'm trying to conduct a drug deal, not just interview her about her cakes!

When Miguelina finally agrees to talk, she tells me she basically does one kind of cake, "dominicano," but the price depends on how much complication you want, how many layers, for example, three tiers with a simple adorno on top (a doll that says "15" or "16") or a more complex cake made up of several cakes with stairs between them and the fourteen couples arranged on the stair steps. . . . There's the $150, $200, $250 one-, two-, or three-tier cake; and the one with multiple cakes with staircases, starting at $500, $600, $800, up to $1,000.

Miguelina says she has been making her cakes for about nineteen years. She makes them at home—she took five classes from a lady, and the rest she has learned on her own. Recently, there has been a decline in demand. Used to be that in a summer, in one month, she'd be making ten of the big cakes. Now she's lucky if she gets one big cake order a year. Why? "People go to the grocery store and order a cake from the deli. Yes, the delis are all making quinceañera cakes now."

This is what happens when our traditions hit the American marketplace, I commiserate. I'm thinking chain bookstores replacing independent bookstores, humongous malls versus downtown shops. "I bet when you had your quinceañera, everything was done by your mami and the familia and friends around you," I observe, prodding her to divulge a little more of her own past.

"What quinceañera?" Miguelina scoffs. "I don't come from people who could be celebrating."

It turns out Miguelina grew up pobre pobre (she repeats the word as if to double the strength of her poverty) in a campo in the Dominican Republic—that much she is willing to tell me. She had never heard of this quinceañera tradition. Maybe people in the city had them. "Or maybe it's something that was taken from here back to our countries."

But then why do I keep hearing about how this is an old tradition we brought with us to this country that we have to honor?

There is a pause as if she can't believe I'm as ignorant as I sound, especially if I'm a person who claims to be writing a book. Finally, she says, "Yo lo único que sé es que el que inventó esto fue muy inteligente." The only thing I know is that whoever invented this was very intelligent.

"What do you mean?" I ask her, wondering if I've finally met up with the little boy who tells me that the emperor has no clothes.

Another long silence and then she says, "I mean just that."

So I try to elaborate for her. Does she mean that whoever invented these quince celebrations knew it was a way to make money? She says she didn't say as much, but think about it, all the things that someone who is going to celebrate a big quinceañera will be buying. Among them cakes, her cakes.

Anyhow, she has to go, another order she has to fill. (For as much as Miguelina complained about business being down, she seemed to be busy baking every time I called.) Besides, she is not the best person to be asking about these celebrations. She advises me to go to the library, there's probably a book that can give me a better answer as to where this so-called tradition came from.

I have to smile at her quaint suggestion for gathering information. Miguelina must not know about Google, postborder cities in a postborder world, virtual communities and chat rooms. She is a near-extinct cultural figure bound for the anonymity she so fiercely maintains. The apparatus is in place and I am part of it, the writer with one foot in and one foot out of a Pan-Hispanic community America is creating out of our diversity, reporting on a curious tradition that supposedly binds us together.

The truth about upper-class quinceañeras

Enrique Fernández, whose byline at the *Miami Herald* reads critic-at-large, is a fund of information and opinions. When I'm trying to connect with quinceañeras in every part of the country and across all social classes, I e-mail him about possibly putting me in touch with that most elusive of creatures, an upper-class U.S. quinceañera.

In part my conversation with Miguelina has made me curious. How does class play into the evolution of this tradition stateside? Back home, Miguelina didn't come from people who could be celebrating. That was for los ricos. But here in the USA, upper-class quinces are hard to find. Which leaves me wondering if there has been a complete flip-flop: working-class Latinos have adopted what only the wealthy upper classes could afford in their native countries; meanwhile upper-class Latinos disparage the tradition as practiced by people who would have been their maids and chauffeurs back home?

These are tricky matters to talk about, even among ourselves. After all, coming to America is about shedding that old hierarchical/oligarchic system. Class is supposed to dissolve in ethnicity. As a Pan-Hispanic group we will always be the *other* here. "To the gringos, we are all spics, white Negroes," one of the characters in

the Cuban film *Memories of Underdevelopment* says in disparage-
ment of the 1961 exodus to the United States. That may be, but a
white-Negro spic with resources is a lot better off than his darker-
skinned equivalent without them.

I figure that if any place is going to have a high-end quinceañera, it will be Miami, where so many of the Cuban upper class
settled in the early sixties, fleeing Castro's regime. And so, before
flying down to the city that has been dubbed—albeit by Miami-
based events planners—"the capital of quinceañeras," I e-mail
Enrique Fernández.

But according to Enrique, what I am looking for does not exist. Upper-class Cubans do not have the kind of ritualized quinces
that have evolved stateside. "They consider them basically tacky,"
Enrique e-mails me back. Instead, they are more likely to have
debutante balls "just like in the U.S. to whose upper classes Cuba's
have always been closely linked, sending their kids to Harvard
and Yale."

I'm inclined to believe Enrique. The only upper-class quinceañeras I've attended have been in the Dominican Republic, where
the family network easily secured me invitations to these exclusive parties. And there, I can report, quinceañeras are alive and
well, across all social classes, as Isabella mentioned, rich and poor.

True, the subdued, old-fashioned fiesta de quince años—the
quinceañera in a ball gown dancing a waltz with Papi at the country club—is dying out. Instead, globalization has introduced a
newer, bigger, blockbuster version of the quinceañera.

At Tanya's quince años at Discoteca Loft, a chichi night spot in
Santo Domingo, ongoing videos played on all four walls. We
were surrounded by larger-than-life Tanyas, dressed in every
imaginable outfit, some of them eye-poppingly skimpy, some of
them downright odd (Tanya in a safari and camouflage minidress

with a rifle on her shoulder visiting the national zoo). Meanwhile, several hot-and-happening musicians showed up over the course of the night to sing her happy birthday and play a set or two or three. There was no formal entrance, no waltzing with Papi in a poufy wedding-cake dress. Tanya was sexy in a turquoise outfit that made her look like a model. A cameraman filmed our hugging and greeting, and when I turned, I saw that one of the four walls featured the Tanya of the moment, greeting guests, dancing, presumably turning into a woman before our very eyes. Meanwhile the abuelitas and tías and older family members had fled to one corner of the pulsing disco where the banquet was set up and where they could barely hear themselves holler, "¡Cómo han cambiado las quinceañeras!" How quinceañeras have changed!

Quinces of this ilk are definitely "in" among upper-class Dominican girls. They have caught the Q-fever from watching big extravaganzas via cable TV, shows like MTV's *My Super Sweet 16,* or from traveling to Miami, a second home for some of the well-heeled families, and learning about Cuban quinces, the true progenitors of the over-the-top parties in this country.

Another spreader of quince fever in our home countries was the vastly popular Mexican telenovela that aired all over Latin America and won Best Telenovela of the Year in 1988, *Quinceañera.* (Reruns still show in some countries.) The soap opera features two quinceañeras who are best friends, Beatriz from a rich family and Maricruz from a poor family, both of whom go through all the travails of growing up and then some. (This is a soap opera, after all.) The biggest threat to both girls is, of course, the threat to their virginity. One of the scandalous aspects of the series, which the Catholic Church hierarchy condemned in several countries, was that both girls tangle with boys and one of them gets pregnant, and not the poor one, either.

This was the first film/TV show to break the pink fantasy bubble and focus on issues of coming-of-age hitherto banished from the airbrushed quinceañera kingdom: drugs, sex, pregnancy, gangs, pressure to conform. (An earlier, 1975 film from which the soap opera was adapted, also titled *Quinceañera*, featured family and economic troubles—poverty, class pressures, and divorcing parents whose marriage is saved by the romance rekindled by their daughter's quinceañera. But there were no problematic hormonic rumbles from *within* the girls themselves.) The later soap opera popularized the Q-tradition, making it a celebration that cool, sexy girls, rich or poor, might go for. The show's party scenes—played at the beginning of each episode—and the accompanying theme song (see epigraph), now often played at quinceañeras, entered the subconscious of a whole generation of Latin American girls whose daughters are now turning fifteen in our home countries.

But does the tradition persist in upper-class Latino circles here? A tradition, of course, can be celebrated only in the context of a community, and though working-class Latin Americans and Caribbeans and Mexicans might emigrate in droves and create barrios and comunidades in this country, let's face it, for the most part the rich and powerful have no reason to leave their home countries and build enclaves in Hialeah or Washington Heights or East Los Angeles.

Except, of course, the Cuban upper class, who were precisely the group to first emigrate in the early sixties, and these are the folks Enrique claims do not celebrate these big, gaudy quinces. Instead, during my visit to Miami, Enrique drives me to a decidedly middle-class quinceañera in a hall in Hialeah. The Styrofoam columns, the poorly choreographed dance of the court with roses exchanged in elaborate patterns, the humongous cake with a trickling fountain under the raised arch of its center, the announcer barking away in an overdone emotive voice that would have embarrassed the hell out of me at that age—all of it seems to prove Enrique right. There's an intrinsic excess in the ritual that does not jibe well with upper-class restraint and horror of "rasquachismo," a kind of Latino kitsch that revels in the vulgar, the vernacular, the traditionally tasteless, as in velvet paintings, lawn decorations, car ornaments, and, yes, quinceañeras.

But when I run this theory by Tony Pouparina, owner of High Performance Designs, a company that stages a lot of events in and around Miami, among them quinceañeras, he is downright apoplectic with disagreement and annoyance.

"You come down here," he invites me—this is several weeks later, I'm back in Vermont—"and I'll show you some high-end quinces, no Mickey Mouse stuff, I mean the cream of the crop." He mentions some wealthy, first-class people, none of whose names I recognize, who are going to unload some serious money on their daughters' quinces. (By serious he means $80,000 and up; the average amount Tony quotes me for a "cheap quince" is $15,000 to $20,000.) "We Cubans, I don't care how rich or poor we are, we love to celebrate life every day. It's in our blood," Tony claims.

For his own daughter Natasha, Tony threw a quince with a *Phantom of the Opera* theme at the James Knight Center. "The biggest production in the history of quinceañeras in south Florida," Tony claims. He hasn't added up the bills ("Too painful," he laughs), but he estimates it cost him in the vicinity of $125,000. It would have been a quarter of a million if he'd had to pay for it retail.

I can hear that Tony is making my same mistake: confusing money with class. The rich are not necessarily the upper-class folks that Enrique was talking about. (Class issues *are* tricky matters.) But I can't get a word in edgewise—Tony, unlike Miguelina, is a talker.

"I'm sorry, but that individual who told you high-class people don't give their daughters quinces does not know the reality of what I work with every day. I'm telling you the truth, the whole truth," Tony concludes. And then, as if reconsidering that high claim, he laughs. "My truth, okay, but I know what I'm talking about. The richest Cubans put out for their daughters. Quinces are special for us. You see, Cuban fathers are very attached to their daughters. The saddest day for a Cuban father is the day his daughter gets married. You're happy for her, but you're heartbroken to be losing her."

So quinces are the perfect solution, I suggest. "You throw your daughter a mini wedding but you get to take her home when the party is over."

"That's the truth!" Tony laughs, even though this time the truth is coming from somebody else's mouth.

The queens of pretty parties

For thirty-two years (we worked out the math over the phone) Esthersita of Pretty Party has been planning, coordinating, executing, and emceeing quinceañeras. Any constructive action verb you want to use before the direct object "quinceañeras," Esthersita has done it, and she has pulled her whole family along with her: her husband, Aurelio, and her daughters, Raquel and Romy, whom she calls "mi versión en inglés," my English version.

"It is a seven-day-a-week job," Esthersita explains, "so it is good that my whole family is into it."

Esthersita actually began what was to be her life's work as a fourteen-year-old girl in Cuba. One of six daughters in a poor family, she was not able to have a quinceañera, but instead she helped several of her friends organize theirs. She found she had a proficiency and a passion for this sort of thing and soon she was in demand. Her skills proved to be transportable when she landed in the United States as a sixteen-year-old, and over the last three-plus decades, she has built a successful business, which she describes as "party planning."

Party planning doesn't quite encompass all that Esthersita does. If Tony Pouparina represents the American Broadway show–style events producer, Esthersita hearkens back to our native countries, the tías and madrinas who knew everything there was to know about every social moment a female human critter would ever have to dress for and in some cases host. There is at least one in every familia, and when she passes, a huge chunk of tradition bites the dust. She is the resource that Will Cain referred to when he said that for many Latino families in this country abuelita is gone.

The Esthersitas I grew up with in the Dominican Republic always knew the correct thing to do and how to do it. They could tell you what to wear to any social event, coordinated with the time of day, the season, the time in your life. They could instruct you on how to keep luto (mourning clothes), when you could begin wearing gray or a piece of jewelry, when you could entertain again. (Quinceañeras are routinely canceled due to a recent death in a family.) They could parse a bloodline so you knew exactly how you were related to fulano, so-and-so, including byways of illegitimacy, widowhood, and the more contemporary divorce. Protocol, etiquette, cuisine, couture, you name it: they were the depositories of all that information for cultures where there was no Emily Post etiquette book next to the *Good Housekeeping* cookbook to consult. They were always well dressed, even if you knocked at their door at ten o'clock at night or eight in the morning (it might take them a little while to make an appearance), redolent with perfume, freshly coiffed and powdered. Actually, when Will Cain called this traditional figure an abuelita, the term didn't quite gel with my experience of such women in my extended familia, because there was nothing grandmotherly about these damas. They were often coquettish even into their late years, exquisitely groomed to the point of almost being a bit vain. The word in Spanish—and I've never found a satisfying translation for it in English—is "presumida," a person who is, well, very well put together. "Dicho de una persona que se compone o arregla mucho" (said of a person who makes herself up or fixes herself up a lot). But so adept were these Esthersitas that just when it seemed they were going to plunge into conceit and caricature, they tipped the balance and turned into exemplars of social graces.

In *The Tipping Point*, Malcolm Gladwell analyzes how social "epidemics" get started. How does a little-known, unique practice suddenly tip and become a fad, a social phenomenon? In very simplified form, Gladwell identifies three kinds of people who are necessary for these epidemics to get started: mavens (who know everything), connectors (who know everybody), and salesmen (who can sell most anything to almost anybody). If you can imagine this trinity put together into one person in the world of social skills, then you have yourself an Esthersita. Luckily for those of us who left ours behind in our home countries, there's one you can hire if you live in or close to Miami and want to throw a pretty party.

I decide to travel to Miami, in large part to interview Esthersita, whose clients have dubbed her "the queen of pretty parties." On the phone, Esthersita speaks only in Spanish with gracious turns of phrases, very impressive and intimidating to me, whose Spanish doesn't get much practice up here in Latino-compromised Vermont. Esthersita cautions me that I must not come on a weekend. Mondays are also bad because she and all her different vendors are recovering from a weekend packed with quinceañeras, weddings, baby showers, and other sundry parties. Thursdays the pace again picks up, and Fridays she won't have a minute to devote to me. So, we agree that we should meet on a Tuesday, midmorning. Already I can tell that this is not going to be the rushed twenty-minute interview that is all I can often manage from Esthersita's Americanized counterparts, many of whom lose interest when it becomes clear I don't have a daughter or granddaughter whose wedding or quinceañera I will be hiring them for. Esthersita, in fact, refers to our meeting with an old-world term, "atenderme." She wants to be free to turn her full attention to me during my visit.

And attend to me she does, devoting a full day to squiring me around to all her different vendors: photographers, seamstresses in the back rooms of studios, a banquet hall, a dj, a makeup artist, a travel agency that does a lot of quinceañera cruises. Esthersita is a large woman, and yet she has a dainty look about her perhaps because she always seems perfectly posed and composed like someone about to have her picture taken. At one point, when I ask to take her picture, Esthersita brightens up, cocks her head, arches her back a tad more, freshens up her smile. "The flash didn't go off," she tells me. "Take it again." And again she strikes the pose. She is dressed impeccably in a black linen pantsuit with large pearl earrings and necklace. Her hair is sprayed in place, there is the scent of my mother's old perfume. Even though she is only a few years older than I am (I've done the math myself this time, as I would never ask an Esthersita-type person her age: she came to this country in 1960 when she was sixteen), I feel as if I am conversing with someone from my mother's generation.

Esthersita is the hub of a widespread network of providers and people capable of fielding any question related to the world of parties, and most specifically quinceañeras. In fact, Esthersita's manual cum etiquette book, *Sólo para quinceañeras,* is the most thorough quinceañera book I have ever encountered in Spanish or English. Where else can you find a list of twenty-five dos and don'ts at a quinceañera? Admittedly, some of these admonitions seem elemental (don't take more than one recuerdo, or party favor, from the table; if you want to say a few words or make a toast be sure you clear it first with your hosts and keep it brief; don't walk in front of the photographer or videographer and ruin a key shot), but you'd be surprised by the number of people that get more than half of these wrong. Esthersita advises that we should all periodically review this list if we want to be the kind of educated person who gets invited to quinceañeras and other pretty parties. The book also has an astrology chapter, the Aries quinceañera versus the Aquarius quinceañera, as well as poems that can be recited by the brother, the father, the quinceañera herself. One especially poignant poem by Luis Mario is addressed to "the exiled quinceañera," who blooms so far from the forlorn native garden where her beauty belongs.

> Este cielo hermoso y libre
> no es tu cielo:
> no te olvides de tu Patria nunca . . . Nunca
> quinceañera del Destierro!

> This beautiful open sky
> is not your sky
> never forget your country, never
> quinceañera in exile!

And yet, for all her old-world social quaintness, Esthersita is remarkably attuned to the younger generation and the problems that arise when a teenage girl born and raised here with Disney and MTV as part of her culture meets head-on with Mami's idea of a quinceañera. Often, Esthersita has to counsel both mother and daughter through some rough spots, which she considers a big part of her job.

What exactly does she do?

"Ir por la parte bonita," go the pretty way to make a fiesta that is special for everyone. She takes each one aside: reminding the mother that this is her daughter's quince, the young girl must be able "to float on the cloud of her dreams"; persuading the daughter to cede to her mami in this or that detail, as this is the quince her mami never had. Oh, yes, many of the mothers of these girls could not afford a quince back in Cuba or as recent arrivals—a statement I've heard over and over again in communities across this country. Now there's more money to spend on extras. But time has moved on, the world has changed, and these American girls don't necessarily want what their mamis never had and now want to give to them.

Besides bridge building and counseling, Esthersita helps families plan, budget, prepare, and execute all kinds of perfect parties, and among her favorites are quinceañeras. "Brides are more complicated," she muses when I ask her why she likes quinces more than weddings. "They are more demanding because they're older. You have to deal with more than one family." She attends every one of her parties, from start to finish, to ensure that nothing goes amiss, "evitando errores y horrores," serving as mistress of ceremony, keeping the guest book, and tending the gifts table. Often she is asked to write the speeches and dedicatorios by parents and girls who feel unsure how to speak in public. Of course, she works only in Spanish. Why forsake the language in which she has learned to say so many pretty things? (When English is called for, Romy takes over and becomes Esthersita en inglés.)

Esthersita charges by the hour, though she admits that each hour she bills for probably represents two or three. From time to time, her services are free. She'll hear of a girl in need, and she'll mobilize all her vendors to donate their services. Periodically, she rounds up old gowns and tiaras and fans and ships them to her native Cuba so that girls coming of age in Communism can have a touch of consumerism. A few years back, she learned about some recent arrivals who had spent their fifteenth birthday in Guantánamo. So she threw them a group quinceañera, fifteen girls—it just so happened there were fifteen of them!—waltzed in donated gowns and tiaras, feasted on cakes and banquet fare provided by the community. In a testimonial included in Esthersita's book, one of these girls, Saimary Rivero, describes Esthersita not only as "my quinceañera fairy godmother, but after that night, she has kept abreast of my studies, worrying over my education, serving as my adviser. She is the best thing that has happened to me in this beautiful but difficult country."

This is a service you could never get from the events production companies, which will indeed provide all the razzmatazz you need for that special night. But at the stroke of midnight (or whenever the party is over), like the Cinderella story so beloved by quinceañeras, they will strike their sets, gather their linens, and vamoose! These community-based party planners stick around, continuing in their role as adviser and resource. Priscilla Mora, who could be called the Esthersita of San Antonio, does a lot of ongoing hand-holding and mentoring. "These kids know that I am there for them, we have a bond somehow, I can't explain it. My quinceañera moms say, 'They listen to you, not me, why is that?'" Her colleague Bisli of Bisli Events Services agrees that quinceañeras are only the beginning, not the end, of a process of accompanying the girl into adulthood. "You see all this family and community energy, time, money, resources mobilized around the young girl for this party. It should not be about just one night, but about the girl and what happens afterward in her life."

Bisli, who is originally from a small town in Panama, first did events management on the East Coast, but four years ago she moved her business to San Antonio. She admits that this is the hardest aspect of her service to transport across distances—this tight relationship with the community she serves. It takes time to develop. It takes trust. But it's the one thing she is sure should not be lost as a business or an ethnic group grows. This familial feeling feeds the soul of who we are as a community and as individuals. It is why, as other events providers climb onboard the big huge quinceañera Hummer-bandwagon, we have to keep hold of the steering wheel, not lose what is valuable.

Pretty parties are more than skin-deep, and the best party planners strike down into the rich soil of a community to provide not just a service but a vibrant transmission of tradition. It's a dying art, which is why the charm of folks like Esthersita is tinged with nostalgia. These throwback figures remind us of the old countries where forlorn gardens have long since recovered and grown new blooms. Meanwhile, so-called "exiled quinceañeras," born and bred here, feel that this is their native home. It's we, the bridge generations, who have that double vision and know these Esthersitas will soon be gone.

Some of them will evolve with the market and new style of doing business. Bisli, for example, now has a highly interactive Web site, and Priscilla Mora is giving up the party-planning part of her business in order to devote her time to being a cyberspace quinceañera planner and provider. ("I just can't keep up with everything. Oh, I'll still do a few local quinceañeras, because I love them, I really do. But God has another plan for me.") At her new Web site, sweet15party.com, Priscilla connects providers with clients across the country. But even in cyberspace, she can't help herself. She adds that personal touch by having a page, "Ask Priscilla," in which she answers individual questions from the girls, as well as a "Parents Corner" for the concerns of parents who want to give their daughters a meaningful rite of passage.

Meanwhile, Esthersita in Miami still works in that old style of attending to each client, visiting with her providers, going to schools and fairs and libraries with her big albums of pictures and handwritten thank-you notes from grateful quinceañeras and brides, educating us all on this tradition, keeping an eye out for those who might fall to the wayside as a community moves forward, and funneling some of the tiaras, ball gowns, and last dolls their way.

These Esthersitas in communities throughout the USA might soon be the has-beens, but for now, long live these queens!

Too many worlds at once

The hall is filling. The soft buzz of conversation has become a loud roar. The guests who got here early are already into their second or third drink. Esthersitas and other party motivators must develop an acute ear for when to move on to the next stage of festivities, and so ride the wave of building excitement. Too soon and the party flops. Too late and everyone's too tired to get worked up into the happy frenzy that means handsome tips and a good recommendation to the next family looking for a place or provider.

In the "green room" area where the court and Monica wait to make their entrance, the girls are practicing their choreographed dance steps while the boys watch. The oldest-looking boy—they all look about three years younger than the girls—wanders too close to this earnest coven and gets drafted into standing still while Raquel demonstrates how they are to spin themselves around their escorts. I'm reminded of Marling's observation that boys next to their young diva-dates in prom pictures are mere props, "the human equivalent of potted palms."

The emcee comes up the steps to make sure it's thumbs-up for the presentation. But what no one had noticed in the commotion of arrivals and dance-step rehearsals is that Monica is prone on the couch, an arm over her forehead, looking very much like a nineteenth-century heroine in distress. It's not just a headache anymore; Monica is feeling too dizzy to stand up. How does information travel like lightning through a gathering? No sooner has Monica bewailed her condition than a battalion of well-dressed matrons is marching up the steps to her rescue, including Monica's mother and Godmother Claire. *Get her a plate of food. A glass of water. Does anyone have un calmante? Maybe there's a drugstore open nearby. Have her lie down. No, no, let her sit up with her head between her legs.* . . . All kinds of remedies are proffered as more and more female guests crowd around the couch, the way people gather at accidents, wanting to see for themselves the awful thing that has happened.

Poor Monica, collapsing just as she is about to make her entrance into womanhood! I hear snippets of explanations: *Nervios, pobrecita. Hasn't eaten all day, imagine.* Meanwhile down in the hall, the intense socializing has abated, and people are now eyeing the aluminum pans warming in their racks as if they might storm the banquet tables if they're not fed soon. But the quinceañera's presentation and the choreographed dance are supposed to happen first. Word goes down to the servers to blow out the warming candles so as not to spoil the already overheated food.

I've taken a spin around the floor, to be out of the way in the waiting room that has now turned into a sickroom. When I head back to my post at the top of the steps, Monica is nowhere in sight, but a half dozen women are bunched up in the narrow hallway that leads to a small bathroom. Briefly, the crowd parts, and I catch a glimpse of Monica kneeling on the floor in her gown and throwing up inside a toilet bowl while her mami and Claire steady her on either side. The crowd settles back and the view is lost, but it is a moment to remember, an image of the wounded heart at the center of so many of our female ceremonies where we witness the actual cost of being always beautiful or pliably feminine, a good girl trying to succeed in too many worlds at once.

Malinche fears

In the course of my own dizzying responses to the quinceañeras I was studying, I would sometimes scare myself sick thinking of what would happen if I didn't fall in line and praise this important tradition of nuestra cultura. The Malinche fear of betraying my own people to the conquistador culture hangs heavy on my heart—Malinche being the indigenous woman in Mexico who supposedly betrayed her people to Cortés. (We Dominicans have our own version of this ailment, el complejo de Guacanagarix, after the Taino cacique who is said to have cooperated with the conquistadores.)

A bigger worry was that of disappointing "my girls," lovely muchachas whose quinceañeras I had attended and who—no matter my explanations—thought of me as a kind of ticket to fame. When at one point I explained to Monica that I would not be using her real name but would, in fact, be disguising her identity—to protect her privacy—she piped up that she wanted to have her real name in my book. "It's an opportunity for her," Monica's father reassured me. I couldn't help thinking of how Monica had introduced me to her priest as "my author."

At first, this desire to be famous surprised me, until I kept hearing it again and again from the girls I interviewed, as well as in the material I was reading. Of course, this desire is part of the gasoline running the whole quinceañera production with its limos and photo shoots and makeup artists and videos of the young girl's life. "I think a lot of girls want to be famous," one girl admits in Lauren Greenfield's *Girl Culture,* a book of interviews and photographs of young girls. "Many times kids whose lives aren't perfect—who live in poverty or have crazy parents—it's like they see this world on television and in movies and magazines, and it looks so beautiful from far away, they want to be part of that. . . . They want to . . . show this world, which doesn't believe in them or respect them, that they're beautiful and special."

But it's not just the have-nots yearning for their Warholian fifteen minutes of fame. Michael Wood, vice president of Teenage Research Unlimited, notes that "there's a universal obsession with celebrity, and teens are looking for their chance in the spotlight." But what if they were to have their wish come true at fifteen? Don't they know that would be terrible? Think of Tom Buchanan in F. Scott Fitzgerald's *The Great Gatsby,* the former football star at Yale, who turned out to be "one of those men who reach such an acute limited excellence at twenty-one that everything afterward savors of anticlimax." Besides, what can you have achieved by fifteen that merits a whole movie about your life, a staged production, your name up in lights? I recall asking a friend's twelve-year-old son that classic question that goes with playing the role of "boring old person" in young people's lives. "What do you want to be when you grow up?" The boy replied, "I want to be famous."

"But famous for what?" I countered.

"What do you mean?" He sighed, exasperated.

I didn't want to turn the boy off completely with a little lecture. *This is getting annoying.* So, I waxed on about the beauty of finding a calling that can be its own reward, and soon he was shaking his head.

"All I know is I'd be really depressed if I was doing something and like nobody knew." ("Nobody" meant the majority of Americans, if not the whole world.) Then my young friend turned the tables on me. "Don't you feel bad that—I know you've published books and all—but that you're not famous like J. K. Rowling?"

"Who's J. K. Rowling?" I said. It was a joke. Of course I knew the name of the author of the legendary *Harry Potter* books. But I could not humor my friend's son or convince him that of the many writers whose talent I envied, J. K. Rowling—no offense— was not among them. George Eliot or Emily Dickinson or Walt Whitman or Pablo Neruda, yes—and what I envied was their talent, not their fame. "When I was growing up," I told my young friend, "fame came at least a hundred years after you died."

Of course, I was exaggerating to prove a point. Ambition will always be a big part of being young, what fuels our finding our way in the world. In fact, when I was just a little older than this boy, at Abbot Academy, I wanted to be a successful writer. But I was deeply conflicted and confused about achieving my dream. I was still enough of a good Latina girl to believe that a public voice was not for girls, would in fact ruin my chances to be successful in that romantic fairy-tale drama which quinceañeras partake of and which I had been taught by mi cultura and familia to want.

This conflict came to the fore in the fall of my second year at Abbot. I no longer had my Miss Stevenson star to steer by: she had left for graduate school; she had left to teach at another school; she had been asked to leave—rumors were rife as to why she was gone. My confusion began to manifest itself in an inexplicable behavior: walking out of exams. I would come to final examinations with one of the highest grades in the course, or, in the case of SATs and achievement tests, with a strong chance of doing well, and as soon as I tried to perform, I would experience dread, a distracting voice would start up in my head. *You can't do this! You're going to mess up! Why don't you get out? Why don't you leave now?* I would try to ignore the voice, to force myself to concentrate, but panic would seize me, my breath would come short, my head would begin to spin. The discomfort was so great that finally I would bolt out of the classroom, leaving behind my dumbfounded teachers and disgusted classmates. After several incidents, the headmistress recommended that I be sent to see "someone" who might help me overcome this problem.

I recall visiting three psychiatrists over the course of the years that I was afflicted by this terror. One of them was just too preciously Freudian—with bow tie and folded hands on the other side of a large desk—to be of any help to me. I visited him twice, and then vehemently protested to my parents that I was fine. But, of course, the behavior persisted. The second psychiatrist I was sent to tried a behavior modification approach—every visit, he talked me through the days before an exam, the hours, the minutes, trying to get a handle on when the panic would kick in and what it was about. "I'm scared all the time," I tried to tell him. I meant all the time beginning with when the teacher first announced an upcoming exam. The last psychiatrist, a Dominican "uncle," a friend of the family's, was mostly flirtatious and disinterested in my angst but ready with a prescription. For years, unbeknownst to my family, I was hooked on amphetamines, legally acquired via a long-distance phone call to my tío, who for reasons I still cannot unravel prescribed speed for terror. (I tried to contact him during the writing of this book, only to find out that he died more than a decade ago.)

Speed only made things worse. At one point it seemed I would have to drop out of school because I could not control these attacks. But my teachers at Abbot persisted and, truly, without their indulgence I would never have made it through high school. They allowed me to write papers or answer take-home questions for my final exam. This somehow got in under the phobia radar, but not altogether. I didn't bolt but I didn't do well. I'd go into finals with an A in the course and end up with a B or, depending on how well speed kept me a step ahead of the furies, a B+ or an A–.

The explanation I remember hearing and believing was that I was too terrified of failure to test well. So much was riding on my older sister and me making it at Abbot Academy, where we had been granted this incredible opportunity. Family pride. We had to prove to these americanos we were good enough. But it's only now, in my fifties and after months of musing on quinceañeras, that I see another part of this puzzling episode in my young adult life. I was terrified not only to fail but to succeed.

For what would happen if I continued on the path of being a woman with a mind and a life of my own? Maybe it was okay for American girls to have careers, though judging from Bette Davis movies in which the ambitious career gal ends up successful, but unloved and alone, I suspected that too much ambition was bad for Americanas as well. But most definitely, female ambition in the public sphere was not encouraged in my Latina family. It was one thing to make my cultura and familia proud, but too much progress up the ladder of success and somehow I sensed the cord would snap, I'd be afloat in that outer space of American culture with no way to get back to a place where I had once belonged.

Girls on the advent of their quinceañeras often talked about experiencing added pressures that they associated with adulthood. "I've got a lot more to think about," Anita in Chicago admitted when I asked her what if anything having a quince had changed for her. "I mean like am I going to go to college and stuff like that." Gabby Castro admitted that until participating in a group quinceañera program in Idaho she had not been planning on going to college. "I was your normal Hispanic girl," she explained. "After high school I was suppose to work to help out the family." A comment that sent a pang through my heart.

It is a sentiment echoed in the popular film *Real Women Have Curves*. When Ana García, the young Latina protagonist, wins a scholarship to a college on the East Coast, her immigrant father explains to Ana's teacher why he can't let her go. "I didn't come this far to see my family break apart." When reminded that he also brought his family to the USA for a better life, Ana's father gives lip service to schooling—up to a point. "Of course, we want Ana to get educated, but we need her to work now. She can go to college later." We all know how easily mañana can morph into never where a Latina's future is involved. As for Ana's mother, she cannot see the need for college for her daughter, now or later: "I can teach her. I can teach her to sew. I can teach her to raise her kids . . . and take care of her husband. Those are things they won't teach her in school."

With these kinds of pressures it's no wonder that many Latinas give up. A recent CBSNews.com article, titled "Tough Road to College for Latinas," noted that "for Hispanic women, the road from the barrio to the college campus can be a minefield strewn with cultural and economic obstacles, as well as ethnic and sexual stereotypes."

And the journey down that mined road begins with that marker of adulthood: her quinceañera.

"It's a time when the young girl is faced with choices that might be pulling her in different directions," Jill Denner, co-editor-author with Bianca Guzman of *Latina Girls: Voices of Adolescent Strength in the U.S.*, commented when we spoke by phone about the quince tradition. "The young girl is moving from girlhood to adulthood in what culture? Does it take her further from her home culture or closer to her home culture, or does the ritual involve a negotiation between her cultures?"

It is an interesting question. On the outside, the young girl is being welcomed as a full-fledged member of her family and community at a time, adolescence, when she might be rebelling and pulling away. She is now expected to take on her traditional female role, in line with Mami and Abuelita. And yet as the young girl and her mother organize the party, make choices, spend time together, argue over details, negotiations are going on, and ever so slightly but significantly, the ground of Latina womanhood is being altered to accommodate the new generation.

But at Abbot Academy, there was no common ground in which my two worlds could come together. Add to this separation the fact that it was boarding school, so there wasn't the daily juxtaposition of worlds to force some key issues into the arena of negotiation. I came home and wham! It was the D.R., the nineteenth century: no socializing with males who were not family members; no going out with anybody, female or male, unchaperoned; no contradicting your parents or correcting the innumerable errors they seem to excel in when you are an adolescent. Meanwhile at school, I was being encouraged intellectually and by the example of my teachers to step up to the front lines of American womanhood. I was smart enough to figure out which was the successful track in my new country, but as Bigi and the nurses reminded me, I had Dominican blood in my veins. I yearned to belong and be loved by my own familia both here and back on the island I still persisted in calling "home."

And so a division set in, one that Ed Morales alludes to in *Living in Spanglish* as "a classic moment in the life of every Spanglish person when one realizes that by adapting or assimilating to the dominant culture, there is a feeling of satisfaction *and* a profound inability to return to where one came from." One experiences "the nausea of transmigration, the onset of vertigo from being pulled back and forth across the border by a desire to embrace a dynamic North Americanism while retaining the deep spiritual sentimentality of the South."

One can see how the quinceañera, the ritual moment at which a young woman begins her own life, can bring these divisive pressures to a head and unleash those forces which are battling for control of who she is going to be—not when she grows up but now that she is being acknowledged as an adult. As Marco Villatoro, a high school teacher interviewed for the CBSNews.com article, concludes about his young Latina students struggling with their families and with stereotypes to continue their education, "There's a lot of tension on them. If it doesn't break them, it makes them stronger."

No wonder poor Monica ended up bent over the toilet, throwing up. Or that girls end up getting pregnant, walking out of exams, or dropping out of school altogether.

Some of us have to break first before we get stronger.

Quinceañera, the movie

Teen pregnancy, homosexuality, drug use, violence—such issues would seem to inhabit an opposite world from that of the fairy-tale kingdom of quinceañeras. But a refreshing new film, *Quinceañera,* shows that they don't. Interestingly, like its predecessor, the Mexican soap opera with the same name, the American film is bound to stir up controversy in the Latino community about conflicts and challenges that our young people are facing, often with no help from us.

Fourteen-year-old Magdalena is a Mexican American girl on the eve of her quinceañera. She wants the cool dress, the Hummer limo, the fancy party, that her rich cousin has gotten for her quince. Class issues are rife in the film—not just within the Latino community but in the quickly gentrifying neighborhood of Echo Park in Los Angeles, where Magdalena and her family live. Wealthier Anglos, many of them gay couples, are moving in and pushing out the working-class residents. This larger context helps give the film a dimension that would otherwise be missing. Dispossession is happening on all levels.

Especially when Magdalena becomes pregnant. Her papi, Ernesto, an evangelical minister, suddenly sees her as the fallen Eve who must be expelled from the garden. Magdalena is no longer his virginal daughter, exemplifying an old-world ideal of womanhood. But the pregnant Magdalena protests that she *is* still a virgin, an assertion that proves to be (technically) true! The movie is so well done that you end up believing an immaculate conception could have happened to her.

Of course, her papi doesn't believe her and casts her out of the house, canceling her quinceañera. Magdalena ends up taking shelter with her loving, tolerant Tío Tomás, who is about to get cast out of his own garden by a gentrifying gay Anglo couple who own the little caretaker's cottage he rents behind their newly renovated house. Tío Tomás has also given shelter to Carlos, whose parents have disowned him, too, because he is gay.

That is a Pandora's box of issues that the film handles with a light touch and a heavy heart. For although the quinceañera ends up happening, Magdalena in a gown let out a few inches to accommodate her situation, her bouquet held coyly before her belly, Carlos in a tux that makes him look like your classic hetero-sexual Romeo, there is a sense that the problematic issues have come to a momentary balance, not a resolution. What will happen when a quinceañera gets pregnant from actually having and enjoying sex? What will happen when Carlos moves in with a boyfriend and is openly gay?

When I interviewed Wash Westmoreland and Richard Glatzer, the joint writers/directors/producers of the film, I joked with them that initially, when I first heard about the film, I groaned at the thought of two white guys let loose in the kingdom of the quinceañera. But I was not just pleasantly surprised but totally won over. I was curious, however, how the Latino community was reacting to the problematic issues their movie brings to the fore. For that was another thought when I heard about the film: better them than me. Two white men can't be Malinches—Corteses maybe, but they can't be accused of betraying their own people.

"Interestingly, the outcry against the film has not been about Magdalena's pregnancy, but about the gay story," Richard noted. "Some conservatives in the Latino press have taken issue with what they see as Carlos's seduction, claiming he's being used and abused by the gay community."

I wondered why the pregnancy of the quinceañera did not cause a stir. "There's a way in which teen pregnancy is now an old issue," Wash explained. (I had to keep asking who was speaking, as this was a stereo phone interview, each one at an echoing extension in their house in L.A.) "I mean the statistics are out there, but the homophobia in the Latino community is still in the closet."

Richard (or maybe it was Wash? Reader, I tried) said many of the actors were local neighbors from Echo Park who, in addition to being in the film, contributed in whatever way they could, bringing tamales for the cast and crew, staying with friends to allow their houses to be featured in certain scenes. One man even let the filmmakers paint his kitchen "a really horrible pink," according to Westmoreland. (The *New York Times* reviewer dubbed this an "it-takes-a-village style of filmmaking.") Among the local amateur actors was an immigrant from El Salvador who cleans houses in the neighborhood. Later, when she was interviewed by Telemundo about the film, she cried. She said that she herself had a daughter who became pregnant at sixteen. She said that the movie made her realize how we worry so much in our community about the material well-being of our children, but lots of times we don't talk to them about what is really important.

We need to talk to our young people about who they are. Why they are feeling divided or overwhelmed or confused or sad.

We need to talk to them about who we are. How we ourselves have felt divided or overwhelmed or confused or sad.

Otherwise, we are Malinches to our children, letting them make their own way in a conquistador-consumer world.

Silence can be a form of betrayal, too.

The quince dream belongs to the mothers

Amazingly, Monica's emcee is on the mike telling everyone to please take their seats; we are about to begin. Magic has been worked in that back room. Those mamis and tías and godmothers heard the alarm—*one of our muchachitas needs help!*—and they flew to the rescue. For months, I've been exposed to the astonishing capacity of a certain-age Latina to get the ball rolling, to single-handedly get things done. The few Anglo women who are here tonight are all accompanied by a spouse, but many of the Latinas, including Raquel's and Alicia's mamis, are here by themselves. I'm reminded that, just as in the African American community, many Hispanic households at the lower economic end are headed by a single parent, and most of these are women. (In 2000, about one-third of Hispanic households were headed by a single parent, usually female, according to the Population Resource Center.) The macho culture notwithstanding, many Latinas wear both the pants and the skirts in their familias.

I love that older Latina woman to whom the descriptive phrase my Disney contact used for Isabella Martínez Wall can be applied: "a full-bodied Latina." I love the flamboyance of their party dresses, the sequins glittering on the wide spread of the hips, the neckline plunging, the rough hands done up with nail polish, the fingers too calloused for rings. There seems to be no shame in displaying a body that has earned its stripes in extra pounds and stretch marks. They have had children, no-good husbands, too many jobs with bad shifts, but tonight they will *echar una canita al aire* (literally, throw a little gray hair to the breeze, that is, let their hair down, have a good time). They dance with one another, with their young daughters (which I find so sweet), and, if need be, by themselves. If the banquet is homemade, they will dish out the food, which they probably helped to make, and if there's a sick girl in the back room, they'll figure out what she needs—a tisana or calmante or just a plate of food—and they will have her back on her feet in no time.

One way or other, they will help us get born and ensure we celebrate our First Communions and quinceañeras, and later, our weddings. They will show up when our lives fall apart, help us give birth, take care of us when we get sick, and, bless them, I do believe they will also be there in spirit to help us die, closing our eyes even if we've pissed them off royally and married the sin vergüenza or published the autobiographical novel against their interdiction or good advice.

Somehow, at the other end of the Cinderella story which many young Latinas first play out publicly in their quinceañeras, there emerges this strong woman, this phoenix from the ashes of a sexist paradigm. It has failed for them—the long-term prince, the happily-forever-after romance, the fairy-tale life as an indulged princess. Why, then, do these mujeres insist on passing on this flawed fantasy to their daughters?

It is a perplexing question. But one thing is clear: quinceañeras are as much about the mothers as they are about the daughters. "The quince dream belongs to the mothers," concludes Liz Balmaseda, who has been reporting for years on quinces for the *Miami Herald*. If Papi is getting to throw his daughter a wedding-type celebration at the end of which he gets to take her home, Mami is showing off her life's work, the girl she raised to be everything she herself might have hoped for but could not become.

Ay, there's the rub! The vehemence of this maternal push for quinceañeras is steeped in nostalgia for the fairy-tale life the mothers themselves never had. Sadly, these women blame themselves for their lack of educational and employment opportunities, their failed romances/marriages, rather than blaming the status quo or the fantasy itself, and so they pass on to their daughters a worldview and a role that will land them in the same hobbled place as their mamis. *Education is teaching our children to desire the right things.* But first, we have to learn this lesson ourselves, which might involve unlearning some of the lessons we brought with us, difficult as that may be.

Not that our new country is free of these paradigms. Ay, there's the further rub! The gender handicap is alive and well in the USA. In 2005, American women, on average, earned seventy-seven cents for every dollar that men brought home; in 2001, women without a high school diploma were 50 percent more likely to fall below the poverty line than men with the same level of education. On a worldwide scale, the majority of the 1.5 billion people living in the world on one dollar a day or less are women—a gap that continues to grow and that is commonly referred to in international-aid circles as "the feminization of poverty." We are steeped in a mind-set that we absorb from even the most enlightened parents and teachers and communities. No wonder most women will play out some version of this story at some point in their lives.

These pervasive, skewed gender relations are further complicated by what have been our traditional roles as Latino men and women. Much has been written about machismo, that cult of hypervirility in which the male is cock of the walk, celebrated for his sexual conquests, his masculine brio and aggressiveness. Less is said about the reverse side of that gender coin, the female counterpart, Marianismo. The Latina woman models herself after that ideal of womanhood, María, the mother of God. In fact, in traditional quinceañeras that begin with a church service, the young girl lays flowers at the Virgin's feet, consecrating her life to the Virgin Mother. Marianismo dictates that the Latina woman is virginal, even after marriage. Sex with her husband is a duty. *Haciéndole el servicio,* my old tías used to say. Doing him the service. She is submissive, self-sacrificing, long-suffering, putting up with her husband's infidelities, devoted to her familia, and most especially to her children.

But if Latinas follow this prescribed gender role, with whom are the men exercising their extramarital macho prerogatives? Reader, that is an excellent question. One that many Latinas, especially around their teen years, begin to ponder.

Remember Cortés's Indian mistress, La Malinche? If María is the virginal ideal of womanhood, Malinche is the violated woman who lets a conquistador man have his way with her and ultimately ends up betraying the homeland by aiding the enemy. You don't have to be fifteen years old to know which of the two role models is the right choice for a nice girl.

So what do we Latinas get from following Marianismo instead of being Malinches? You might be thinking of that old bumper sticker: BAD GIRLS HAVE MORE FUN. That might be true in the USA, where bad girls are on their own, living in apartments far from home, but not so in countries that until recently were steeped in Catholicism. A bad girl would be banished by her familia, which in a tribal culture that continues to be the modus operandi in many of our native countries, amounts to a kind of societal death.

What we girls get from Marianismo is the high road, moral clout, spiritual superiority. We get to be the "good guys," who know that men are children whose infidelities and peccadilloes have to be forgiven because they can't help themselves. What's more, we exercise enormous power from our pedestals, especially at two pinnacle points in our female lives: when we are at our most virginal and most desirable (why quinceañeras are important) and when we become mothers, especially mothers of sons who worship us. Well, most of the time. A Dominican friend once illustrated Marianismo-that-never-quits with this story:

A saintly mother had a son who got mixed up with an evil, possessive mistress. (You got it. The bad girl, Malinche.) The mistress was very jealous of her lover's devotion to his mother. She demanded that he prove his love by bringing her his mother's heart torn out of her breast. The son was swept up by passion. (Crimes of passion, by the way, are treated much more leniently in our Latin cultures—a man who murders his philandering wife can get off scot-free. Not so for murdering your mother, which is one of the worst crimes you can commit. In fact, during his thirty-one-year dictatorship in the Dominican Republic,

Trujillo tortured enemies by killing their sons and violating their daughters and wives. But there is no instance of his raising a torturing hand against somebody's mother. In fact, this murderous dictator visited his mother without fail every afternoon, even though this predictability set him up for ambush by the underground.)

The impassioned son of my friend's story could not help himself, and, weeping apologetically, he pulled out a knife and tore out his mother's heart. As he was running furiously back toward his mistress's house, he stumbled and fell, and the heart slipped from his hands. From it issued a worried voice, "Son, did you hurt yourself?"

It's easy enough to reject this extreme version of Marianismo. But as Evelyn Stevens points out in her excellent article "Marianismo: The Other Face of Machismo," there are perks and protections in this system that operate below the radar of an outsider's cultural biases. As an example, she cites the dilemma that American working women often face when a child is ill. It's a dilemma their Latin American counterparts seldom face. "The granting of sick leave to the mother of a sick child is not so much a matter of women's rights as a matter of the employer's duty to respect the sacredness of motherhood that the individual woman shares with the Virgin Mary. Try telling that to your American boss the next time you are scheduled to do an important presentation but your little boy has a high fever and neither Abuelita nor Mami is nearby to pitch in and take care of him. But one thing we can say is that the Marianismo model might have served us well in our native countries, but it definitely does not do us service here, not without some reworking.

Monica's full-bodied battalion are now back in their seats. The word goes out: *Todo bien, todo bien.* They have that triumphant glow of women who have got the world back on track. Such un-acknowledged power they have! No wonder the United States Conference of Catholic Bishops issued a statement in support of quinceañeras, even if it is a rite just for girls. "In the Hispanic community, traditionally it has been the women who hand on the faith. Hispanic women are the evangelizers and teachers of values, yet their leadership has often gone unrecognized. The Quince Años blessing publicly acknowledges this historic role." Hallelujah! If only the Catholic Church would take that a step further and let there be female priests to minister to those largely female congregations!

Monica is indeed revived, sitting on the couch, eating a piece of bread, again with her gloves on. The color is back in her face, the smile only a little dimmed by the ordeal of an evening that keeps coming apart at the seams. But the trials and tribulations are over. *Todo bien, todo bien.* Let the fiesta begin!

No drumroll. No schmaltzy intoning of Spanish verses by the emcee. No mariachi singing "Las Mañanitas" at five hundred dollars a shot. This is a working-class quinceañera, after all. The emcee reads from the paper Monica wrote out for him: each couple is introduced. They stand for a moment at the top of the stairs, then descend, walk across the dance floor to the other end of the hall, where the swing awaits.

First, Mr. and Mrs. Ramos: she, radiant in a pale yellow gown with spaghetti straps; he, elegant and relieved in his tuxedo, not at all the heavyset man sweating in a T-shirt whom I met this afternoon.

Next, the brother and sister, Joselito and Silvia. The emcee mentions that Joselito is in the air force, here for his sister's party, then back to fixing planes for the war in Iraq. Applause. Silvia, in hot pink with spiked heels that make her as tall as her short older brother, is given no other introduction than the mention of her name. Knowing what a trouper she has been all afternoon, trying to keep the party from unraveling, I applaud. A few others join in.

The court is next, and because I've met all the girls, I know the emcee is screwing up. Raquel is introduced as Alicia, "playing the role of Belle from *Beauty in the Beast.*" But Raquel is supposed to be Jasmine! I don't know the boys by name, but later, they, too, will complain that the couples' names were all mixed up. Cindy especially is miffed. Not only did she have to wear a dress she didn't like because she was Snow White, but after all that, she gets introduced as Aurora! I know it is no consolation to tell her that it didn't make a bit of difference, as the court did nothing but come down the stairs, then, at the bottom, turn to face each other, the young man bowing, the lady curtsying. No sooner is the choreographed performance over but Cindy hightails it to that back bathroom and comes out in a little black number that transforms her from a girl playing pretend to a foxy lady who might not have had one herself but is going to have a damn good time at her best friend's quinceañera.

The final member of the court is now introduced: Franz, Monica's escort, comes down the steps in his white tuxedo. I've got to hand it to this young man who has stood by Monica through all the snafus of the evening, a calm presence, checking and rechecking his cell phone. The latter seems to be the accessory de rigueur for most of the young people here. Never have I seen Franz actually make a call or talk to someone, but he keeps consulting his cell phone the way men of an earlier generation might have consulted their pocket watches. Later, I will see one of the young female guests walking around the dance floor, not with the little sequined party purse I recall from these sorts of parties when I was young but with her cell phone in her hand. I wonder if among the garbled instructions Monica wrote down for the emcee, she made a note for all cell phones to be turned off during the presentation. But no phones ring, no vaguely familiar melody plays, announcing a call. Things are really, finally, looking up.

Franz finds the heels that someone has deposited in the middle of the dance floor. He picks them up and studies them, and then slowly, so the full drama sinks in, he makes a 360-degree turn—hey, this guy's good!—looking for the owner of these dazzling high-heeled silver "slippers."

As he comes round full circle, she appears at the top of the stairs, the princess of the evening, Monica Altagracia Ramos! Franz pulls back in astonishment, then comes forward and stands to one side, awaiting her descent, a man who is seeing a vision. We all are! Monica is radiant and lovely as she sweeps down the steps, enjoying this moment when all eyes are on her and her pretty dress. The emcee does not have to ask us to give the young lady a round of applause, for we are all on our feet, clapping wildly and welcoming this newest girl into womanhood. And again, though I've seen the behind-the-scenes ropes and pulleys, often frayed or snapping, that are holding this moment in place, or maybe because I've seen them, my eyes fill with tears and I am crying for Monica, for her beauty and brains and her sturdy spirit. May she thrive, oh may she be the queen of her own life!

Lulled by old stories

I myself kept failing at being the fairy-tale princess in the happily-forever-after story I had been raised to want. But like the stepsisters, I was determined to make the shoe fit. To prove I was indeed the real Cinderella, worthy of the love of a handsome prince.

Actually, after a few years of Abbot, I now called her by another name. I wanted to be a romantic heroine, straight from a George Eliot or Jane Austen novel, but it was still the same story. A love story in which a man took care of me, a man who would heal the divisions, make me whole and happy.

Notwithstanding my wonderful training at Abbot Academy and the examples of teachers like Miss Stevenson, this story was still the operating system in my head, and, most important, my heart. In fact, this confusion was coming to a head in American culture itself. My dose was just stronger by virtue of being reinforced by a home culture that didn't even allow for these educational ambitions to exist past a certain point. As Miami sociologist Lisandro Perez notes, quinceañeras traditionally marked the end of a girl's academic education. "You might send your son to college, but this is what you did for her . . . a way of announcing her entry . . . into courtship."

And so, my Abbot education not only put me in conflict with my parents and mi cultura, it put me in conflict with myself. I did not know how to integrate the competing selves inside me. What models were there of women in my family who had done this? What models were there of Hispanic women doing this? (It was the mid-sixties; the civil rights movement was just getting under way. Chiquita Banana and Ricky Ricardo were the only two Hispanics I ever saw on TV, both embarrassing to me.) My Abbot teachers were Anglo women, facing their own sets of challenges to be sure, but none that they shared with my classmates and me. In fact, the only way I might have detected the presence of these pressures in their lives was by the extra vehemence they brought to bear in discussions of why the Bennet sisters must find suitable husbands in *Pride and Prejudice* or why Tess in *Tess of the d'Urbervilles* is doomed once she lets herself be seduced by Alec.

The books we read—the canonical texts by white British and American mostly male writers—were no help to me either. Literature by ethnic writers, a multicultural curriculum, which might have presented other options or given me a vocabulary and framework with which to at least name the problem—all of that was at least twenty years in the future. The help I got was: *Now let's go back to the very moment that final exam is being announced* . . . Or, a renewed prescription for speed with which to outrun the furies.

School had provided a holding pattern. But Abbot was about to end. College was supposed to be the next step, but I kept crumbling under pressure. The headmistress at Abbot suggested to my parents that I take a year off. After all, I was younger than most of my senior class, having just turned seventeen in late March. Then, too, none of the colleges I had applied to had accepted me. No doubt my Abbot teachers had felt compelled to address my perplexing behavior vis-à-vis exam taking, even as they presented extenuating circumstances or mentioned improvement at the time of the writing of their letters of recommendation. And of course, since I had walked out of SATs and achievement tests, I had terrible scores. Connecticut College for Women—as the all-female school was then called—did put me on its wait list. This had a lot to do with the fact that my older sister had just completed her first year there, was popular, and had done fairly well.

I was in a quandary over what to do—especially when my status changed from wait list to acceptance at Connecticut College. I had a few weeks to decide whether to accept or take a year off. As usual at these junctures when a choice had to be made, my several selves clamored inside, urging me in divergent directions. I was torn with indecision. That's when the invitation arrived from my parents' hometown of Santiago. Could they send my older sister to represent la familia at the presentation ball for young ladies? My older sister, now a cool soon-to-be college sophomore, adamantly refused. My father begged me to go. Having one of his daughters presented at the annual ball was a way of showing off how well he had done in the United States. He even offered to pay me what I would earn if I stayed and worked at El Centro Médico instead. Meanwhile, my mother, swayed by the headmistress's advice, suggested I go for the summer and see if I might want to stay for a year, or longer.

Santiago in 1967 was a sleepy little city with a small-town atmosphere. I felt as if I had entered a Jane Austen novel, a nineteenth-century world, but without Austen's liberating sense of irony. Abbot had been strict, but this was ridiculous! We had chaperones, serenades from young men at night to whom we could not show our faces at the window, afternoon gatherings hosted by local matrons at which we were to hone our social graces. One visit I recall was to the town poet so he could get inspired and write a poem to each of us to be declaimed the night of our presentation as we made our entrance. Here's the second verse from the poem he wrote for me:

Va llegando. Reluce su cabellera.
Su pie madrigaliza en la alfombra al pisar.
La arrullan viejos cuentos de hadas y quimeras
y se inclinan las rosas al sentirla pasar!

She is arriving. Her hair shines.
Her steps make madrigals spring from the ground.
She is lulled by old stories of fairies and fancies
and the roses bend down when they feel her go by!

I can assure you, reader, that this was not a case of a round-faced americanita launching a thousand ships. Each young lady got two similar hyperbolic stanzas, which we might have traded with one another. Really, I don't know why the poet had to see us at all.

Perhaps to avoid the mistake of describing a pair of brown eyes as sky blue or a dark girl as having skin white as new-fallen snow he had never seen.

There were twenty-seven young ladies in all, between the ages of seventeen and eighteen—many of whom had also had quince-añeras. But only Dilita and I were not currently living there. As such we got a lot of extra attention from the young men in town who had grown up with all the other girls in our group and so were no doubt ready for new faces. Not only that, but by virtue of our having arrived from allá, we were deemed to be wilder, less provincial, more fun to be around.

It was a misapprehension that Dilita and I played up, wearing our jeans and skimpy tops, our hair long and loose. Originally, I was supposed to stay with an uncle in the countryside, but I soon petitioned to stay with her at her aunt and uncle's house in town. The porch of Mamacán and Papá Rafael's house on the main drag became the gathering spot for our presentation group and their escorts, brothers, cousins, and male friends.

Of course, Mamacán was always there as our chaperone. She and Papá Rafael were indulgent but not lax when it came to the rules and our reputations. Poor Mamacán kept giving us consejos on how to behave ourselves, what was expected of us, so as not to meter la pata, not take a false step and end up booted out of the presentation ball. Maybe if her niece Dilita had been alone, which had been the original plan, Mamacán might have succeeded. But together, we two were far bolder than we would have been had there been only one of us.

This annual debut at the Centro Español was an event for the daughters of the best families, which in that small city meant mostly middle-class girls whose fathers were professionals, doctors, lawyers, businessmen. Although I saw myself as an outsider, along with Dilita, there was a part of me that yearned for what I saw as a simpler life without the complications and divisions that had come with emigration. It was alluring: the attention, the courting, the fuss made over our group. Several times, desserts arrived at the house from the mothers of young men, a signal that they considered us good catches for their sons. At a time when I felt totally powerless, I was waking up to a new kind of power, sexual power, which for a number of reasons, including a gender-segregated education, I had never experienced before. It was a heady feeling to think that I could turn heads and win hearts. For a few weeks, anyhow, it turned my own head, made me think that maybe this was enough to make me happy.

Dilita soon had a steady beau, Eladio, tall with jet-black hair, the best-looking guy in town. Lucky Dilita! I got the Sancho Panza to this Don Quixote—his short, stocky sidekick, Manuel Gustavo, whom I teasingly nicknamed Mangú, a popular mashed plantain dish served with fried onions and hunks of cheese. Initially, I was not the least bit attracted to this fellow, but after several serenades, bouquets of flowers, desserts from his mother, I began to convince myself that I was falling in love. I was. Totally smitten with the idea of being a romantic heroine.

I ignored little signs that should have been red flags waving left and right. His proprietariness, his not liking me to talk to someone else of the male gender unless I was related to him and he was under twelve or over forty, his insistence that I call him first before leaving the house with an explanation of where I was going. Of course, I disobeyed, enjoying the dramatic scenes that resulted, mostly because I was growing bored.

I had arrived mid-June and the presentation itself would not take place until the end of July. There was not much to do besides visit family and attend the round of parties at which the guys mostly got drunk and the girls gossiped. No one seemed to read a book. No one seemed to want to discuss the meaning of life or a poem by e. e. cummings. Maybe it was my bad Spanish. After seven years away I couldn't put my thoughts and feelings into that childhood language. I couldn't really communicate with Mangú or family members or the other girls. But even with Dilita, with whom I spoke that mixture of English and Spanish which would later be termed "Spanglish," all we talked about was Eladio and Manuel Gustavo, and the other girls and their beaus and what they were up to, as well as every and any detail of personal groom-ing—what we would wear to a party, how our hair looked, what color polish for our nails.

I felt an unsettling vacancy. My Abbot education had peopled a whole mansion in my head, now the rooms lay empty, haunted by heroines homesick for me to come back and open up the win-dows, let in light and air, peel back the lid of the piano, talk about e. e. cummings, about the meaning of life. But I could not seem to get back there, couldn't seem to entertain a single thought; reading was beyond me. The effort of having an inner life in the midst of a family and a culture where that kind of solitary enter-prise was discouraged was beyond me. I felt I was losing my mind, leaving my American self behind.

From Queens came phone calls from my parents, who had heard through the grapevine that I was dating Manuel Gustavo, whose family were old friends of our family's. I felt the waters closing over me. "I hear you're having a wonderful time!" Mami probed.

Yes, I was having the time of my life, I told her. "Tell Maury." (The rivalry with my older sister was still strong.)

"Maybe you should stay on, take a secretarial course?" my mother suggested. "I mean since you're liking it there so much."

"I don't want to be a secretary," I snapped. I didn't understand my own anger. I *was* having a good time. But the moment my mother had mentioned staying, I felt a stab of panic, not unlike what I felt when I had to take an exam. *Why don't you get out? Why don't you leave now?*

"Well, you still have a few weeks to decide."

Things came to a head one afternoon when Dilita, Eladio, Mangú, and I snuck off to the beach. I can't imagine how we slipped past Mamacán's watchful eyes, but we did. Some rehearsal we'd gone to with our group, which we ditched, jumping into the car Mangú had borrowed from a friend and heading for the beach at Sosúa. The thought was that we would be home by dark and be dropped off around the corner to walk back to the house pretending to have just left the rehearsal.

You could tell that Dilita and I had been living anonymously allá, "over there" in the United States, thinking we could get away with a secret escapade. Santiago was a small town. Someone was bound to see us and report back to our families. But Eladio and Manuel Gustavo should have known better. Then again, they were guys. *Los hombres son de la calle; las mujeres de la casa,* Mamacán often reminded us. Men belong to the street, women in their houses. Ha! We were proving her wrong! We laughed at our naughtiness, the boys drinking their Presidentes straight from the bottle, offering us swigs, all of us feeling worldly and wonderful. At least for the first half hour, and then I, anyhow, began to have misgivings.

Eladio and Dilita had slipped into a whispery conversation in the backseat, interrupted by long, smoochy silences. Not wanting to miss out, Mangú reached over and pulled me to his side. I remember the perfumey smell of his cologne, the broad band of his gold watch on his brown arm, the feeling that he was strong and could overpower me if he wanted to. At this point in my life I had been only chastely kissed by a couple of dates at Abbot mixers, but that was it. For all the flouting of my wild Americanized ways, I was a total prude.

Once at the beach, Dilita and Eladio wandered off who knew where. Mangú, who now had two free hands, corralled me in his arms, his eyes on my lips as I kept yakking—a Scheherazade strategy I had worked out, keep talking to save your life.

He wanted me to go for a swim, but I refused. I didn't have my bathing suit with me, and I was not about to take *anything* off in front of this horny guy. Finally, he gave up, slipped out of his pants and shirt, and raced down the beach in his underwear, diving into an incoming wave. I sat on the hood of the car with his clothes and the gold watch he had left with me, trying to imagine being married to this fellow. And I knew with a certainty I'm not often blessed with that I would not be happy if I stayed there and tried to take up the life I had left behind seven years ago when we emigrated.

By the time we returned to Santiago it was after dark and Mamacán and Papá Rafael were beside themselves with worry about what might have happened to us. Several people had called them to say they had seen us in a car with men, heading out of town. Our escapade turned out to be quite the scandal, culminating in both Dilita and I attending confession and going to Communion the next morning in order to restore our tarnished reputations. There was the threat, I don't know how real, that we might be eliminated from the presentation group. Later that day, when my parents called, I was sure the gossip had reached them in Queens about their daughter's appalling behavior. But no, it was Mami, reminding me that the deadline was next week. Did I want her to send in the deposit to Connecticut College?

I felt like a person drowning who hears the reassuring plop of a lifesaver landing beside her. Of course, I grabbed it.

Playing and replaying the tape

Looking back over my life as a young woman, I've wondered if I was psychologically dense. Why did I have to learn the same lesson again and again? And again. I'm convinced that we are hardwired during our early years, and it takes a lot of playing and replaying the tape before we inch past those glitches that snag us every time. At each new stage in life, all the stuff we learned back when we were dumb has to be transferred to this new stage—and in that transfer, we can so easily be pulled back into the old divisions, make the same mistake yet one more time.

After three and a half years of college, as graduation was coming round again, I found myself in the same muddle. Who would I be now that I was grown up? And again, it was not just me feeling the division between mi cultura Latina and my American culture. Many if not most of the female members of my senior class were experiencing a similar confusion. We were the generation on the cusp of the women's movement. Our mothers, for the most part, were traditional homemakers, their example no help to us. Our education supposedly had prepared us for the working world. But given the actual opportunities out there, not to mention the glass ceilings and gender wage differentials, it sure looked like a trumped-up version of "the Dominican secretarial course" option, dressed up as a bachelor of arts. In fact, job prospects being what they were, we would not be able to afford the lives we were used to, which our fathers had paid for thus far. Tellingly, during that last semester of college, many of my classmates were getting serious with their boyfriends, getting engaged, as if we all knew that beyond this bubble of academe, the world was not a friendly place for a woman without a man.

This idea of romance being the quick-fix-it option is, of course, embedded in the Cinderella aspects of the quinceañera. The danger lies in young Latinas actually trying to play out the story in their post-quinceañera lives. Angela Fajardo, who grew up in East L.A. and now teaches there, confided in me that many girls end up pregnant and drop out of school after their quinceañeras. She wonders if the tradition, originally meant to signal that a young girl was now marriageable, gives young Latinas a mixed message: now you can be sexually active, now you are a grown-up and can do as you please. Nicolás Menjivar, the pastor at Iglesia El Buen Pastor, a 100 percent Spanish-speaking parish in Durham, North Carolina, agrees that many times the young girls treat their quinceañeras as a "quasi boda," an authorization to shack up with their chambelán de honor. It's a way of being grown-up, or so they think. I'm reminded of how out of the seven girls who Jaider Sánchez coached in Denver, four invited him to their baby showers only a year after their quinceañeras.

But I had already learned my lesson with Manuel Gustavo in the D.R. Falling in love and getting married, as many of the girls in my presentation group had done or were doing, was not going to resolve the internal divisions and make me happy. Perhaps learning that lesson once would have been enough if I hadn't felt so trapped and forced into a corner as graduation from college approached. *Who was I going to be now?* I wondered.

Some of my girlfriends were talking about moving to Boston or New York, getting jobs, sharing an apartment. It seemed there was a little more wiggle room for girls in American culture. But that wiggle room was not an option in my familia. There were the two states of Latina womanhood, the virgin-mother of Marianismo and the Malinche-whore. Actually, my parents allowed for a third, scholar, which made them more progressive than some Latinas' families. Since all of these states of female being were in reference to male control, good girls remained under their fathers' roofs until they were wed. In other words, no apartamento con tus girlfriends if you want to be part of this familia. Punto. End of discussion.

By virtue of being a year ahead of me, my older sister sometimes took the slings and arrows of outrageous fortune full force and, therefore, opened paths for me. This time she was of no help as she had chosen to prolong her freedom by going to graduate school, something I did not want to do. (More pressure, more exams!) Going home to Queens, on the other hand, was out of the question. After living away in dorms for almost eight years, I was used to a certain—if clandestine—measure of self-determination and independence. My parents' old-world rules coupled with my mother's need to have her daughters under her total control would make living in that house impossible for all of us.

Enter my first husband, late fall semester of my senior year. A young musician, he and his older brother came to play a gig at the college. What a beautiful young man! And Lord, could he ever sing! I was smitten and I suppose he was flattered to have a college girl paying attention to him. And so it went. We started seeing each other. I invited him to come down during Thanksgiving break to meet my family. My parents went through the roof. Was I crazy? Loca de remate? I was a smart girl with a college education. He was a high school dropout. He was Jewish. I was Catholic. (A totally lapsed one, as were my parents, but still, Latinos of my parents' generation tended to be culturally religious long after they had stopped listening to the pope or going to church.) He was poor. What on earth did I think we would live on?

They were right, if not necessarily for the reasons they gave me. But even if they had presented me with the best arguments, I doubt they would have succeeded. As Yeats notes in "A Woman Young and Old," it is an age-old problem, girls falling in love against their parents' better judgment with a man who will break their hearts, no doubt about it:

> She hears me strike the board and say
> That she is under ban
> Of all good men and women,
> Being mentioned with a man
> That has the worst of all bad names;
> And thereupon replies
> That his hair is beautiful,
> Cold as the March wind his eyes.

My parents pulled out every stop they knew. They threatened to send me right then and there to the Dominican Republic. By force? They couldn't do that! This was America. I could call the police. So, I had turned into a girl who would call the police on her parents, ay Dios santo! What a monster they had raised! Finally, they delivered an ultimatum. Either I stopped seeing this fellow or they would not pay my last semester's tuition and I would have to drop out of college. Furthermore, I was on my own. Not to bother to come back home ever.

And so I did what good girls do when confronted with disapproval they don't have the character to withstand: I went underground. I snuck out with my boyfriend for weekends away at his older brother's house. One such weekend my parents, who must have sensed I had caved in a little too readily, called the dorm. After four or five calls, whoever was working the switchboard got annoyed and told them it was no use calling. I was out for the weekend with my boyfriend. By the time I got back on Sunday there were several urgent messages that I call home immediately. It was late when I reached one of my sisters, already home for Christmas break. I was in deep trouble, she told me. In fact, Papi was ready to drive up the next morning and kill this guy.

What to do? What would make it okay that I had gone away overnight with my boyfriend? Of course, I knew the choices: virgin-mother-scholar. I had just destroyed the last option and the first with my disobedience. I packed my bags and we drove over to his parents' house. His parents agreed to sign a legal permission for their underage seventeen-year-old son to marry me, a very young twenty-year-old. (It still baffles me that they would go along with this.) As soon as the disappointing "ceremony" was over—in the kitchen of the local justice of the peace, his chained dog barking away outside—I called home with the good news. I was a married woman! I don't know why I thought that a license would make it all right that I had married the wrong person.

At first my parents carried through on their threat: they cut off all communication and funding. But later, realizing that now more than ever, married to a musician, who was a high school dropout to boot, I would need that degree, they agreed to pay for my last semester in college. Just the tuition. I'd have to take care of my living expenses myself.

Fair enough. We rented a tiny apartment within walking distance of the college. My friends would come over and we'd spend hours in one of the two rooms discussing our poems and stories. My husband would sit by, silent and sullen, feeling left out of a conversation that was over his head. After my friends left, a fight would inevitably erupt, my husband berating my friends as snobs, I defending them. The fights left us both shaken, bruised, bewildered. It wasn't working, but I had to make it work! After all, I had burned all my bridges back to the only world I knew besides school, mi familia.

After graduation, at the beginning of the summer, we tried to renew the lease, but the landlord refused. Our neighbor said she couldn't abide our constant arguments. And so we kept moving, living in motels that offered weekly rates, barely getting by. I got waitressing jobs wherever and whenever my husband and his brother had a singing gig. When we couldn't get by on his singing and my waitressing, I took another job at a home for the severely retarded. Second shift, working from two to eleven p.m. Feeding the mostly bedridden patients, changing their diapers, cleaning up their messes. The checks at the end of the week were not enough to pay our expenses. So we took cheaper digs, did without, got food stamps. His parents were too poor to help us. My parents had cast me out. And the worst thing for me about the whole situation was the failure of imagination it represented. There was no redeeming love story to offer some relief from that deepening sense that I had made a big mistake and now would have to live with it.

But I got lucky, a way out presented itself. My father called me from his office and asked if I would come home for Thanksgiving by myself to give the familia a chance at a reconciliation. I decided to go, despite my husband's threats that if I went where he was not invited, I should not bother to come back.

And yet when the time came, he drove me over to the Greyhound bus stop several towns away, kissed me when we said good-bye as if, like my parents, he would not make good on his threat. I looked out the window as the bus pulled away. He was still achingly beautiful, his eyes as cold as the March wind. I felt the same mixture of feelings as when I walked out of exams and looked back at my classmates bent over their blue books. Regret and shame not to be like them, succeeding; immense relief to be leaving.

That Christmas I went back to the same sleepy city of Santiago, where a lawyer uncle helped me get a quickie divorce. The government had just passed a new law to drum up tourism. "Divorcio a vapor," it was called. You could come for a long weekend, be released of your wedding vows with time left over to go to the beach, get a tan, meet a new man. But I didn't go out at all, didn't contact Manuel Gustavo or any of the girls in my group. I was twenty-one years old, a fallen woman, without the option of coming back "home" anymore except in a very straitened role. And so I returned to the States, and for a while lived with my parents and worked in the city, trying to make it up to them. I had ruined my chances, my mother kept berating me. I never thought to ask her, What chances? Or to ask myself if those were chances I even really wanted anymore.

Stumbles make you pick up your feet

Why am I revisiting these places? I suppose I am hoping to understand the places that tripped me up as a young Latina woman in an effort to save somebody else some heartache. Not that someone else could learn from my mistakes. *Nadie aprende en cabeza ajena,* the saying goes. No one learns in somebody else's head. But over time I believe generational wisdom does trickle down. That seeing as clearly as possible what can happen trains us to keep a sharp lookout. That we can feel less alone and encouraged in our efforts to put the pieces together into the larger versions of ourselves. Even when we are going against the current of what our familia, cultura, and mainstream culture are telling us.

After half a year living with my parents, I followed my older sister's footsteps and applied to graduate school. Academia was turning out to be our harbor and home in this country. And the good thing about a master's in creative writing—all the exams would be take-home! I thrived at Syracuse University, falling in love, but not losing my focus, and therefore losing my lovers. Over time I found that if I stayed true to what I loved to do, most men fell away on their very own. Given their druthers, men—at least of my generation—seemed to want a woman to be preoccupied with them, not with her poems and novels.

After graduation, I landed a job in Kentucky as a poet in the schools, a two-year post in which I traveled all over the state giving writing workshops in schools and prisons and nursing homes. It was a low-paying job, but I didn't need much. I was happy, I was writing, I was free. It seemed like my life was back on track. Unfortunately, I got lucky-unlucky. I met *the* perfect prince, just not the one meant for me.

My new beau was an Englishman, who true to the British tradition for second sons had come to the colonies and landed a managerial job in a telephone cable company. With his Brit accent, his boarding school education, his good manners, he was eminently suited for the role of prince. I was amazed that he could be interested in me, a divorced woman, a sort of bohemian, a poet wandering about the state in a yellow Volkswagen. Again, I felt that head-spinning giddy rush of sexual power.

And so, I took my prince home to meet the family. I needed to show my mother that I was not a ruined woman, a nice man could still love me.

After my divorce, my mother and I, who had been having a rocky time since adolescence, were at war. Everything I did she criticized. Everything she did infuriated me. But unlike my American friends in similar situations who just cut the tie with their parents, I couldn't seem to do that. As I mentioned, I was hardwired to familia. My operating system didn't work on "sole individual." And there was my father, who, under the overlay of patriarchy, always came through with phone calls, moral support, emergency checks I was not to tell my mother about. And my sisters, who would be left on the front lines of the collision of two worlds, needing my shielding and sharing. And finally, there was Mami, whom I yearned to win over. The beautiful storytelling Mami with the tender touch I remembered from when I was a small child. How I yearned to hear her croon, like the Aztec mother, *My dove, my little one, my daughter, my child.*

As I had anticipated, my mother was delighted with my new suitor. In her eyes was that loving look I hadn't seen in ages. "I can see you've really learned from your mistakes. *Los tropezones hacen levantar los pies,*" she praised me. Stumbles make you pick up your feet. "This is the kind of man you need. Trust me. He will make you happy."

Over time, I started believing that I was in love with him, too. His mother was the only one who saw through the romance, for even I and my lover were caught up in it. It was during a trip we made to England so I could meet his parents. At some point during our visit, my lover asked his mother what she thought of me. She's lovely, he told me his mum had said. She's funny, she's smart, but she's not in love with you. I was hurt. She was so wrong, I protested. She just didn't like me and this was a way to blame it on me. But ah, the years have proven Mum right. I was not in love with her son, but in love with the chance to make good on the story I had once gotten so wrong.

Besides, my mother and he got along famously. They started cooking up a business scheme for the Dominican Republic. It turned out my mother had always wanted to start a pharmaceutical import company, bringing affordable medicines to people back home. How come I didn't know that? How come no one at home knew that? She had kept files with information from drug reps from when she had worked at my father's office. Meanwhile, my lover was getting bored with his job in Kentucky. Here was a chance to explore another former colony. Soon they were doing the numbers at the kitchen table on a calculator.

Papi and I sat by. Periodically when our eyes met, he'd wink. The war was over, we were both thinking. But actually what Papi didn't know was that trouble was about to start for him. Mami was beginning to spread her wings, and here was a successful young businessman aiding and abetting her. After sending her daughters off to boarding schools, my mother had spent years running Papi's office, doing all his paperwork, hiring and training his Spanish-speaking staff. She had boundless energy. Her own life had been circumscribed by her family and culture. Now, having learned a thing or two from her headstrong daughters, she wanted more.

How odd that my lover should bring out a side of my mother that my father, my sisters, and I had ignored. If he could liberate Mami and make peace between us, surely he would do the same for me, or more.

He would have been delighted if I'd joined him and my mother in setting up a business. But I was totally bored by these planning sessions. I'd wander off to read or work on a poem. Why did he put up with me? In the first flush of romance and sex I had probably seemed exotic to him with my artsy friends, my island family, my poems and stories. Why did I put up with him? Contrary to what one would expect, he was totally familiar to me. If my first husband appealed to my American hippie side, this second one was a throwback to my Dominican uncles and male cousins, men who ran things, men who were in charge. My mother was right: my lover was an excellent match for the woman I might have become had my familia stayed back in the Dominican Republic.

By the end of the year, we were living together—not openly, though surely my canny mami must have guessed as much since my lover was always "over" when she called. One afternoon, he brought home the news that he had accepted a job across the country in California. I was flabbergasted. No discussion? No consideration that I had a job, too? His theory, oft repeated during our time together, was that as the one earning the higher salary he called the shots. *He who pays the piper calls the tune.* If I loved him, I would come.

I was angry. No, I would not come. We parted. Perhaps it would have ended there if I'd stuck to my guns. If my mother had also not begun that litany: *You're making a big mistake.* I started to second-guess my decision. To feel that I was being selfish by not following a man I supposedly loved to California. Besides, my two-year post would soon end. As a writer, having my spouse be a steady wage earner was not a bad idea. Patronage of sorts. (My lover, in fact, kept saying to come out there; I could write full-time; he would support me.) I was figuring all this out with my head, not my heart. But that's what can happen when the cultural paradigm doesn't fit. You talk yourself into it.

The night before the wedding, we sat in my tío's house in the Dominican Republic, watching a television that had been carried into the living room. I had gone back "home" to marry the right way this time, in a Catholic church with the sanction of the family. The next day was election day, and the pundits were all weighing in on what would happen. The country was only recently rid of its dictator, but a strong military was still in place. Depending on whether the army's candidate won, there might be trouble tomorrow. In fact, several of my uncles had wondered about the advisability of planning a wedding on election day. It's as if even current events were beaming me a big sign that read: WHY DON'T YOU GET OUT? WHY DON'T YOU LEAVE NOW?

I slipped out onto the terrace and walked down a path into the dark garden. A moon must have been out because the water in the swimming pool was shimmering. There were tall ferns surrounding two sides of the pool. Beyond the high stone walls lay the eerily quiet city, punctuated now and then by a preelection burst of fireworks and what might have been gunshots. I wanted to scale those walls and run! But where would I go to get away from the revolution brewing *inside* me?

My mother and older sister came out to see what I was up to. I started to weep. I couldn't go through with it. It just was not fair to my lover to marry him when I felt so unsure.

As I spoke, I remember shredding those ferns, wanting to tear up this supposed tropical paradise that the people on television were predicting would blow up tomorrow. "If you feel you're making a mistake then we should call it off," my mother said. I could hear disappointment in her voice. I knew her theory. That this was just cold feet, understandable after a first failed marriage. My older sister, who was working on her doctorate in psychology and had spent long sessions talking things over with me, tried again to help me. "What does your heart tell you to do?"

The truth was that my heart was telling me *yes, no, yes, no.* Why do we think that our hearts, our guts, our psyches somehow remain free of the disquieting training and conditioning we get socially? For months I had been torn apart by indecision; I was spent, exhausted. Trying to decide anything was like sinking deeper and deeper into the hole in my own gut. And so I chose what I knew the significant people in my life, my parents and family, thought was right for me to do. I married my lover the next morning in the middle of a military takeover.

We survived the wedding—my tío found a friend who was a general who came over in his army tank to marry us. (Under martial law, a general could do this. So much for my Catholic wedding with a priest in a church full of family.) What amazes me now is that even with all these very real obstacles, I forged ahead. We spent a horrible honeymoon in the interior in a borrowed house, my new husband fretting about whether we'd be able to leave the country at the end of the week. By the time we got back to the capital, the coup was over; a tentative truce had been reached.

But our situation went from rocky to rock-bottom. Though we were both well-meaning, there was no overlap on which we could build a life together. Our inclinations, friends, dreams led us in different directions. I wanted a soul mate who loved literature and gave me just the right measure of support and autonomy. My husband wanted what most men wanted back then, a devoted wife, not without her own interests and hobby-jobs, which it was understood she would soon set aside to start a family. Who can blame him? My old-world culture and familia had taught me to want that as well.

But my education had breathed new possibilities into me. And so, I did and didn't want to be what I was supposed to be. As my husband said when we parted: he never knew what he was going to encounter on any given day, the women's libber or the Spanish Inquisition.

Ten months into the marriage, my hippie friends in Berkeley told me about a fabulous new play in town I had to go see: *for colored girls who have considered suicide when the rainbow is enuf.* I was surprised that my husband agreed to go with me. Never before or since have I attended a performance that turns into a ritual, but that's what happened. Six women, each dressed in a color, recounted their stories: they told of falling in love and making the wrong choices and hurting and falling apart and not knowing where they were going, whom they should love or be or become. They danced and chanted in a circle:

i waz missin somethin
something so important
somethin promised
a layin on of hands . . .
makin me whole . . .
i waz missin somethin
a layin on of hands
not a man
layin on
not my mama / holdin me tight / sayin
i'm always gonna be her girl . . .
a layin on of hands
the holiness of myself released . . .

At the end of the performance, the colored girls came off the stage, singing and dancing, and beckoning the mostly female audience to join them. We did, swaying and weeping and singing: *i found god in myself/ and i loved her/ i loved her fiercely.*

My husband did not know what to do with himself—surrounded by women, many of whom were undergoing a cathartic experience. I felt a surge of tenderness and sadness at how unwittingly I had misled him. But then, I, too, had been trapped by a story so enchanting I could not tear myself away. Until this moment, when I understood viscerally what it meant to find god in myself. Isn't this what ritual can do for us, connect us to this power in ourselves, and by doing so empower our families and our communities as well?

This is the potential embedded in the quinceañera, what folks like Isabella Martínez Wall, Priscilla Mora, and Sister Angela see in the tradition, which is why they want the practice to become more universal.

Maybe that is why so many quinceañeras mouth the same old

platitude like a mantra: *I'm going from girlhood to womanhood.* Why the old poet's verses were so generic, so hyperbolically nonspecific. It was not about me or Dilita or the twenty-five other girls. We were joining that river of time, connecting to that eternal part that runs through our communities and families and selves down through the generations. That old dance whose steps we learn from those before us and which we have to adapt to our particular time and place, then pass on to the next generation.

"That old fandango," Mami used to call it, at which I kept stumbling, learning and relearning how to pick up my feet.

Speech with candles

Out on the floor, there's a line dance going on. All the young people are up and at it. The mix of music is perfect. Periodically, an old canción is thrown in for the older folks, a bolero, slow and romántico; then, a merengue or bachata, something everyone can dance to; finally, for the young people, a few contemporary numbers, rock and rap and line dances.

We've all eaten—a long buffet line, paper plates, the food overdone from being warmed too long, shells stuffed with a creamy cheese sauce, eggplant parmigiana, chicken cacciatore, salad, and dinner rolls. Nothing Dominican about this food—the Dance Club's caterer is Stallone's, a local Italian restaurant. But this seems to raise the caliber of the meal to a fancier level. The man ahead of me on the line heaps his plate high. "Comida de novelas," the food of soap operas, he calls it, a compliment to be sure.

I've assumed my post on the steps, looking down at the dancing, at the cozy camaraderie of the different tables, feeling that pang of the proverbial kid with her nose against the glass case in the candy store. Periodically, Mr. or Mrs. Ramos invites me to come down, but I can't figure out how to insert myself into the boisterous clusters of happy guests. There is a rich history here that a few interviews by phone and an afternoon and night trailing Monica can't begin to tap. I'm reminded of one of the chief reasons that many parents cite for why they decide to throw their daughters a quinceañera: it's a chance to reunite their family and friends at a happy life-marker event. Doubtless the next big gathering will be a grandparent's funeral, or perhaps, if she is a good girl, as they hope this party will encourage her to be, she will marry un hombre serio and they will gather again to celebrate her wedding. But then it won't be the same: half the people will be strangers, the groom's family and their friends.

Just when I think the ceremonial aspect of the night is over, the music stops. The emcee is on a portable microphone which he walks across the dance floor, announcing that a very special part of the night is about to start. Two of his staff pull out a stand with seventeen tall tapers arranged in a circle. He would like to introduce the young lady of the evening, who now will be lighting her candles and dedicating each one. Monica comes forward, unfolding several sheets of paper. I had almost forgotten! The speech that Monica had confessed was one of the major reasons she opted for having a quinceañera, the culmination of her special night.

Monica takes the mike from the emcee and thanks everyone for coming. "You guys are soooo special to me! I want to thank each and every one of you in this room soooo much for coming!" The room goes utterly quiet, overwhelmed by this onslaught of gratitude. Amazing how these tonal shifts happen at such gatherings. All the carousing and shouting above the loud music has stopped. Even Tavito sits down by his mother's side and leans into her. I, too, lower myself on the steps and watch the room turn into a listening ear.

The usual suspects are called up—Monica's parents; her sister; her brother; her fairy godmother, Claire; uncles and aunts and family friends. Monica thanks them, describing their roles in her life. Each one gets a candle he or she lights and places on the rack. It's an intimate look at the people who are important to her, though I can guess who are her favorites by the way Monica addresses them, prolonging her "so's" and sprinkling her speech with an extra serving of adverbs.

The sixteenth candle is reserved for the boyfriend, or so I've heard from the court in a hush-hush way. There seems to be some secrecy around the fact that Franz and Monica are no longer just friends. Romance has sprung up between them, which is not surprising. For months they've been rehearsing being a prince and princess, tonight's public performance seeming to sanction their romance. I'm reminded of how the actress Geena Davis, speaking of a project she started, *See Jane,* to increase the percentage of strong female characters children see in the media, admitted that there's no way to totally protect little girls. "That princess stuff just comes like a fog under the door—you can't keep it out." As Franz goes up to take his candle from Monica, I notice the bulge in his breast pocket and hope he has turned his cell phone off. Monica's hand trembles slightly as she dips her candle to light the one she has given him. The couple smile down at their candles, no doubt afraid to look up and betray their feelings for each other.

The final candle ("for someone absent") is dedicated to God. Given that no priest was present to deliver grace before we ate or a blessing to the young lady before her first waltz, this serves as a kind of prayer. Monica wants to thank God so much for all He has done for her, bringing all these wonderful people into her life. She hopes He will be with her for the rest of her life. But she will never ever forget all the people who have helped her out.

As she stands there, flanked on both sides by family and friends who love her, I'm convinced that Monica will take wing, achieve her dreams, make us proud. The lights are dimmed and for a few hushed moments we watch the long tapers burn; not one falters or goes out.

There should have been more light

One of the Web sites I happened upon in my research, miss-quince.com, features a virtual quinceañera. Verónica Muñoz has posted her 2003 quinceañera in full detail, allowing the viewer to experience every stage of her celebration from shopping for the dress to practicing with her court to attending la misa and partying at the fiesta. On the welcome page a musical score plays loud strains of the Blue Danube, which almost immediately morphs into a pulsing Latin-rap number, "La quinceañera, la quinceañera, como la baila, como la goza, whooo . . ." In the chat room attached to this site, where guests can comment, there is a forlorn little entry posted by Maira on Thursday, August 4, 2005: *there should of bine more light.*

At first, I thought Maira meant that Verónica's photos were too dark. So I clicked back to Verónica's album, and the pictures were quite clear and bright. What could Maira have meant? I wondered. Her e-mail address was provided below her entry so I wrote asking her if she would explain her comment, but I never heard back.

There should have been more light.

After spending a year reading and researching and interviewing girls and their families as well as mulling over my own young womanhood, no single phrase sums up the welter of feelings about this tradition and time of life better than Maira's. As women and Latinas, we have inherited a mixed bag of cultural roles and practices. Many of us grew up in the dark as to the contradictions and problems this legacy presented to us. Just consider two of the emblematic gifts that the young lady receives in a traditional Mexican American quinceañera ceremony: a tiara or crown and an esclava, which literally translates "slave," the name for a type of "identity bracelet" with one's name engraved upon it. Queen *and* slave?

Spanish Inquisition and women's libber?

No wonder my husband was confused, along with my mother, my sisters, and many of the young ladies I interviewed, when I persisted beyond the platitudes in asking them questions. *This is getting annoying.*

No wonder I was confused as I struggled to make the passage from girlhood to womanhood, a process that lasted way past my teens—why I haven't concluded the story of my coming-of-age with my fifteenth year or my twenty-first or my twenty-ninth year, for that matter. No wonder I felt drawn to the topic of quinceañeras. The young Latina girls I met in my research reminded me of being that age, filled with hopes and dreams, girls at the cusp of making or not making it, the latter the bigger pool according to the statistics, female fallout being more often than not the rule among the poorer, darker female members of the American population. Meanwhile, at this critical moment in their lives we doll them up and waltz them out.

But there is a further turn of the screw: la familia and the comunidad are gathered together to walk with our girls into their womanhood—what potential for affirmation and solidarity! If only we took them somewhere other than this dubious reenact-ment of certain key oppressions.

There has to be more light.

Memoried light

For several years after my second marriage broke up, I felt like Maira, wanting more light so I could see why I kept messing up. Sometimes when one culture failed me in a certain arena, the other one offered an alternative. But in terms of being female, both cultures seemed to be failing me, or, I should say, I seemed to keep failing both at being a successful female. Something had been damaged, perhaps in the transit between cultures?

The first month after leaving my husband I stayed with my sister, sleeping on her couch, avoiding talking to my mother or my soon-to-be ex-husband on the phone. I was afraid their voices would drown out my silence. My sister let me tag along on her cooking jobs, not asking much of me except to dice those onions, peel that pile of potatoes. I was grateful to be kept busy, not to have to account for myself. She was the sibling I'd been closest to growing up, the one who came right after me, thirteen months later, to be exact. The "nurturer," as she was known in the family, who had been her own kind of maverick, dropping out of college to go to chef school. *(We came to this country and made all these sac-rifices for you to become somebody's cook!)* It wasn't just the daughter who kept divorcing who was the problem in our family.

One of the things I found heartening during this dark time was that my instincts were intact. A wounded animal, I somehow knew enough to lay low, stay out of harm's way, revisit past wa-tering places in the hope that the springs were still running.

And that's where I got the idea of returning to Abbot, to that memoried light at Miss Stevenson's window. Actually, the 145-year-old school had disappeared, having recently merged with its "brother school," Phillips Andover. "Merger" was not the word most diehard Abbot teachers would have used. My former history teacher Mary Minard, never one to mince her words, declared it "a takeover." Jean St. Pierre, another of my beloved Abbot teachers who stayed on after the merger/takeover, saw trouble ahead. "Everyone kept talking about the upcoming change as a wedding, but those of us at Abbot saw it as a death." The strong, vibrant, small, and nurturing all-girls community was suddenly thrust into a man's world. Perhaps it was not unlike an immigrant girl suddenly finding herself in an alien country, adrift, and in need of guidance, a safe harbor, a light left on. I had found that harbor at Abbot, so that was the straw I grasped for when my life fell apart.

I called the school and surprisingly was asked to come to the campus for an interview. When I was offered the job, which included residential responsibilities and a heavy teaching schedule, I did not hesitate. It was the academic equivalent to dicing the carrots and peeling the potatoes; I would be kept busy. At the time, I thought of myself as a modern-age Latina, breaking away from tradition, pursuing a career, earning my own way. (I had learned the high price of having someone else take care of me. *He who pays the piper calls the tune.*) But in fact, my choice turned out to be much more traditional than I thought. Historically, women who have made mistakes, defied some social code or other, end up in a convent: *Get thee to a nunnery.* And Andover, at that time, was the pedagogical equivalent of a convent, a gated academic community—even a burned-out lightbulb in my faculty apartment would be taken care of by the grounds crew.

And so I journeyed back to an Abbot that was no more. It was only six years after the merger, and things were still rocky, especially for the girls and female faculty. We were very much aware that we had been granted privileged entry into what one male faculty member described as "the Harvard of secondary schools." The pressure was palpable, the support system minimal, and though efforts were made to accommodate the new female population (whilst not compromising the lofty Andover standards), the truth was the old-boys academy network didn't have a clue as to how to make us ladies feel welcomed. "I didn't have a lot of experience with women as real people, as opposed to dates," Meredith Price, one of my new male colleagues in the English Department, reminisced a few years later. Meanwhile, Zanda Merrill, one of three school counselors, was seeing a surge in depression, eating disorders, breakdowns—all the ways in which females register their bafflement at finding themselves like the canary in the mine shaft in a noxious environment.

Enter one English teacher in shaky shape herself. I was as much affected by the pressure-cooker atmosphere as my students. I had no training as a teacher; I was terrified in the classroom. I was sure my students could see right through my bluster to the heart of my self-doubt. When they came knocking at my office door, I'd march out Rilke (*Letters to a Young Poet* was a favorite), quote Rumi ("Do not go back to sleep!"), share the Inuit fear poem I had taped above my desk. All I had to offer was second-hand light, strings of words that I myself was using to navigate my way through the labyrinth:

> I think over again my small adventures
> when with the wind I drifted in my kayak
> and thought I was in danger
> My fears
> Those small ones that seemed so big . . .

For all the vital things
I had to get and to reach
And yet there is only one great thing
The only thing:
To live to see the great day that dawns
and the light that fills the world.

That great day was not to dawn for a while for me. I was full of doubts and worn-out with trying to keep it together enough to hold on to my job. At one point during my first semester at Andover—before I had connected with Zanda—I was in such a state of anxiety, I sought help from a local psychiatrist. I confessed how insecure I was feeling, how sometimes in class I kept writing on the board, too terrified to turn around and face a classroom of ten or fifteen fourteen-year-olds! On and on, I spilled my guts to the doctor, weeping as I recounted incident after incident of my incompetence. Finally, I was done. I looked up—and the face I wore must have been that of the drowning dog in Goya's painting by the same name. "Do you think I'm crazy?" I asked the psychiatrist. No, he assured me, he did not think I was crazy. "Okay, but would you want your child to take a course from me?" He hesitated. "No, I would not," he admitted.

The hour was almost up, but I could no more get out of that chair in one piece than I could fly. The judgment, which albeit I had asked for, was the final straw. The doctor realized too late that his had not been a useful answer. In the few minutes left us he apologized, explaining why he had said what he said. It turned out he had a son at Andover, and as I spoke, he had been thinking how my depression and self-doubt might affect his shy, sensitive boy. This was supposed to be soothing?! He was a parent of a student! Soon, there would be a confidential call to the headmaster, saying, *You must get rid of this crazy loca woman.*

Somehow I found my way back to my apartment, to my classrooms, to my students. I worked even harder at class preparations in order to be worthy of teaching at this elite institution. I was so overprepared that each class was a concentrate out of which ten lessons could have been distilled. I suppose that made them intense and in their own adolescent way exciting to my young students. It was not uncommon for my colleagues in the English Department to call me the night before to ask what I was planning to do the next day in my classes. Could I share my "lesson plan" with them? And so, within months of leaving my husband, I was back at it again, performing for those who paid the piper and so had every right to call the tune.

Don't get me wrong. There was nothing wrong with trying to do a good job. But there was an element of having to prove I was good enough, which made the whole colossal effort exhausting and self-defeating. Finally, an incident occurred that made me stop and take stock.

Every fall, Andover hosted a parents' weekend, during which parents of our students were invited to sit in on our classes. You can imagine what little sleep I got the week before, worrying about my performance before parents I imagined as the equivalents of the psychiatrist dad. Thankfully, the classes went off well, and so I was surprised when the following Monday the head of our department called me into his office. "Relax," he said, grinning, when he saw the grim look on my face. He just wanted to share with me a comment that a parent of one of my students had made to him. My heart slowed; my stomach stopped churning. Finally, someone had recognized my hard work! Praise would be lavished on my classes! The department head then told me that the father of one of my students had expressed "surprise" that with so many excellent teachers available, a fine school like Andover had to get a Spanish woman to teach his son English.

I felt angry, but instead of showing it, I did the female thing and burst into tears. Finally, collecting myself, I thanked my department head for his support. Or so I understood it until recently, when a guest at my dinner table heard me recount the story— obviously a little narrative bump I still need to keep going back over. My guest wondered why the head of the department felt he should deliver this disheartening bit of information. Sure, it was a way to show solidarity with my struggles. But wasn't it also a way to keep me in line, to say, *There but for the grace of my good word would you remain, relegated to the margins?* And yet, this was the same department head who had hired me on the strength of very little published writing. I've come to believe that both possibilities might have been contained in his disclosure, the mixed bag of a Latina woman's heritage I have been talking about.

I ended up in Zanda's office, an inspired choice. It was a small back room full of lush plants and pillows and colorful fabrics and crystals—a totally different universe from the buttoned-down New England campus with its parlors presided over by stern portraits and its stark Quaker-style meeting rooms. Zanda herself had the look of someone who didn't belong here with her abounding long skirts, her mane of yellow hair, and eyes so light you felt a beam coming from them. She seemed tribal, centered, a woman who drew other women to her. Later, I came to understand that this is what female power might look like, nurturing and fierce and untainted by seduction, submission, or combativeness—all the ways in which we women go astray in reaction to a male world.

I was not the only woman having a hard time surviving at Andover, Zanda assured me. What's more, I was not the only woman having trouble putting the pieces of her life together. This was a totally confusing time in history for many women, not just Latinas: we were trying to reinvent ourselves. So there was another way of looking at my failure at being a girl-woman: evidence of a vibrant and questing spirit.

All you need is one person to see it, a person you admire or look up to, a Zanda, a Miss Stevenson. And then the great day begins to dawn—that is, a small but significant light starts to fill up your world.

I began to spot them in my classes. Soulful girls with that special passionate intelligence which did not register on the tough grading scale. I recognized the hunger in their eyes, an ardent yearning for what George Eliot describes in her prelude to *Middlemarch* as "an epic life wherein there was a constant unfolding of far-resonant action." These young girls needed a muse, female wisdom they could tap as they made their way in that achievement-oriented male territory.

I decided to initiate a ritual for these, my special girls. I selected five of my female colleagues with whom I felt a strong bond—of mutual displacement, of terror!—to prepare a meaningful story and a symbolic gift. I would take my girls on a sort of Joseph Campbell journey of the hero(ine). (Campbell's *Hero of a Thousand Faces* was required reading in my English classes.) We would stop at five watering places where we would be met by helpers who would offer up ancient wisdom. (*You're making stuff up,* as Monica's priest would say.) Jean St. Pierre was one of our stops. My dear friend Carole Braverman was another. Zanda, of course. The fourth I'm almost sure was a chemistry teacher, and the fifth I cannot remember, having filed the memory away in a drawer retrospectively marked THINGS I'D LIKE TO FORGET.

The girls arrived at my faculty apartment, giggling self-consciously, but intrigued. There had been a private invitation in an envelope; a request that they not divulge their invitation to anyone—the idea was not to make others feel left out. I gave each girl a stick and some red yarn. We would be making power bundles out of gifts we would gather in the course of the night. My gift was this stick and this story: I told them about Fatima, the Sufi version of the tale in which Fatima goes through several adventures, which all end tragically but from each she learns a skill that ultimately allows her to triumph. "All along the journey of your life there will be challenges. We're going to enact that journey tonight."

Off we went, traversing the dark wood, to Zanda's faculty house down the hill on the nearly deserted Abbot campus. Of course, we could have gone by sidewalk down School Street, but the whole point was to infuse drama into this rite. Zanda greeted us with the story of Proserpine and handed out pomegranates. (How do you put pomegranates in a power bundle?) The chemistry teacher wasn't sure what I meant by "a power story," but she had made a batch of chocolate chip cookies, boarding school antidote for anything. (Ditto for how to put chocolate chip cookies in a power bundle.)

As we proceeded from stop to stop that night I had the sense of being a madwoman whom friends had decided to indulge. You can't just make up a ritual from whole cloth and expect it to work overnight even if it's based on ancient ceremonies you read about in Joseph Campbell. (Part of the controversy surrounding Kwanzaa has to do with how authentically African it is.) This is why the quinces that seem made in Hollywood or in Disneyland do not have the spiritual and mythic heft that distinguishes a rite from a big production (à la MTV's *My Super Sweet 16*). Our failure as Americans to understand that distinction speaks volumes as to our spiritual poverty.

Maybe if I had stayed on teaching at Andover and at the end of each semester I'd conducted this ritual, I might have connected it with some older, meaningful ceremony that might clothe it in legitimacy—as Kwanzaa has done by linking itself to "first fruits" harvest rituals, which are truly ancient, inarguably universal, and authentically African. Or maybe from the start, the problem was not with the ritual itself, but with its not-so-wise creator, foundering in her own life. I now know enough about ritual to understand that it involves a surrender to cosmic time, so that one is safely, symbolically ferried past those jolting transitions of our mortal life. I also now know enough about myself to understand that a part of me will always remain outside any such surrender— seeing, recording, noticing the pomegranate juice staining everybody's clothes, the mosquito bites and bruises (the dark wood's only challenges), the failed ponderousness, the bittersweet humor of that not-yet-forgotten night.

Women's way

The spring of my second year at Andover, I turned in my resignation letter. I felt guilty, leaving my special girls behind to fend for themselves, but I knew if I stayed, I would never become the writer I still dreamed of becoming. But no way to recast it: I was abandoning my babies. Again I felt that I had failed at my female role of nurturing and accommodating others.

By leaving my job at Andover, I was burning my last bridge to a life that made conventional sense even to me. Also, little by little, I was removing the safe ground from under my feet. Just short of terrifying myself, I was pushing myself out there into thin air. It was a tricky maneuver—as I said, my instincts were intact. If I wanted to be a writer, damn it, I had better risk it and try to fly. Lucky for me, a great day was beginning to dawn in American literature. Ethnic writers, who like their earlier Afro-American counterparts had been eating in the kitchen, were starting to be welcomed to the big table of American literature.

I had taken a one-year job in Vermont filling in for a writer friend who had won a Guggenheim. In my initial euphoria all I could think was, I'm free! Having totally failed at the fairy tale—and its alternative convent denouement for girls who mess up—I could now write my own life. Sounds good. But it's lonely out there in that literal and metaphorical no-man's-land, and unless you have pretty sturdy internal shoulders to carry it off, you're going to keep falling apart under the weight of all that personal baggage you don't know how to discard. To be totally free of any entrapping relationships—the only kind I seemed to know how to make so far in my young life (thirty-one years old)—is to be rootless and alone and, let's face it, storyless. Narrative needs a local habitation and a name and some kind of human interaction, by which I mean a love story. Not necessarily the heterosexual type, but some sparks flying between human beings. Or the fire goes out. The page is cold. Kris Kristofferson had it right when he sang, "Freedom's just another word for nothing left to lose." Or anyone left to hold.

Lost and lonely that first winter in my Vermont outpost, I was invited by Zanda to join her Women's Way workshop, a nine-day retreat with twenty other women. I quote from a more recent letter about this workshop—which is now into its fourth decade—about what goes on:

> You will be in the company of kindred women, all of us looking into the mirrors of the cultures we live in and represent. Carrying the internalized mirrors of our mothers, sisters, grandmothers and women friends, all of us are seeing that the contemporary women's myths offer us cruel and distorted mirrors. We have to look backwards into the images from the cultures that

precede us. . . . We are looking for more compassion-
ate mirrors, ones that reflect us as we really are rather
than as others would have us be.

Frankly, I was terrified to go to this workshop. I was sure that
this group of what I imagined would be hard-hitting feminists
would clobber me for my unenlightened life and opinions. Or I'd
find myself trapped in an oppressively earnest coven with no
moderating sense of humor. Man haters—I worried about that,
too. I was not going to spend nine days trashing the guys, no way!
Freedom off the backs of other people did not interest me, even
if those others were bullies, machos, or male chauvinist pigs, because you know what? Those bullies-machos-pigs also happened
to be fathers to daughters like me. Indeed, my very patriarchal-
macho-sexist Papi had been a far more nurturing parent to me
than Mami. As I drove the four hours south in the middle of the
snowstorm, I kept wondering, why was I setting myself up for
feeling even more left out? I had packed my makeup in rebellion
because if I wanted to wear eyeliner at this retreat, I WOULD
WEAR EYELINER! The adolescent commotion going on in my
head! It was a wonder I didn't end up in a snowdrift.

The specific memories of what happened during those nine
days have faded in the ensuing twenty-five years. But a significant
inner shift took place because of what I experienced there.

Coming together to share stories, to recast the metaphors—I
had not known that this in itself can be so empowering. Oh, I
knew it intellectually, because, of course, these gatherings of
women happened often enough in my own family back in the
Dominican Republic, but those were gatherings to get a job done
in the midst of which stories were told, gossip exchanged, advice
shared. But the focus at Women's Way was our own female selves.
To shine the light of story on what was going on for each of us,

across cultures and generations. Zanda was right. Confusion was rife among us women. But we were beginning to pick up the shattered pieces from stories we'd been given by family, culture, training, and puzzling how we could fit them together into a larger, more satisfying version of being female.

This doesn't necessarily happen to everyone who attends one of these workshops, but perhaps because I was prime for this sort of reenvisioning, the workshop filled me with a heady and hopeful knowledge: that we need not keep acting out or reacting to the old stories, that we could get off the grid. And we could do this within community; we need not be exiled because we were not going to play by the old rules. There were women out there who had survived their fairy tales, who were a step ahead of us: Miss Stevensons, Zandas; there were strings of words, poems, and stories we could use to navigate our way through the rough waters.

In his book *The Songlines,* Bruce Chatwin tells of tribes on the northwest coast of America who lived half on the islands and half on the mainland. They would travel over the sea and navigate their canoes up the current from California to the Bering Strait, which they called Klin Otto. The navigators were priestesses. Chatwin quotes an old woman talking about a tradition close to fifteen thousand years old:

> Everythin' we ever knew about the movement of the sea was preserved in the verses of a song. For thousands of years, we went where we wanted and came home safe, because of the song. On clear nights we had the stars to guide us, and in the fog we had the streams and the creeks of the sea, the streams and creeks that flow into and become Klin Otto. . . .
>
> There was a song for goin' to China and a song for

goin' to Japan, a song for the big island and a song for
the smaller one. All she had to know was the song and
she knew where she was. To get back, she just sang the
song in reverse.

What was my song? For years I had been listening to other people's songs and ending up adrift and lost, shipwrecked on their
shores, angry at them for being sirens when all they were doing
was standing their own ground, being themselves. The piper's tune
was not bad, it was just that it was somebody else's song. To know
my own song was to know who I was, where I'd come from, and
how to get beyond to the big islands and the small ones, the rich,
adventurous, and scary life I was now consciously embarked upon.

Maybe younger women—younger than me, say, and I'm now
in my mid-fifties—know all this from the get-go because they've
been raised by women of my generation and so have absorbed
this knowledge with mother's milk: it can be done—being your
own person. Not that it's easy. In fact, maybe our daughters never
expected that it would be anything but difficult. All I know is that
when I and many of the women of my generation were the age
our daughters are now, we were totally at sea in a new world
where the old paradigms our mothers and grandmothers had
passed on to us were not helpful. And for those of us who were
also Latinas, those paradigms given to us by our mamis and
abuelitas were not only not helpful but to reject them was to reject nuestra cultura, to desert our ethnic group, nuestra comunidad, sagradas tradiciones y familias.

What happened to me at Women's Way allowed me to find
my way back to that culture, to tap that mujer strength that I saw
in full force at Monica's quinceañera. It was one of those aha!
moments where things inside get ever so slightly shifted around,

but that shift allows for new possibilities to enter into one's consciousness. Heady claims, I know. And it didn't happen just like that. It was a seed, a beginning, a laying on of hands.

It was a lot like what happened when as a young writer I read my first "ethnic novel," *The Woman Warrior: Memories of a Girlhood Among Ghosts,* about a Chinese-American girl caught between her parents' old-world culture and her new life in America. Before Maxine Hong Kingston's magical book, I had not known that I could put my own experience into an American story. I don't mean that I thought a writer couldn't use autobiographical material: I had read James Joyce, Sylvia Plath, F. Scott Fitzgerald. But I didn't know that nonmainstream narratives in which there were Spanish words and Latina/o characters could be part of American literature. Such material, I had been taught, was folklore, the province of sociology. And then I read Maxine Hong Kingston's book.

When I think of how the quinceañera can do something more than or other than affirm and codify the old paradigm of being a princess, a heroine of a fairy tale, I wonder what would happen if the ritual could do for our young girls what Women's Way did for me much later in my life, after many hard knocks and a lot of wrong turns and burned bridges and painful mistakes. If only it had come earlier, that laying on of hands.

The stories in our heads

Quinces definitely have the potential of introducing a new story into the imagination of the next generation, one that might indeed help them live happier, more productive lives.

Why else would companies like Maggi and Kern's Nectar

choose the quinceañera as the target tradition at which to aim their public relations campaigns? They know a powerful cultural icon when they see one.

But others are drawn to the tradition not as an advertising tool but as an opportunity to truly empower young people to believe that their dreams for their lives can come true.

Enter the fairy godmothers.

Isabella Martínez Wall, Priscilla Mora, and Sister Angela we have met: Isabella, dispensing advice from her Web site, bellaquinceañera.com, and committed to making each girl feel like the queen of her life; Priscilla Mora, organizing expos to educate Latinas on financially responsible and culturally meaningful quinceañeras; Sister Angela, using the tradition as a teachable moment for Catholic youth, boys and girls, Latino or not. A fourth fairy godmother, Ana Maria Schachtell, founded the Stay-in-School Quinceañera Program, which could well become a model for such programs elsewhere.

In Idaho, of all places.

But, then, Ana Maria is the kind of self-powering dynamo to which you constantly find yourself applying versions of the phrase "of all places." As in, of all people, this Mexican immigrant mother of two sons started a program for what is traditionally daughter territory. But, if you spend more than five minutes talking to the bubbly, charismatic Ana Maria, you think, *Of course!*

Ana Maria grew up in a family of five girls, two boys. She laughs when I ask if she had a quinceañera. "We were too poor," she says, echoing any number of mamis of present-day quinceañeras. Ana Maria came to this country in 1965 when she was eighteen, worked hard at everything from waitressing to packing eggs, but kept going to school at night. Eventually, she met and married her German husband, and they moved to Idaho, following one of her sisters who told her there were jobs out there. Ana

Maria ended up in Nampa, where there was a growing Mexican migrant community.

Which is how Ana Maria got involved in quinceañeras. One of her sons was invited to be in a girl's court up in Caldwell. So, every Saturday, Ana Maria would drive him to the rehearsals at Memorial Park. "I'd sit under a tree, watching these thirty or so kids practicing their waltzes and dances. And then one day, I had this revelation!"

She looked out at this group of kids and all she could think was, *Oh my God!*

Ana Maria felt a surge of desperation. "I wanted to rush over and stand in the center of this group and just tell them: 'Do you realize that thirty percent of you girls will be pregnant by next year? Do you realize that thirty percent of you boys are going to end up in jail by the time you are twenty-one? Do you realize that the majority of you will drop out of school?'"

Ana Maria pauses as if in revisiting that moment she is again feeling that mix of hope and dread at seeing the fragile possibilities gathered before her. It is a mix of feelings I've gotten to know well this last year, attending quinceañeras and talking to young girls. Such potential for flight; such likelihood of broken wings, crash landings.

"Here they were, kids having fun, kids eager to learn, kids open to experiences, and we leaders of the community were missing out royally, not taking advantage of this amazing learning opportunity."

So, she decided to do something about it. Four years later, when her son went off to college, she began mobilizing the community to establish the Hispanic Cultural Center and the jewel of the center was her dream, the Stay-in-School Quinceañera Program.

"We start in January, twice a week, one school night and then one Saturday, thirty to forty fourteen-year-old girls and boys," Ana Maria explains. "We have them until the end of school in June. Most of them have just started high school or are going to start in the fall." She figures she has a small window in which to make a difference about how their lives are going to go. "Most of these kids come from poor migrant families. Their parents haven't had much education. They need to hear it can be done. So, we bring in teachers from the high school to talk about what to expect there. We bring in community leaders to encourage them to think about their future and make them proud of their past, their roots, their traditions. Judge Gutierrez, our only Hispanic judge in Idaho, has come to talk to them, and this last year we brought in Loretta Sanchez!" This is obviously a big fish and I'm embarrassed not to know who she is. Later I Google her and find out she is a congresswoman from California.

"We bring in artists and dancers and writers to do workshops with the kids." Suddenly, Ana Maria pauses. A loaded pause. "Want to come talk to our kids?"

I'm off the hook because it's May, the program is almost over. But no doubt about it, next winter I will be in Idaho. There is nothing more fierce than a fairy godmother who needs a pair of wings for a young heroine or hero in trouble.

According to Ana Maria, the kids have a lot of fun—"or they wouldn't keep coming back, week after week." Much of that fun comes from doing things that affirm their sense of pride in their culture. "They learn old cerámica techniques. We brought in an eighty-nine-year-old woman to teach the girls how to make their traditional coronas out of wax flowers, a Mexican handiwork that is being lost because of the cheap plastic crowns around. And for the boys, we bring in a charro, that's the original American cow-

boy. A lot of people don't know that. The charro tradition represents the best of machismo, how to be a real hombre, responsible
to your familia and community. The boys eat it up."

I bet they do. How could they not, with Ana Maria cheering
them on? The whole program culminates in a gala night, a fund-
raiser for the Hispanic Cultural Center. The center has a stock of
thirty gowns for the girls and it rents tuxedos for the boys. The
governor comes, the senators, the mayor. (The Hispanic population of the state is growing at four times the rate of the non-
Hispanic population. No doubt, these elected officials have done
the numbers.)

What is inspiring about Ana Maria's program, which is now in
its eighth year, is that it takes the tradition of the quinceañera, acknowledging its power as a coming-of-age ceremony, but recasts
it with new content, including a strong emphasis on education.
What does it mean to be a man, un hombre, un charro, in this
new country? What does it mean to be una mujer who knows her
tradiciones, can make the old-country wax flowers for a corona
but can also run for Congress? In other words, the Stay-in-School
program takes the occasion of the quinceañera to revise the limited narrative the rite has traditionally endorsed.

It's the same approach taken by a group of health professionals and researchers in a study outlined in an article, "Latina Adolescents' Sexual Health," included in *Latina Girls*. The project,
SHERO (female version of "hero"), involved a group of Latina
adolescents in Chicago, ages twelve to twenty-one, who were at
high risk for unplanned pregnancies and HIV infections. How to
empower these young girls to take better care of their sexual
health? The group of five researchers and health professionals
(Harper, Bangi, Sanchez, Doll, and Pedraza) used "a narrative
ethnographic approach," in which they worked collectively with

the girls "to reveal the range of community and cultural narratives that serve as barriers to sexual self-protection."

In other words, as I discovered at Women's Way, there are stories in our heads about who we must be and what we can do, and these stories drive our lives. The girls in the SHERO group learned to recognize these narratives, most especially Marianismo and machismo in all their subtle and not so subtle forms. They then went on to create their own "new healthy stories and narratives," incorporating admirable qualities of mothers, aunts, grandmothers, as well as whatever was valuable in their traditions.

But the fact that these old restrictive narratives about womanhood persist in our young Latina girls speaks to the need for retooling. And the quinceañera tradition—as a number of fairy godmothers have discovered—can provide that amazing learning opportunity.

No hairs on their tongues

One of the things I found curious was how some of the Latina women I identified as hard-hitting, groundbreaking compañeras seemed to get dewy-eyed and reverential around the idea of the quinceañera.

Part of it, I surmised, was the same ambivalence I felt toward the tradition. I, too, got weepy and hopeful at the celebrations I attended, even as I also deplored certain aspects that seemed to endorse a princess-in-the-patriarchy fantasy, which was at best useless, at worst harmful, to the young girl.

Were we Latinas closing ranks around our own comunidad, refusing to allow for a division among ourselves by criticizing a tradition of nuestra cultura, as if solidarity involved checking our brains and forgetting our battle scars at the door of our Latinahood?

Was there an element of campy condescension among those who embraced the excesses of a ritual that had become so popular, especially at the grassroots level?

Or perhaps we feared being called Malinches, betraying our own people by finding fault with what some claim is "an ancient Aztec tradition"?

So, it was heartening to come across the work of Latina scholars who—to use an expression in Spanish—*no tienen pelo en la lengua*—do not have hair on the tongue. In other words, Latinas who do not mince their words, who will tell the emperor *and* the empress that he/she has no clothes, if need be. In her previously mentioned study, "La Quinceañera: Making Gender and Ethnic Identities," the cultural anthropologist Karen Mary Davalos readily admits that there are a lot more sparks flying than are acknowledged in the public discourse about this tradition.

Among the Mexican American women Davalos interviewed there was ongoing "negotiation and contestation surrounding the event." Sometimes the conflict was over a seemingly petty issue like the color of the dress. One quinceañera and her mother fought over whether her gown could be red; the girl won and came of age in the traditional ceremony her mother wanted but dressed untraditionally in flaming crimson. Claudia, a member of the junior varsity softball team at Lawrence High School, insisted on wearing her high-top sneakers for her papi to change into heels. Her mother and grandmother did not take to this idea at first, but finally conceded because, in fact, Claudia would be symbolically putting aside this ugly-duckling tomboyish phase to become the docile swan in high heels, as per Papi's agency.

For Davalos, these surface squabbles were evidence of "various often conflicting views about women, family, and mexicano tradition." It's as if the quinceañera itself were a cultural Rorschach test that allowed conflicts and contradictions embedded in Latinahood to surface. So although the ceremony seemed a way of "holding on to your roots" and creating and displaying your mexicana identity, "this construction of identity was not based on carefree choices that produce harmonious images of whole mexicanas." Instead these women came face-to-face with "contradictory presentations of the self . . . through an event that is imagined as highly 'traditional' within a patriarchal institution." Davalos concluded that the quinceañera inhabits that "uncomfortable territory . . . [where] two or more cultures, multiple meanings, and complicated constructions" of latinidad come together. In short, the quinceañera is the site where the young girl meets the complex legacy she is inheriting as a Latina woman head-on.

This being so, the quinceañera tradition does present an amazing opportunity. It offers a space where we Latinas can view, review, articulate, and perhaps even reframe some of these contradictions. Just this fact makes *me* get dewy-eyed about the tradition. As I learned in Women's Way, having the occasion to speak and understand our stories can be transformative. Part of what made my own passage to womanhood so difficult was that there was no talking about the conflicts inside us and inside our families and our communities. It takes a trailblazer to answer Maira's cry and shed more light. Maxine Hong Kingston's memoir, *The Woman Warrior,* published in the mid-seventies, turned on the light for a generation of Latinas, myself included, and not just at the level of craft as I mentioned earlier. Even though the author's experience was Chinese-American, so much of Hong Kingston's borderland experience reflected our own. The interdiction that opens the book could well have been uttered by any of our mamis: *You must not tell anyone,* my mother said, *what I am about to tell you.* That was the mandate, silencio!

Seven years after the publication of *The Woman Warrior,* as if echoing Hong Kingston, Cherríe Moraga subtitled her memoir *Loving in the War Years: lo que nunca pasó por sus labios,* "what never passed her lips." Moraga closes her book by acknowledging those profound and simple messages that never passed our mothers' lips but which nevertheless are deeply imprinted on our brains:

> It has always been like this
>
> profundo y sencillo
> lo que nunca
> pasó
> por sus labios
>
> but was
> > utterly
> > > utterly
> > heard.

Just reading the Latina writers who began to emerge in the mid- to late eighties helped me feel encouraged and less alone. Cherríe Moraga, Lorna Dee Cervantes, Sandra Cisneros, Gloria Anzaldúa, *que en paz descanse,* were articulating what I utterly, utterly knew to be true in my experience. Writing about her own stormy passage into womanhood in *Borderlands/La Frontera: The New Mestiza,* Anzaldúa describes the borderland world many Latinas were trapped in: "Alienated from her mother culture, 'alien' in the dominant culture, the woman of color [is] caught between los intersticios, the spaces between the different worlds she inhabits."

But Anzaldúa refused to stay stuck there, battered by opposing forces. This is what makes her 1987 memoir seem prophetic and more timely than ever. Anzaldúa believed in the evolution of a new Latina consciousness based on a tolerance for the contradictions we have inherited. That painful borderland world can also be the place "where the possibility of uniting all that is separate occurs." Anzaldúa's analysis is too good not to quote in full:

> This assembly [of disparate cultural traditions and selves] is not one where severed or separated pieces merely come together. Nor is it a balancing of opposing powers. In attempting to work out a synthesis, the self has added a third element which is greater than the sum of its severed parts. That third element is a new consciousness—a mestiza consciousness—and though it is a source of intense pain, its energy comes from continual creative motion that keeps breaking down the unitary aspect of each new paradigm.
>
> *En unas pocas centurias,* the future will belong to the mestiza. Because the future depends on the breaking down of paradigms, it depends on the straddling of two or more cultures. By creating a new mythos—that is, a change in the way we perceive reality, the way we see ourselves, and the ways we behave—la mestiza creates a new consciousness.

And a Latina shall lead them—I love it! Why not? Hybridity is what being Latino/Spanglish is all about. "In every Spanglish family, one can find a black person, a white person, an Asian person, a Semitic person, or an indigenous person," Ed Morales explains in *Living in Spanglish.* Unlike their Anglo counterparts, the Spaniards, who brought few of their own women to the New World, mixed with the natives and slaves. "We are a miscegenation-happy people," Ed Morales concludes.

And this same mixing continues among us *here* in the USA. Ironically, as Ed Morales points out, Simón Bolívar's dream of a Latin-American unity, which fell apart because of national and regional rivalries in the nineteenth century, is happening now in the twenty-first century within—not in opposition to—the United States. We are becoming that Pan-American group on American soil. And as we mix, not just with one another but with other Americans, we are transforming our new country. *E pluribus unum,* all right. Out of the many, one hybrid nation.

But it's hybridity as a state of mind that interests Ed Morales, that intrigued Gloria Anzaldúa, that inspires me now. A state of being betwixt and between, "of belonging to at least two identities at the same time, and not being confused or hurt by it," according to Ed Morales. Being Spanglish, he calls it. John Keats called it the quality of negative capability, "ideal for the poetical Character . . . the camelion Poet": that ability to entertain dualities and "to be in uncertainties, Mysteries, doubts without any irritable reaching after fact & reason." Mike Davis in *Magical Urbanism* notes that Latinos could well be the ones who teach America how to be—of all things!—American:

> To be Latino in the U.S. is rather to participate in a unique process of cultural syncretism that may become a transformative template for the whole society.

Again, why not? Statisticians predict that by the year 2050 one out of every four Americans will be of Hispanic origin. More and more Spanglish people! But immigration into a new culture or into a mainstream—being Spanglish, being a hybrid—is no longer an experience exclusive to Latinos. Globalization brings the "immigration experience" beyond our borders and makes the collision of cultures a reality everywhere. And so when we wonder about how to deal with these confusions and contradictions, we are really addressing how to evolve a new kind of world consciousness that is transformative and synthesizing. Anzaldúa was right. The question is no less than how to be a new kind of human being!

That is a tall order, but, like all such orders, it breaks down into teensy millimeters of understanding in the present moment, the here and now, that tricky ground. How we go about our daily lives, make choices about what we buy and who we vote for, and, yes, how we nurture and help our young people in their passage into adulthood. They especially are at ground zero of these collisions of worlds; their identity is being formed in the crucible of these encounters. And the quinceañera is as good a place to start as any.

The writer and critic Norma Cantú thought so. Having had a traditional quinceañera, which reflected the limited roles available to her as a young Latina, she decided to throw herself a second quinceañera at fifty! Her "cincuentañera," as she called it, included a traditional court, with forty-nine (instead of fourteen) godmothers of such items as madrina de queques, madrina de AARP, madrina de hierbas y remedios caseros (godmother for cakes, for AARP subscription, for herbal and home remedies). The celebration was a chance to affirm what had been only potential thirty-five years earlier as well as to reframe the tradition from a place of power, intelligence, humor, and experience.

I read about Norma Cantú's cincuentañera in her article "Chicana Life-Cycle Rituals," included in her anthology *Chicana Traditions: Continuity and Change.* The book itself is a gathering of Chicana scholars who are studying and sharing stories and thus helping to create that new Latina consciousness. An anthology of mujeres without hairs on their tongues. I was so tickled by Norma

Cantú's zany and wonderful recasting of the tradition I decided to call her. For years I'd been hearing about Norma Cantú from my Latina friends, reading her work. But as happens when one is slightly in awe of a person, I was a little afraid of her. Even her name sounded fierce. Her first e-mailed response mapped out a schedule that would wipe out a much younger man or woman— there seemed to be only a handful of hours in the next few months when she might be free to take a call. But after batting a few e-mails back and forth, we fixed on a time.

"There's a need in all of us for ritualized expression in the context of community," Norma explains when we finally connect by phone. The absence of rituals in our lives makes us powerless to withstand the pressures of our times. Norma cites the anthropologist Solon Kimball's assertion that the increase in mental illness in the mid- to late twentieth century may be due to how many individuals are forced to accomplish life transitions alone and with private symbols.

But we also don't have to be hamstrung by a tradition. "It's a live critter, tradition." Norma laughs. Her voice is softer and prettier than I thought it would be. "It's in the nature of ritual to evolve according to the needs of a community." She tells me the story of an anthropologist who was surprised that the Mexican migrant community he was studying in Wisconsin did not celebrate the Day of the Dead—a big feast day in Mexico when the community turns out in all the cemeteries, feasting and celebrating with their buried ancestors. When he asked the migrant workers why they had abandoned their tradition, they said, "None of our dead are buried here!" "Besides," Norma adds, "imagine spending a night outdoors in a cemetery in Wisconsin in November. It's too cold for the dead, not to mention the living."

Norma, who is the oldest of eleven children, grew up in a working-class family that somehow found the resources to celebrate the milestones of each of her siblings. "I myself was honored with piñatas at one, five, ten, and, of course, then I had my quinceañera. I really believe in celebrating milestones and also expressing gratitude to the universe for all the blessings that come into my life." In fact, Norma is already planning her sesentañera.

"These celebrations serve to draw us together, keep us going," Norma asserts. "Really, a ritual is transformative for the whole community, not just for the individual going through it." She elaborates how in her own cincuentañera when her aged parents stood up and emotionally wished her happy birthday and expressed their pride in her achievements, they were, in effect, acknowledging a change in their own thinking. They were celebrating a life that had not gone the traditional route they had anticipated. For them to publicly "bless" her successful academic and literary career was important, not just for her but for the younger women in the community. "Those who defy the patterns as set forth by society require affirmation."

After our talk I e-mail Norma to thank her for helping to shed more light on some of the confusing behaviors encoded in our Latina women's bodies and brains, and, like Anzaldúa, refusing to stay stuck there. We are rewiring ourselves with our writing and our talking and our sharing of stories. Now that we, mujeres of my generation, are becoming the elders of the tribe, we want to pass on some of what we have learned from the struggles we had to take on.

I am reminded of my trip to Miami to interview quinceañeras and events planners. On one of my visits to a one-stop quinceañera store, I asked if I could go into the stockroom and look at some of the dresses. I wound my way through a dressing room and found myself in a windowless back room where three Latina women not much older than myself were working on quinceañera gowns. All around them, finished gowns hung from pipes in the ceiling. I had the feeling that I had entered a mythic world where the three fates were spinning the thread of our Latina lives.

I explained what I was doing. I was writing a book about our tradition of the quinceañera. For some reason, this introduction made them all laugh merrily.

"Well, you are at the right place," the one who seemed the oldest of the bunch said. Her white hair was disheveled, her smile revealed several missing teeth. She had been eating a sandwich, but quickly slipped it to her lap when I entered. No doubt the shop had a rule about eating while working on the fancy gowns.

We chatted for a while. The woman who had been doing most of the talking was from Cuba, as was another quieter woman with a helmet of gray hair that looked sprayed in place. She was the one who most matched my idea of a seamstress, a kind of librarian in the fabric world, tidy and proper. The third woman seemed a few years younger, dark-haired and perky, and proud to be from Nicaragua. It turned out that not one of them had had a quinceañera. "We were too poor in our family," the woman from Nicaragua explained. The other two concurred.

"Are you sorry you didn't have one?" I wondered out loud. That made them all fall silent. "I didn't either," I added in case they thought I was suggesting a credential they were supposed to have.

The white-haired one again broke the silence. "To me it makes no difference. To me," she said, lifting what was left of her sandwich, "I'd rather spend the money on something necessary. But I am glad they are doing it because it keeps us all working."

Among them they counted up more than sixty years in this business of making quinceañera and bridal gowns.

"Sixty years!" I exclaimed. My surprise made them laugh.

"We are the veteranas of the wars of the quinceañeras and brides," the white-haired one proclaimed.

That made me laugh. "What do you mean, veterans of the quinceañera wars?"

"They come, they want a certain dress, the mother wants another one, they fight because she wants a short dress, or a strapless or a halter top, you let the dress out for the gorditas, take it in for the skinny ones." The women laughed again.

Somehow they have stayed with me, those three old veteranas of the quinceañera wars. Now, every time a quinceañera makes her magical entrance or sits on her throne while Papi changes her shoes and Mami crowns her with a tiara, I catch a glimpse of them in my mind's eye, working away in the back room. It's a longer, more useful view, the bookend at the other end of the quinceañera. A view that makes me wonder: what can we give our young girls that will carry them all the way through to this last stage of their womanhood?

Liberating quinceañeras

It's a question that began to haunt me again as the time neared for completion of this book, but in a negative form: what were we *not* giving our young girls that was causing them to fail?

It was the question that, in fact, had gotten me interested in the topic of quinceañeras. Reading the dire statistics in *The State of Hispanic Girls* had made me curious about this odd disparity between the fantasy the ritual enacts and the facts of these young girls' lives. But during the course of my research, I had met so many successful and focused young women! Of course, I was encountering a select population as quinceañeras are often given to girls by their parents as a reward for being "good girls." But maybe the reports of failure were an exaggeration, and there was a sunnier side of the story that was not getting as much press?

Just as I'd begin to bask in the pink glow of a Pollyanna Latina-hood, a shadow would fall on the happy kingdom.

I had put a Google Alert on the topic of quinceañera, and so, besides reviews for the new movie *Quinceañera* and feature articles spawned by the film about specific quince parties, I kept getting articles about violence at quinceañeras. In Wellington, Florida, a quinceañera ended in "a mini-riot" between guests and deputies who had been called to the scene when a fight erupted on the dance floor. A headline from San Diego read: A MAN SHOT TO DEATH AT GIRL'S FIFTEENTH BIRTHDAY PARTY. In San Bernardino County, California, a guest was shot and died after a fight broke out at a quince party. At a West Sacramento quinceañera, a nineteen-year-old guest was gunned down and two others wounded. In Oakland, the victim at a quince party was a fourteen-year-old. In Fitchburg, Massachusetts, it was a seventeen-year-old boy who opened fire and shot four men at a quinceañera, one of whom died. What was going on?

Of course, this is in part how journalism works. As I like to remind my writing students, stories are about trouble. Still, the constant reporting on quince fatalities made me feel defensive: trouble breaks out in the Latino community, and it gets a lot of media attention. But the reports were a pebble in my shoe. As for a pattern: quite a few of the fights began over uninvited guests being turned away, or, if they somehow snuck in, being asked to leave. Young males wanting entry into an intimate female space; gangs feuding for territory with alcohol thrown in: these are all tried-and-true triggers for tragedy—all you have to do is read *Romeo and Juliet*. But these quinceañera tragedies presented an old story with a very new twist: there was no love story involved. This was violence, raw and coming to the surface, entre nosotros, among our own.

The articles mentioned the names of police departments that had responded to these disturbances. I decided to make a few calls and ask the officers what they thought was going on.

Dave Farmer, the lieutenant with the West Sacramento Police Department who responded to the party where one guest was killed and two wounded, admits that he gets concerned every time a quinceañera is coming up. Will there be enough security and monitoring to avoid trouble? He himself has been married to a Hispanic for thirty-six years and really appreciates what he calls "the festiveness of Hispanic people." But what happens at these quinceañeras is you have a young population, you have rivalries, you have gangs. "Depending on the community situation at any given time, if there are tensions going on, they will tend to flare up during a quinceañera."

Arden Wiltshire at the San Bernardino County sheriff's department agrees. As a deputy, she gets hired to do security at quinceañeras. "You've got to have two, not one, but two of us, armed," she explains. "It's a requirement anymore for insurance purposes." She has done four to five dozen quinceañeras in the last six years, and though she admits "I don't know a lick of Spanish, except for Alto! [Stop!]," she does know that every incident—and there have been quite a few on her beat—has involved alcohol. "People get drunk, then some rivalry issue arises, and forget it."

But it isn't until I call the Fitchburg Police Department following the incident in which a seventeen-year-old killed one guest and wounded three others that I begin to understand that the shadow falling in the form of violence at these parties is part of a much larger problem. Chief Ed Cronin, who sounds avuncular and wise, says that when he got started in his Fitchburg precinct in 1982, he had seven murders in the first eighteen months, and six of them were Latinos killing Latinos. He also had eighteen officers under lawsuits from the Latino community.

"And here's some more bad news," he adds. "Just in Fitchburg our Latino high school dropout rate is forty percent. When you think that fifty percent of the kids entering kindergarten are Latinos, then we are facing big-time failure here in central Massachusetts."

Two years ago, Chief Cronin decided that running a vigilant police department was not enough. "I started asking myself what in my behavior was failing them." He joined a Latino Coalition group and began what he calls "a listening process, not judging, just listening. I tried to see the world through the eyes of Latino people. And I don't mean generically."

So what did he see?

"I saw wholesale systemic racism down the line in our institutions. It's a dual system, which works to bring some folks success, and a lot of others failure." A lot of those others—in his community anyhow—are Latinos and it's during adolescence that they begin to see the writing on the wall. Violence in quinceañeras is just a symptom. "Disenfranchised people are going to blow up at quinceañeras. They're going to blow up on the streets, in their homes."

Chief Cronin sends me to talk to Sayra Pinto, who is the executive director of the Latino Coalition, a young woman, about half his age. Fierce and passionate, Sayra tells me hers is "our typical story." Her father was not around. Her mother left her behind with relatives in her native Honduras to come illegally to el Norte, seeking a better life. "By the time she was legal and sent for me, I was twelve, and it was like meeting a stranger." Things did not go well between them, and soon Sayra was out on the streets. But some aunts and uncles took her in. "I guess I don't have to ask if you had a quinceañera," I remark.

Sayra laughs. "Actually, I could have had one. I was offered one by my aunt. But I didn't want to be displayed like that."

That fierce sense of integrity led her in a different direction.

Sayra got herself into college. "None of my relatives wanted to sign off on my application. They were afraid they'd be liable. I had to do a lot of convincing." Again the "typical story": a girl did not need so much education. ¿Para qué? When Sayra graduated from college, she decided she was going to be there for young people in the way that no one had been there for her.

Her job in the coalition is to help combat the systemic racism that Chief Cronin spoke of. "We are the big boom in the population. We can begin to build bridges, create a new template, transform an educational system that is failing our young people. It's a critical time," Sayra goes on with an urgency in her voice that sets me to doodling hearts pierced with arrows on the margins of my page of notes. "We have a historic opportunity to shape what this country will become."

Sayra estimates a window of opportunity of ten, fifteen years. "There is a confluence of crises occurring in the world as we speak: environmental degradation, increased nuclear armament, failing democratic systems, et cetera. We are facing challenges on a world scale that have not been faced before." The system that is in place needs to be drastically changed. It's a system that fails to recognize the integrity of the feminine. "So to liberate women through a true quinceañera ritual would mean creating and affirming a consciousness in our young women about the sacredness of the feminine, the connection between their bodies and the natural world and the body politic," Sayra explains. As for the violence that so typically erupts at quinceañeras, Sayra believes that "it is almost a poetic and deeply unconscious subjugation of women, their newfound sexual power, to a system that uses violence to perpetuate itself. Redefining this tradition, much like we redefined the term 'Hispanic,' will require that we work very hard to own the best of us and bring it out into the light."

There has to be more light. There it is again.

If this seems a grim prognosis, with scales tipped by someone who has spent eleven long years working in the urban trenches, a recent series in the Spanish language New York newspaper *El Diario/La Prensa* corroborates Sayra Pinto's and Ed Cronin's urgent sense of mission. Reporting on a 2005 national survey on dangerous juvenile behavior among high school students by the Centers for Disease Control and Prevention of the U.S. Department of Health and Human Services, *El Diario/La Prensa* concludes that we are facing a mostly ignored national crisis among one of the fastest growing segments of the American population, young Hispanic girls. According to the study, one in six young Latinas attempts suicide, a rate more than one and a half times as high as that of non-Hispanic black and white teenage girls. In addition, this vulnerable population has the highest teenage pregnancy rate and one of the highest dropout rates—one-quarter of Latina teen girls drop out of high school—a figure topped only by Hispanic young men, one-third of whom do not complete high school.

"Latina girls are in crisis, and if we deny it and ignore it, we will doom them with our complacency," an editorial in the same issue of *El Diario/La Prensa* warns. "When these young women try to kill themselves it is a cry for help. We must listen and act. These are the daughters of our community, and they need us."

"This is a public health issue," agrees Dr. Luis H. Zayas, a licensed psychologist and professor at Washington University in St. Louis who spearheaded the 2005 survey. "Whenever you have rates at this level, we should all be concerned."

Not only are the present levels high, but when you consider that one in four women in the United States will be Hispanic by midcentury, then we are facing not just a community crisis but a national one. "The time to help is now," concludes a *New York Times* editorial responding to the *El Diario/La Prensa* series. An Op-Ed piece in *Críticas* following release of the survey agrees: "If we want our quinceañeras and mujeres healthy and productive, ready to conquer the world, we have to take action now."

But why are our young girls in such despair in such high numbers?

"It's a million-dollar question as to why this is happening," Dr. Zayas explains in one of the *El Diario/La Prensa* articles. "There's a combination of forces that are coming together as the girls are moving into the American social experience."

Dr. Zayas cites as chief among these forces the cultural divide that begins to form between girls and their parents as the girls enter adolescence: the parents expect their daughters to live by their strict traditional values and the girls want to be a part of a contemporary American society that allows them far more freedom. At the same time, these young girls are unsure where they belong ethnically, racially, and culturally in this new American world. They know they will need a good education to succeed, and yet they are pressured by their home cultures to be caretakers, self-abnegating females steeped in Marianismo. And all these pressures are exacerbated by the fact that many of these young women have few resources, many come from low-income backgrounds. A feeling of intense and oppressive isolation sets in.

"We were all adolescents once," the *Críticas* editorial concludes. "We know how intense and confusing that period is. Imagine adding to that mix two major forces, American culture and Latino traditions, and you might understand why growing up Latina in the United States is shocking and difficult."

And further, imagine this: becoming aware of the racism that even a white middle-aged police chief found rampant when he set himself the goal of seeing the world through Latino eyes. When that kind of vision hits a young girl already floundering between worlds, it's no wonder that suicide seems a very real possibility. When that kind of vision hits a young Latino, no wonder he explodes when yet one more person tells him he's not invited to the party.

The shadow that keeps falling on the quinceañera fantasy every time a fight erupts is a grim reminder that many of our girls and our boys are in trouble. And they need our help more than ever, so that they do not keep failing. The time to act is now. "Being with our young people, accompanying them into adulthood, is exactly what I believe is the work for our leadership right now," Sayra explains. "I hear from our own people that I'm wasting my talent working with gangs and kids in trouble. I guess it all depends on whether or not you take the long view. But I refuse to leave our inner cities . . . with all our children in them alone."

As for the quinceañera shootings that wracked her small community, Sayra says it was so difficult. After all the work and progress made by her coalition, to have a coming-of-age birthday party turn into a funeral! "And what was really disappointing was how little help we got afterward. No grief counselors in the schools, for one," Sayra recalls. But even so, "in the midst of multiple systemic failures to support our community from all sides, I experienced justice. Just when we thought we were alone at a funeral, Ed [Cronin] showed up and I found myself sobbing on his shoulder. Perhaps it was the first time in my life that I actually experienced safety."

A police chief can never make up for a long-lost father, and crying in his arms is no kind of waltz. Still, I couldn't help thinking that Sayra Pinto had experienced a kind of liberated quinceañera after all.

Wishing on a quinceañera

It's getting close to that witching hour, the party has crescendoed, Monica has cut her cake and gone from table to table handing out small Cinderella dolls, the recuerdo or bolo, a commemorative party favor usually in keeping with the quinceañera's theme. She is radiant, especially as everyone has told her what a beautiful speech she gave. "She made me cry," Mr. Ramos admits when I go up to him to say good-bye.

"I know," I agree. What I don't tell him is how I cry at every quinceañera, how I keep seeing my old crones in the back room spinning the thread of our Latina lives, how I wonder what Monica will find helpful from having had this special night.

"She wrote that speech all by herself," Mr. Ramos boasts, dabbing his brow with the decorative handkerchief he has pulled out of his tuxedo's chest pocket. He launches into a résumé of all that Monica has accomplished in her short life: her As in English, her posts in student government. "She's going to go far," he says. He is sure of it. My presence serves as proof. Already she is getting national attention, a writer covering her quinceañera!

Mrs. Ramos spots us and hurries over; I've noticed this before, her discomfort whenever she catches sight of me talking to her husband. I suspect that she is afraid that Mr. Ramos, who has something of a loose tongue, and now even more so since he has been drinking, will tell "the writer" something she shouldn't know. Well, the danger is over. I'm headed back to my hotel. "Thank you for letting me be here tonight, " I say, kissing her good-bye.

"What? Leaving? So early!"

"Early?" I laugh. She has to understand I'm one of the viejitas now. "My husband and I are usually fast asleep by ten." Mrs. Ramos gives me a long look. I can't be more than a few years older than she is, if that. She doesn't buy it. Didn't I like the party? There were a few problemitas but everything came together at the end. Didn't I think so?

"It was a lovely celebration," I assure her. "You have a beautiful daughter, two beautiful daughters."

Her face softens, relieved. She has had such a hard time these last few years, she confides, a brush with cancer, other problems. Mrs. Ramos herself never studied, never had a chance. "Yo no soy nadie, nadie." She is nobody. She tells her daughters that she doesn't want them to end up nobodies also.

"You're not nobody!" I protest. The music is so loud I have to raise my voice to be heard. How can she say that? This handsome woman has raised two lovely, smart daughters, a successful son. But as we talk to, or rather holler at, each other, I realize that Mrs. Ramos doesn't really think of herself as a nobody except around women like me, who seem to her to have risen above our common lot. How odd at this stage of life, knowing the mess I made of things, to see that past reframed by a measure of success as a path I traveled to a happy ending, a published writer, una profesora, a woman other women might look up to. If only she knew what "my life's journey" amounts to: my conveyance, the seat of my pants; my road map, a series of detours around burning bridges.

I find Silvia laughing with her cousins, finally released of all her responsibilities. "Hope you had a good time," she says in parting. Later, by phone, Godmother Claire will tell me that all night Silvia was comparing her younger sister's extravagant coming-of-age to her own more subdued party three years ago. "I told her, 'Yours was special in its own way.'" I bet a lot of people tell Silvia that, and it must get old: being the sister of the princess. Maybe someday soon she will realize that there's a freedom in not getting the starring role. You can get out from under, follow your own star.

Monica has been nonstop occupied by people taking her out to dance. It's part of the quinceañera tradition that the young lady dances with all the male guests at the party. It brings good luck to take a spin with the princess of the night. Even her girlfriends haul her out to the dance floor, form a circle around her, dancing and clapping. The moment has an ancient, tribal feel to it, women alone celebrating one of their own. But soon, someone thinks to improve things and Franz is pulled inside. The old story. But maybe these young girls will be living it differently, inventing their own unique ways of putting the pieces together. One would hope. Certainly they will need more light to find their way in that tricky borderland world where many of us got lost. Hopefully, like the old navigator-priestesses, we left some road signs, wrote books, taught classes. *Everythin' we ever knew about the movement of the sea was preserved in the verses of a song. For thousands of years, we went where we wanted and came home safe, because of the song.* And we are still around, spinning new tales in that back room, las veteranas.

When the dance is over, I hurry forward to say good-bye to Monica. I hand her the little shopping bag with two small gifts I brought from Vermont before I even knew who this young quinceañera would be. "Open them later," I tell her since I can see she is distracted by the commotion around her. "Thank you so much," she says, throwing her arms around me. The gifts fall to the floor. Oh, no! Inside one of the boxes is a ceramic figurine of a girl with wings holding a heart she is about to set free. I hope she has not been broken by the fall. The other gift is one of my novels, since Monica has told me she loves to read. Later I call Monica to thank her again and to reminisce about her special night, and I ask her if the winged girl was okay. "Oh, thank you so much," Monica croons.

"No," I correct her misunderstanding. "I mean, was she broken or anything?"

"No, she was perfect," Monica tells me. She seems to have forgotten that we dropped the box as we were embracing. "I put her with these Dominican dolls my mom has in our living room."

The seven ceramic figurines without faces on the Ramoses' coffee table! And here I thought I was giving Monica a unique, contemporary American gift. At this later stage in my life, I'm often surprised and heartened by how my cultural and biological genes have survived, intact. So the damage was not so bad. Finally, in my thirties I began to weave together the narratives: the immigrant girl; the Latina woman; the American writer; the tentative teacher; the childless madrina-godmother, helping to raise all our children. With Maxine Hong Kingston as guide and other Latina writers as compañeras on the journey, I began to write my way through all the contradictions, to make a new narrative out of the weaving of these old threads. I began to send out my poems and stories, and not just wait to be discovered, the writer's version of the princess-waiting-for-her-knight-in-shining-armor syndrome.

Love, too, proved true, the third time around. In my late thirties, I fell in love with a true companion, a marriage that is now almost two decades old and flourishing.

There is a Spanish saying about what to do with the troubles you experience, cosas de la vida you live through: *Hacer de tripas corazón* (Literally, to make heart out of guts, a more visceral version of *If life gives you lemons, make lemonade*). One of the quinceañera sites I visited—poorgirlsquinceañera.com—has for its home page the following logo: "The quinceañera you were too poor to have: a celebration of art fueled by deprivation." Poet Gwen Zepeda, who founded the Web site and hosted a quinceañera in Houston for all those who had never had one, feels that her event specifically and the tradition in general is a magnet for all kinds of unfulfilled longings. The best thing to do with that longing, she decided, was to make art. *Hacer de tripas corazón.* Thus this book. Thus Monica's winged girl belongs next to her Dominican mothers and grandmothers whose wombs, now hollow, and wounds, now healed, she came from.

I drive back to the Pan American Hotel from Monica's party via the instructions the front desk gave me. My heart beats strong in case I should get lost. *All she had to know was the song and she knew where she was.* If I could pass on one wish for all my girls that would be it. *All you have to know is your song and you'll know who you are.* This song takes a lifetime to learn and relearn, as the old women in the back room can tell you. As I can tell you.

Usually, I turn the radio on for company, but not tonight. I keep an eye out for the landmarks—Catalano's Bakery, Amore Laundromat, Gaspar's Quality Meats, New China Soft Taco, a library, the Lutheran cemetery, then a right on Sixty-ninth, past Mt. Olivet Cemetery, under a banner that reads MASPETH IS AMERICA, all the way down to Queens Boulevard.

La Bendición

S PENDING A YEAR trying to understand a tradition focused on young Latina teens, I often felt like an adolescent myself, subject to the swings of contradictory feelings about the subject of my study.

But never about the subjects. This I want to make clear. Over and over what I felt toward the girls themselves was a tenderness and protectiveness that surprised me. I had just met many of them. I was not their mother or grandmother or godmother or aunt. But their youth and their vulnerability, their hopefulness and their beauty, touched something womanly and profound in me that—for lack of a better name—could be called the maternal instinct.

Driving home from their quinceañeras or hanging up the phone after our interviews, I wanted to continue at their side, accompanying them, advising them, and protecting them, but mostly listening to them, cheering them on. Those feelings, I came to realize, are what coming-of-age ceremonies are meant to ritualize and affirm in a community over time. Somehow, as a nation we've dropped the ball in this regard, leaving our young girls in the lurch, as Mary Pipher warned more than a dozen years ago in *Reviving Ophelia*. Perhaps our leaving them on their own was based on a well-meaning desire to let our young girls experience the freedom and autonomy we ourselves had not been allowed at their age. Many of us, Latina women, especially, grew up with so many prohibitions and inhibitions. Of course, we want our young girls to be free, free, free at last of all the bonds that hobbled and divided us!

But by celebrating their quinceañeras these Latina girls are letting us know that they want something more than freedom. They yearn to connect with their history. "It's like part of my Hispanic culture," many responded when I asked them to tell me about this tradition. I appreciated the "like" in their descriptions because it signaled that this tradition is being transformed even as it is being codified by their descriptions.

The quinceañera as practiced today in the United States is *like* a ritual that came from the native countries of grandparents or parents, countries many of these young girls have never been to. But through this tradition, they are reaching back to that old culture, out of a need for community and meaning, continuity and direction. A way not to get lost. A way to be and belong: a Latina girl stringing her bead of self in the necklace of the generations.

Not all of us older Latinos and Latinas are first-generation Americans, but *all* of us are the first Hispanics, a group created in 1973 by a stroke of the pen. It is important that we not let another stroke of the pen, metaphorically speaking, define our traditions for us. By this I mean the danger of a runaway consumer culture re-creating and distorting our traditions in order to sell us something. Change is necessary but it should be change based on the needs of our young people, not a corporation's bottom line. Neither should we allow ourselves to be circumscribed by a sacred-cow mentality about native country traditions just because "they are one of the few traditions we have left." Traditions are made of sturdier stuff, and our ongoing responsibility is to revise and renew them so that they continue to fulfill their authentic purpose, to empower us.

Which is why this journey into the world of quinceañeras proved to be richer and more complex than I initially suspected. Why I come out of this year feeling a deeper understanding of the challenges facing our Latino community as we come of age in the United States as well as the challenges facing our daughters and granddaughters as they come of age as young women. We need to be there with them at this important passage, profundizando and deepening their sense of what this journey entails. In order to educate them, we have to educate ourselves, as Plato reminds us, about who we are as a community and as new Latina Americans.

This book has been an attempt to do that through the lens of one tradition, the quinceañera: to review and understand this evolving ritual with all its contradictions, demystifying its ideology, dusting off the glitter that is sprayed over the ritual in order to be sold back to us by an aggressive consumer market as the genuine article, handing it down in as clear and conscionable a form as possible. My hope is that from the vantage point of this ritual we can begin to understand both our personal past and our collective present, as well as our evolving future as a diverse community within an ever more Latinized nation.

꧁ꙮ꧂

But the swings, dear reader, the swings in my feelings toward the tradition were downright dizzying and baffling. Did I believe in this Q-tradition or not? Yes and no. Sí y no. Back and forth. At dinner parties, I'd relate the details of some Q-extravaganza I'd just been to or heard or read about, and as my friends shook their heads and compared quinceañeras to the runaway Bar and Bat

Mitzvah parties, I'd find myself backtracking, wanting to defend nuestra tradición. "On the other hand," I'd tell my friends.

On the one hand: quinceañeras are expensive, especially as they are evolving in our U.S. consumer culture. It is outrageous to throw the house out the window for a one-night party. Money that could well be spent by a working-class family on education or mortgage payments. Then there's the whole issue of a ceremony that encourages young girls in the dubious fantasy of being a princess, a fantasy most of our young girls cannot afford to indulge in. In fact, to revisit Ana Maria's vision under a tree in Memorial Park in Caldwell, Idaho, the percentages are telling us an altogether different story about what lies ahead for our young people. How can we let ourselves be conned into thinking a hyped-up, supersized production has anything to do with an authentic tradition that can empower our young girls as they become women?

On the other hand: there were times as I sat in a kitchen, watching the women in the family, the mother and grandmothers, the tías and madrinas, making the recuerdos while the court of fifteen young couples practiced their choreographed dances in the living room or backyard, periodically dropping into the kitchen for a snack and to listen to the old stories that inevitably arise when women gather together—those times, I'd feel a special transmission going on. I was a part of something timeless, hard to name or contain. "Something was growing inside of me," says Estrella as her special night approaches in *Estrella's Quinceañera.* "A feeling I hadn't had in a long time. I was part of something bigger. I truly belonged." In that kitchen, I, too, felt a part of a rare and true experience, one I had mostly missed in my own growing up. "We need symbolic action to draw us together and keep us going," Norine Dresser writes in *Multicultural Celebrations.* "That's what these life-cycle celebrations do. They make us feel that we belong. This feeling comes through the creation of *communitas*—a feeling of oneness. . . . Life-cycle celebrations furnish creative outlets for the human spirit . . . confirm spirituality and authenticate life."

That oneness, that empowering feeling of being a part of an ongoing transmission, is what the tradition ritualizes, why quinceañeras are not just about the girls but about community, why they can enrich all of us.

⚜

In wanting to hand down a tradition that truly empowers young women, I, of course, worried about the charge of sexism. As traditionally practiced, the quinceañera enacts and, therefore, subliminally affirms a patriarchal paradigm, the sexuality of the young girl controlled and monitored by a macho culture. How can any woman who calls herself a feminist want to pass on such a ritual to her daughter?

Over the course of the past year of attending them and immersing myself in their lore, relishing the new, liberated variations, I thought a lot about this charge against quinceañeras. Was it a sign of my own corrupted feminism that I felt the hypnotic pull of this ritual?

What I came to understand about myself and most of the women and girls I interviewed is that there is a hunger in us for this kind of ritual expression that truly respects and honors our female sexuality. In her wonderful essay "Brideland," Naomi Wolf describes experiencing similar baffled feelings as a young feminist preparing for her wedding, a ceremony "that leaves no doubt as to the naked patriarchialism of . . . its origins." In fact, Naomi Wolf feels herself lulled and deeply attracted to this bridal world. Why would a young feminist want to submerge herself in this world of "Brideland"? she asks herself.

The reason has to do with the modern era's denigration of female sexuality. We live in an age in which female sexuality is held incredibly cheaply; it is on tap; you can gain access to it at the flick of a switch. While few people want the bad old days of enforced virginity to return, I think there is a terrible spiritual and emotional longing among them for social behavior or ritual that respects, even worships, female sexuality and reproductive potential. We are no longer Goddesses or Queens of our own sexuality.

Paradoxically, swaddled in the white satin of the formal bridal gown, we take on for a moment that lost sexual regalness. . . . We are made into treasure again, and jewels adorn our breasts. In white, we retrieve our virginity, which means metaphorically, the original specialness of sexual access to us. . . .

Who wouldn't want to drift in those currents for a while. . . .

The quinceañera offers a young Latina the opportunity to drift in these currents as well, and not because she is marrying someone. This is precisely what Isabella Martínez Wall meant by wanting each girl to feel like a queen of her own life. Of course, none of us older Latinas and feminists would want to go back to the "bad old days," when our rights were curtailed and our hearts and minds divided by either/ors, as my own long and rocky passage to adulthood attests to. But as Wolf concludes, "perhaps the knowledge that we have lost the sense of the value of female sexuality . . . will lead us to find new rituals, new experiences, new ceremonies in which we can announce to the world that we are sexually priceless—and not just for one expensive day."

The quinceañera is just such a ritual, but it needs revamping, as I can affirm after a year of feeling as if I were drowning in pink clichés and watching working-class parents dish out dollars "to show off rather than show off their daughters," a distinction a guest made to me about one such party. As the generation passing on the tradition, we need to divest it of its entrapments while at the same time recognizing that beneath them lies a living spring. Mimi Doll, one of the researchers involved with the SHERO project mentioned earlier, made a wonderful observation about tradition. (Given how this book began with dolls, I loved that her last name is Doll, and her comment is helping me to close this book.) Hearing me grumble about traditions that entrap us and prevent us from full flowering—it was one of my days of swinging into Q-con territory—Mimi Doll reminded me: "Our traditions are meant to take care of us and protect us as a people. So we can't just dismiss them. The challenge is to ensure that we recast them to our present-day context so that they continue to take care of us."

Mimi Doll went on to cite the example of Marianismo, that ideal of Latina womanhood with its heavy emphasis on virginity. The girls in her SHERO project had identified it as one of the powerful behavioral forces in their lives. How can this old paradigm be useful now? "Originally, Marianismo was all about chastity as a sign of the purity of the female and the honor of the family. Our SHERO girls are now talking about chastity in order to protect themselves, so they don't get pregnant, so they can finish high school and go to college."

Our young Latinas should feel free to reimagine the old stories so that they do not feel divided by their dual cultures, as many in my generation did, so that they feel our blessing on their particular expression of their traditions, as many of us did not, to our detriment.

This expansive attitude toward our inherited cultures is, in fact, being embraced by young feminists today. In her introduction to *To Be Real: Telling the Truth and Changing the Face of Feminism*, Rebecca Walker explains why many young feminists have rejected an earlier generation's feminist label: "For many of us to be a feminist in the way we have seen or understood feminism is to conform to an identity and way of living that doesn't allow for individuality, complexity, or less than perfect personal histories." *Third wavers*, as these young feminists call themselves, are "broadening our view of who and what constitutes 'the feminist community,' staking out an inclusive terrain from which to actively seek the goals of society equality and individual freedom we all share. We are accepting contradiction and ambiguity . . . using *and* much more than *either/or*."

In our first and second waves of feminism as well as in our first and second generations as immigrants and as newly minted Latinos, we sometimes trap ourselves in too-rigid definitions of what it means to be who we are. As Rebecca Walker reminds us: "The complex, multi-issue nature of our lives, the instinct not to categorize and shut oneself off from others, and the enormous contradictions we embody are all fodder for making new theories of living and relating." So, yes, Rebecca Walker assures her young fellow feminists, you can be a feminist and shave your legs, get married, want to raise three kids on a farm in Montana, still speak to the father who abused you.

How these young feminists are redefining and enlarging the ground of feminism is applicable to our young Latinas as they negotiate and expand the ground of their ethnicity. The very hybridity they inherit because of their dual cultures in addition to the global culture in which they are coming of age means that the traditions we pass on to them have to take into account a more complex and multifaceted and contradictory young person than we ever were at their age. And the quinceañera offers them an opportunity to explore that variety and contradiction within the supportive context of family and community, of custom and ceremony. As W. B. Yeats reminds us in his poem "A Prayer for My Daughter," traditions are a society's way of cultivating, protecting, and passing on the things that are important to the new generations:

> How but in custom and in ceremony
> Are innocence and beauty born?
> Ceremony's a name for the rich horn,
> And custom for the spreading laurel tree.

Perhaps out of the same impulse that led me to rouse up some wise women at Andover and construct a ritual that might empower my special girls, I decided to end this book with a gathering of wise women.

I would invite fifteen mujeres sin pelo en la lengua to join a court of wise women, truthsayers. I envisioned a kind of virtual quinceañera for my readers, who would encounter these madrinas here at the close of this book, each one proffering a consejo, or piece of advice, that might prove useful to them in the future.

One morning, listening to National Public Radio, I felt affirmed in my decision by a report about a group of elders who dispense advice online. Elder Wisdom Circle was founded by a forty-four-year-old "youngster," Doug Meckelson, who felt there was a need for guidance among the young and not so young as well as a fund of untapped wisdom in our elders. At the time of the report, Elder Circle was up to 250 volunteers, spread all over the United States, representing eighteen thousand years of experience! (I was tickled by the response to one letter from a thirteen-year-old girl, worried about her older sister's drinking, which began, "Hi, Thirteen Ladies and four gentlemen are responding.")

One of the not so surprising revelations was that the majority of letters seeking advice come from teens. "A lot of them write in saying, 'nobody listens to me,'" Sharon Morrison, a member of the circle, told the NPR reporter. Then, musing over why, she sighed. "When you're young you need an authority of age to help you find your way."

"It used to be that how we learned was based on dealing with people who had already experienced something," Doug Meckelson elaborated. In fact, his immediate inspiration for founding the circle was his late grandmother, "who gave me advice on everything." But now, as Will Cain, the founder of *Quince Girl*, reminded me about the quinceañera, "La abuelita is not always a resource." Emigration from our native countries and mobility within this country have forced us to seek advice and knowledge elsewhere, online from Elder Wisdom Circle and from manuals and books like this one.

All the more reason to gather some of those abuelitas and wise women here and ask them what piece of advice they would give a young or not so young person who might feel the need for wisdom in today's world.

And so, I began making a list of wise women I knew. The plan was to send out a first round of letters to a handful and wait for a response before sending out a second round. After all, I didn't want to invite too many wise women into the circle and then— in the interest of keeping to the thematic number fifteen—boot anyone out. But how to decide? There were so many. The only way to make any kind of a selection was to remind myself that each woman in my circle was representing a heck of a lot of absent ones. A representative congress, more than an oligarchic coven.

Some of the wise women on my list were figures you have met in the pages of this book, women who served a guiding role in my own life, Zanda Merrill and Ruth Stevenson and Cherríe Moraga and Maxine Hong Kingston. Others were figures who serve leadership and inspirational roles in our Latino community or in the larger culture, women like Isabel Allende and Dolores Huerta, the female face of United Farm Workers, and Mary Pipher, author of *Reviving Ophelia*. Some were fellow journeyers like Sandra Cisneros and Norma Cantú and María Hinojosa.

"I am writing you because you are one of the wise women in my life," I explained in my letter. "We are now the elders of the tribe, and as the Hopi elders reminded their tribe during a difficult time, 'We are the ones we have been waiting for.' What can we pass on to our young people as they come of age in today's world? I'd like you to consider that question and join my sacred circle."

"Let me think about it," Ruth Stevenson graciously wrote back. In a later e-mail she admitted, "I'm usually suspicious when I hear the word 'should.'" She did try a couple of times, but what she sent back were not nuggets of wisdom but stories of times when as a young woman she felt the winged life stirring inside her. I had to smile. Of course, my English teacher would tell stories! She knew, as did the Sufi masters, that the best "answer" to give a student is to tell her a story that allows for multiple interpretations and from which she can garner wisdom commensurate with her ability to absorb and understand.

I began to wonder if my great idea was a truly useful way to close this book. But then some "answers" started to trickle in, often prefaced by "Oh my god, only *one* piece of advice?" Or conversely, "Oh my god, I don't know if I believe in *any* advice." Still, many of these big-hearted mujeres indulged me and went on to offer what did seem to me very wise advice. But what I realized as I culled these responses and began to draft a second round of letters was that when I was fifteen, what I would have found most useful was not a piece of advice, no matter how wise, but a relationship with the person who was modeling that wise advice in the way she was living her life. Someone who might have listened to me and helped me access the strength and wisdom in myself and apply it to the particular challenges I was facing at that stage of my own life.

Perhaps not surprisingly, the advice I got even from such a varied group of women fell along the same lines. The strongest emphasis was about realizing the power in you. It would seem that in the pantheon of my three little Papo dolls—princess, fairy godmother, woman warrior—the key figure among my wise women is the woman warrior. "Learn your strength," María Hinojosa wrote. "Eat your fear and self-doubt for breakfast!" Isabel Allende agreed. "Take risks," she advised, "because a life without risks is no life at all."

"Don't forget your powers," Zanda Merrill echoed, and went on to list them. Wishing power, staying power, going power, healing power, power to make a change in the world.

During a face-to-face interview in my hotel room in Los Angeles on the eve of a big immigrant march she would be leading, Dolores Huerta responded to my query for advice with a question. Who did I think was the more fierce of a species in the animal kingdom, the male or female?

I could guess the right answer, but I wanted to give her the pleasure of enlightening me. "The male?"

As expected, Dolores answered gleefully, "No! It's the female!"

"That's why I tell young girls, you have to stand up for yourself. Be bien preparadas. If you can't fight for yourself, how can you fight for your family, your community, your country?" It seemed odd to hear such a battle cry from a petite, very pretty seventy-six-year-old woman, dressed daintily in a black pantsuit with a flowered blouse. But her blue black eyes were wise, the eyes of an old soul with a young heart. The beaded necklace ("made for me by a prisoner") with the eagle (águila) logo of the United Farm Workers was also a reminder of the long, hard struggles she has fought and continues fighting.

The other major emphasis in the advice received from this first round of my wise women involved finding your magic: the fairy godmother figure in my trinity of dolls. "Use your talents," Norma Cantú advised, and then went on to use hers by proffering fourteen other consejos, from the high-minded (set goals, take risks, forgive) to the mundane (exercise, be on time, keep a diary). When I asked her to pick just one, she went back to "celebrate your gift and share it." Sharing was a key component of Cherríe Moraga's conversation with me. "Remember you live in community. You have a responsibility to be accountable to your family and your community as well as yourself." Cherríe laughed, explaining she had lost her mother in the summer at ninety years old. "And although I was a rebel, I find my mother's words coming out of my mouth."

Finally, some of the advice was addressed specifically to the princess in our young girls—the last one of my Papo dolls. "Don't become drunk when a pretty (or famous) man pays attention to you," Sandra Cisneros wrote. "Pretty (or famous) men who come after you like gangbusters come after ALL women that way. If I had known that then, I wouldn't have been so naive to think I was selected among all women and honored by their attentions. I thought I had incited them to 'love,' but for men I was simply another four-letter word, which, to be kind here, I'll call 'lust.'"

"No te dejes," Cherríe Moraga echoed. "Don't abandon your-self. If you find yourself in a place where you've betrayed your-self, get out!" Again, Cherríe laughed. Something else her mami used to tell her.

Perhaps because Cherríe kept bringing up her mother, I felt a yearning to call my own mami and find out what she would advise.

I had not intended to ask her to join my circle of wise viejitas. Like most daughters, I felt I had had enough maternal advice to last me all my life, thank you very much. Then, too, Mami and I had had such a rocky relationship since the very years I was writ-ing about in this book on quinceañeras. Not to mention that in the past she had taken issue with some of my autobiographical writings. She did not buy my defense that my novels were fiction, that I had used what I knew in the service of story, not as a tell-all tabloid would. Beyond the veil of fabrication, she saw the shad-owy shape of our own family, our struggles, our failures, and what she refused to see in her rage, our triumphs.

During the height of her hurt feelings toward me, she had been hospitalized following an ankle fracture, and I had hurried down to New York City to be at her side. My distress and unwav-ering allegiance—despite my "disobedience"—were reminders that this woman was part of my heart's core, not an appendage I could remove and continue living without.

After visiting her in the hospital, I stayed overnight in the small apartment my parents had moved to in Manhattan after they sold the house in Queens. I slept in her bed, next to Papi's bed. On the small tray on her bedside table was a small jar of Vicks and a tube of face cream, just as on my own bedside table back in Vermont. Below the drawer in a cubbyhole, I found a copy of my first novel, which came as a surprise since I knew my mother had banned my fiction from her home.

I opened it, and what a sick and pained feeling! She had gone through the whole novel highlighting certain passages—some pages literally glowed. Their offensiveness seemed to stem from the mention of sex or drugs or mental illness or flawed mothers. I closed the book and stroked the cover—my first novel, my grand achievement that I had hoped would reclaim my standing in the family—and set it back in the cubbyhole where I had found it.

Fifteen years later, to be serendipitously exact, I was going to contact her about being in a book with no pretense that this was fiction! No, I am not a masochist. As it happens, we had found each other again in the last few years. My mother had asked my husband, an ophthalmologist, to remove her cataracts, and she had come up to Vermont and stayed with us during the two procedures. She was grateful to me for welcoming her into my home, to him for "giving me back my sight." Afterward, it was as if her vision—as well as mine—had been figuratively cleared. I heard a new tone in her voice. *My dove, my little one, my child, my daughter.* Meanwhile, I picked up an old-country habit that my sisters and I had discarded over the years. In saying good-bye to our parents, in person or by phone, we would ask for their blessing, "La bendición, Mami, Papi."

"Que Dios te bendiga, mi'ja."

But it was not just nostalgia that was the impulse for my wanting to call my mother and ask for her consejo for ending this book. In fact, there had been a sea change not just in our relationship but in our family's story. After forty-two years in this country, she and Papi had moved back to their hometown of Santiago. Soon after the move, my father began the long good-bye, descending into Alzheimer's, forgetting whether or not he had eaten supper or if beyond the windows lay New York City or Santiago, the now very urban, bustling city of his birth, the city where he had chosen to die.

In this most difficult transition, my mother's uncomplaining and tender care of my father, her resilience and joy in life have amazed and impressed her four daughters. It turns out we had underestimated Mami's capacity to handle adversity, to take the lemons life gives you and, as she would have said in her mala-propping, mixed-metaphor English, find the silver lining in them. *Hacer de tripas corazón.*

But we can sense she is lonely. The calls come more often; she welcomes our visits as she never did in the past when we would arrive from boarding school or college or our own lives with our noise and demands and our messy ways and our worrisome stories. She has also become an avid baseball fan, rooting for the teams with the most Dominican players, watching the games on cable TV. My mother, who couldn't sit still for a long talk because she always had to be moving. Talking made her nervous, especially talking with her daughters, who had so many strange ideas. Most especially talking with this daughter with her divorces and problematic autobiographical novels.

We are tentative with each other. Our conversation stays within the safe confines of her health and Papi's condition, as if we're still unsure how far afield to wander from our newfound closeness. Sometimes she asks about my writing. When I told her I was working on a quinceañera book, she lined up a bunch of great-nieces for me to interview during one of my visits to Santiago and threw a "tea" for all the "girls" who had been presented with me back in the summer of 1967.

So, I was both encouraged but a little nervous to ask her to join my circle of wise women. What would she offer as a consejo to a young girl today, a girl who would inevitably wear my teenage face in her imagination?

I sent her an e-mail suggesting the idea to her. A few days later, when I hadn't heard from her, I followed it up with a call.

She was watching a baseball game, the Red Sox against Cleveland—the TV blared in the background—and eating saltines, a new habit because the tension of the game made her want to munch on something and chewing gum was no good as it stuck to her dentures.

She would love to join my circle of wise women if I wanted her to, she said somewhat shyly. But she wasn't sure she had any good advice to give a young girl.

My mother at a loss for advice?! "Of course you do, Mami," I encouraged her. "You've got eighty years of experience! *Más sabe el diablo por viejo que por diablo.*" I quoted the saying she used to quote to us, endorsing her authority. The devil knows more because he's old than because he's the devil. "And besides, you've raised four daughters."

"Okay," she agreed, taking a bite of a saltine. Now it wasn't the game but my question making her nervous. "I guess I'd tell her she better be prepared. You have to be able to take care of yourself. You don't know if you're going to be divorced someday and have to raise kids on your own. Don't depend on anyone but yourself!"

Again, as with my other wise women, the woman warrior was being summoned.

"Another thing is that if there's something you love to do, do it. Like if you want to spend ten hours in a room writing, do it, and don't let anyone tell you you should be giving it up or keeping your husband company. It's the quality time that counts."

Cheers and the excited voice of the announcer. Big Papi was up to bat, Mami informed me, nervously biting into another cracker.

I, too, was feeling the need to chew on something so as not to blurt out, "Mami!!!" You see, during my last visit, she had cautioned me that I had better get ready to let go of my writing.

"You're going to get old, you know. You can't keep doing that writing day in and day out."

Although we hardly ruffled each other's feathers anymore, this comment had ruffled mine. "Well, I am not going to give it up, Mami," I informed her. "Writing is how I live my life." She had shaken her head as if she knew better. "It's a calling, Mami, not a job. The best thing I could wish somebody is to find their calling, not let anyone make them give it up!"

Somehow my impassioned defense of my writing months ago had dissolved her absolute certainty of what was right for me. In fact, the wisdom my wise-woman mami was now handing down she had gotten a few months earlier from me!

But because of talking to Mami, I do get wiser. How could I think I could round up a bunch of women and harvest wisdom from them for everyone's use? Wisdom is not a fixed quality. It circulates among us. No wonder I found it so hard trying to decide whom to include in my circle of wise women. Wisdom happens in relationship, in a context of the back-and-forth. Aniana Vargas, a very wise Dominican woman who stayed on working with campesinos after her companion revolutionaries went down the mountain to their plush jobs and comfortable lives, once told me that everything that is known in the world is known among all of us. *Todo lo que se sabe en el mundo se sabe entre todos.* Our joint wisdom is the great river into which our little rivulet lives and books flow, and it is that river that we can help our young people learn about and access and navigate on their very own.

Mary Pipher, whom I contacted right before my call to Mami, had begun to steer me toward this realization. She had graciously agreed to be interviewed but declined to offer a consejo. "Sage advice all starts sounding the same," she explained. "Be true. Follow your North Star. Listen to your inner voice. I'd much rather approach my reader as a fellow learner than as a teacher. But here's a thought about your book," she added, as if wanting to give me something. "Think of it as a canoe, and steer us back into the Big Water, into a richer experience of this tradition, with what you have to say."

I had to laugh (my mother's laugh) because here I was getting the most personal and touching consejo from the wise woman who had declined offering advice.

And so, I decide to disband my circle of wise women. Because, wise reader, as you've probably realized: it has been my very own quinceañera at fifty-six that I've been setting up here at the close of my book! Inviting my favorite women to be part of my court. Asking for their wisdom and their stories, their bendición to cherish and preserve and now pass on.

Acknowledgments

To the madrinas and padrinos,
godmothers and godfathers, of this book

In the Mexican American community, every detail of a quinceañera is sponsored by a relative or friend. I have seen invitations that list more than forty names: godmother of the cake, godfather of the limousine, godmother of the tiara, godfather of the dj. From the decorations to the dress to the last doll, there is a madrina or padrino whose investment in that particular gift represents a larger investment in the girl herself. The gift is a pledge and a promise to the quinceañera: her godparents will stand by her, protect her, and nurture her in any way they can as she journeys into adulthood.

I am reminded of these sponsorships here at the end of a book I could not have written without the help and generosity and encouragement of so many madrinas and padrinos. My research took me inside the homes of dozens of girls and their families, into churches and hotel ballrooms and recreation halls, into businesses and establishments that provide services to quinceañeras. So many of you welcomed me into your lives and homes and stories. From the bottom of my heart, I want to say gracias.

In addition, the book itself went through several evolutions along the way, beginning as a short, commissioned manuscript to be packaged with a DVD, an idea that dead-ended when the imprint folded. At which point several godmothers from the Penguin family stepped in to rescue a project that by then had become a passion, not an assignment. And all along the way, my tireless warrior-woman–godmother agent provided encouragement and kept faith through some rough passages in the coming-of-age of this book. My measureless gracias.

Below is a partial list of some of the madrinas and padrinos of this book. Since I've chosen to respect the privacy of girls and their families, I do not list some of the people who were most significant to me in the writing of this book. Know that my heart is full of gratitude, and any critique of certain aspects of the tradition is not intended in any way to diminish your specific celebration or mitigate my deepest gratitude. Thank you for helping me understand this key ritual and the evolving community in which it is celebrated.

First and foremost, to la Virgencita de la Altagracia
gracias
for so many blessings,
not least among them the privilege and pleasure
of having met so many wonderful people in the course of writing this book,
some of whose names are listed below:

CHAMBELÁN DE HONOR
Bill Eichner

MAMI
Julia Tavares de Alvarez

PAPI
Eduardo Alvarez

MADRINA DE HONOR
Susan Bergholz

CORTE DE HONOR
Isabel Allende, Ana Rosa Alvarez, Maury Alvarez, Norma Cantú, Maria Hinojosa, Dolores Huerta, Tita Jensen, Zanda Merrill, Cherrie Moraga, Grace Paley, Mary Pipher, Shannon Ravenel (who is also a madrina of many of the categories listed below), Ruth Stevenson, Judy Yarnall

MADRINAS TO THE RESCUE
Kathryn Court and Alexis Washam

MADRINAS FROM WAY BACK
Emily Haynes and Trena Keating

MADRINAS AND PADRINOS OF INSPIRATION
Gloria Anzaldúa (*que en paz descanse*), Boodramsingh family, Graciela Fonseca, Maxine Hong Kingston, Ledesma family,

Isabella Martinez Wall, Ana Maria Schachtell, Donna Vasquez,
Vendela Vida, Gwen Zepeda

MADRINAS OF NETWORKING
Ofelia Barrios, María Battle Pesquera, Liz and Maria Bueno,
Maris Callahan of Lippe Taylor, Inma Carbajal, Arlyn Davich,
Suzanne Kelly, Zoa and Zoa Izanet Mendez, Priscilla Mora,
Esthersita Pentón-Nodarse, Christy Rivera, Michele Salcedo,
Mari Santana, Maria Rosa Tavares de Bogaert

MADRINAS AND PADRINOS OF
PHOTOGRAPHY, FILM, AND MEDIA
The Benavides of Tilde Photography, Inés Espinoza, Emily Ríos, Franklin
Bencosme, Will Cain, Richard Glatzer, Enrique Muñoz, Higinio Muñoz,
Payret Studios in Miami, Salvador Suriano, Wash Westmoreland

MADRINAS AND PADRINOS OF
EVENTS PRODUCTIONS
Bisli of Bisli Event Services, Yolanda Martos, Priscilla Mora of
sweetfifteenparty.com, Esthersita Pentón-Nodarse of Pretty Party,
Luis Molina, Denny Nicholas, Tony Pouparina, Oscar Suárez

MADRINAS OF THE DRESS
Lisa Chang of Mary's Bridal, Trina Chartier of House of Wu,
Cindi Freeburn of David's Bridal, Tonya Gosselin of
Needleman's Bridal Shop

MADRINA OF THE CAKE
Miguelina, wherever you are

MADRINAS AND PADRINO OF
RESEARCH AND HISTORY
Rachel Manning, Joy Pile, Charles Mann

MADRINAS OF FURTHER INFORMATION
Jill Denner, Mimi Doll, Bianca Guzmán, Cettina Larrow,
Evelyn Rodríguez, Bernadette Sánchez, Sunita Trevino

MADRINAS AND PADRINOS OF RELIGIOUS INSTRUCTION
Reverend Cathie Caimano, Daysi Caro, Sister Angela Erevia, Josette
Goldish, Yvonne Konig, Esperanza Monterubio, Heske Zelermyer, Rabbi

Isidoro Aizenberg, Eli Cohen, Rabbi Oisiki Ghitis, Reverend Nicolas
Menjivar, Father Jorge Reyes, Rabbi Ira Schiffer, Father Carlos Urbino

MADRINA OF THE MUSIC
Monique Alvarado (lead singer in a youth mariachi group out of San
Antonio, known as la muñequita de oro for her golden voice)

MADRINA AND PADRINO OF
ACCENTS AND TRANSLATION
Lyn Tavares, Roberto Véguez

MIAMI MADRINAS AND PADRINOS
Dulce Goldenberg, Esthersita Pentón-Nodarse of Pretty Party,
Enrique Fernández, Maurice Mompoint

LAWRENCE MADRINAS AND PADRINOS
Daysi Caro, Zoa Mendez of Mendez Flowerloons, Peralta family,
all the girls at Lawrence High School who helped me out—
you know who you are!, Lou Bernieri, Richard Gorham

MEXICAN AMERICAN MADRINAS
Ana Barrios, Norma Cantú, Gabriela Castaneda, Sandra Cisneros,
Lorena Flores, Leticia and Heather and Apolonia Hernández,
María Hinojosa, Monica and Juanita Lepe, Angela Mosqueda,
Norma Pérez, Marisela Ramos, Juliana Santillan

PUERTO RICAN MADRINAS
Andrea Español, Melissa Parada, Carolyn Ramos

DOMINICAN MADRINAS
Carolina Alba; Karla and Mauri Alvarez; Yajaira Blanco; Ivanna Bogaert;
Paulina Estepan, "Pali"; Patricia Franco; Mariana Franco de Miess; Lidiana
Fuente; Amantina Grullón, "Titi" (who has passed on, que en paz descanse);
Yanique Grullón; Sandra Haddad de Estrella; Rose Mary Lora; María
Antonia Pichardo; Redondo family; Astrid Trujillo Cabral de Idigoras;
Ameriquín Valázquez; Zaidy Zouain

CUBAN MADRINAS AND PADRINOS
Vitalina Alfonso, Celita Gómez, Carmel Rodríguez,
Eduardo Béjar, Roberto Véguez

MEXICAN, SOUTH, AND CENTRAL
AMERICAN MADRINAS
Inés Espinoza, Angela and Verónica Fajardo, Gloria González,
Loren Michelle Mejía, Mercedes Peralta, Patricia Saldarriaga

MADRINAS AND PADRINO OF AUTOBIOGRAPHY
Judy Sherman, Ruth Stevenson, Bruce Holsapple

Suggested Reading

For those interested in learning more about the tradition
of the quinceañera and about Latina girls in general

NONFICTION

Anzaldúa, Gloria, *Borderlands/La Frontera: The New Mestiza* (San Francisco: Aunt Lute Books, 1987).

Cantú, Norma, and Olga Nájera-Ramírez, *Chicana Traditions: Continuity and Change* (Urbana: University of Illinois Press, 2002).

Denner, Jill, and Bianca L. Guzman, *LATINA GIRLS: Voices of Adolescent Strength in the U.S.* (New York: New York University Press, 2006).

Dietrich, Lisa C., *Chicana Adolescents: Bitches, 'Ho's, and Schoolgirls* (Westport, CT: Praeger Publishers, 1998).

Dresser, Norine, *Multicultural Celebrations: Today's Rules of Etiquette for Life's Special Occasions* (New York: Three Rivers Press, 1999).

Erevia, Sister Angela, *Quince Años: Celebrando la vida: Celebrating Life* (San Antonio: Missionary Catechists of Divine Providence, 2000).

King, Elizabeth, *Quinceañera* (New York: Penguin Putnam Books for Young Readers, 1998).

Lankford, Mary D., *Quinceañera: A Latina's Journey to Womanhood* (Brookfield, CT: Millbrook Press, 1994).

Marling, Karal Ann, *Debutante: Rites and Regalia of American Debdom* (Lawrence: University Press of Kansas, 2004).

Morales, Ed, *Living in Spanglish: The Search for Latino Identity in America* (New York: St. Martin's Press, 2002).

Napolitano, Valentina, *Migration, Mujercitas, and Medicine Men: Living in Urban Mexico* (Berkeley: University of California Press, 2002).

National Coalition of Hispanic Health and Human Services Organization, *The State of Hispanic Girls* (Washington, D.C.: COSSMHO, 1999).

Pentón-Nodarse, Esthersita, *Sólo Para Quinceañeras* (Miami: Colonial Press International, 1999).

Pleck, Elizabeth, *Celebrating the Family* (Cambridge: Harvard University Press, 2000).

Salcedo, Michele, *Quinceañera!: The Essential Guide to Planning the Perfect Sweet Fifteen Celebration* (New York: Henry Holt & Company, 1997).

Vida, Vendela, *Girls on the Verge: Debutante Dips, Drive-bys, and Other Initiations* (New York: St. Martin's Press/Griffin, 1999).

FICTION

Alegría, Malín, *Estrella's Quinceañera* (New York: Simon & Schuster Books for Young Readers, 2006).

Alvarado, Lisa, Ann Hagman Cardinal, and Jane Alberdeston Coralin, *Sister Chicas* (New York: New American Library, 2006).

Bertrand, Diane Gonzales, *Sweet Fifteen* (Houston: Arte Publico Press, 1995).

Canales, Viola, *The Tequila Worm* (New York: Wendy Lamb Books, Knopf, 2005).

Chambers, Veronica, *Quinceañera Means Sweet Fifteen* (New York: Hyperion Books for Children, 2001).

Osa, Nancy, *Cuba 15* (New York: Delacorte Press, 2003).